Acclaim for Curtis Chin's

EVERYTHING I LEARNED, I LEARNED IN A CHINESE RESTAURANT

"Coming out and coming of age are hard enough for the average teen, but when they're happening in a Chinese American family, in a city in conflict with itself, the result is an epic journey of self-discovery. For a kid who also ran around in the back of a Chinese restaurant, this book is literary comfort food, so delicious and good for the soul. Curtis Chin's story is endearing and unforgettable."

—Jamie Ford, author of *The Many Daughters of Afong Moy*

"Vivid, moving, funny, and heartfelt, Curtis Chin's memoir show-cases his talents as an activist and a storyteller. This is one man's story of growing up gay, Chinese American, and working-class in 1980s Detroit; finding a place in a large and loving immigrant family and in a changing city; and, in doing so, carving out a place in the world for himself." —Lisa Ko, author of *The Leavers* and *Memory Piece*

"A candid, sometimes funny reflection on growing up Chinese American and gay in Detroit in the '70s and '80s." —Associated Press

"A charming, often funny account of a sentimental education in a Cantonese restaurant...Curtis Chin is a born storyteller with an easy manner, and this memoir should earn him many readers."

—*Kirkus Reviews* (starred review)

T0384064

"Curtis Chin's vivid writing makes it easy to imagine him and his siblings hanging out at Chung's and observing all the people who come in and out. Chin brings a combination of earnestness and levity even to more serious topics, such as experiences of racism or denying his sexuality as a kid."

—*Eater*

"Curtis Chin's movable feast of a memoir dishes out everything you might want in a literary meal: savory reflections of our recent history, the sour-sweet tang of adolescent nostalgia, a little sauce, a lot of heart—and, yes, plenty of hot tea. The real magic is in how a book that's so fulfilling still leaves you hungry for more."

—Jeff Yang, author of *The Golden Screen: The Movies That Made Asian America* and coauthor of *Rise: A Pop History of Asian America from the Nineties to Now*

EVERYTHING I LEARNED, I LEARNED IN A CHINESE RESTAURANT

EVERYTHING I LEARNED, I LEARNED IN A CHINESE RESTAURANT

A Memoir

CURTIS CHIN

BACK BAY BOOKS
Little, Brown and Company
New York Boston London

Back Bay Books / Little, Brown and Company
Hachette Book Group
1290 Avenue of the Americas, New York, NY 10104
littlebrown.com

Originally published in hardcover by Little, Brown and Company, October 2023
First Back Bay paperback edition, October 2024

Back Bay Books is an imprint of Little, Brown and Company, a division of Hachette Book Group, Inc. The Back Bay Books name and logo are trademarks of Hachette Book Group, Inc.

The publisher is not responsible for websites (or their content) that are not owned by the publisher.

The Hachette Speakers Bureau provides a wide range of authors for speaking events. To find out more, go to hachettespeakersbureau.com or email hachettespeakers@hbgusa.com.

Little, Brown and Company books may be purchased in bulk for business, educational, or promotional use. For information, please contact your local bookseller or the Hachette Book Group Special Markets Department at special.markets@hbgusa.com.

ISBN 9780316507653 (hc) / 9780316507752 (pb)
LCCN 2022950494

Printing 1, 2024

LSC-C

Printed in the United States of America

Contents

Note to Diners

This is a memoir. It's how I remember and believe things happened. Sometimes, I changed names and descriptions. Other times, I reordered or combined events and reconstructed scenes and dialogue to the best of my recollection. Please be kind. It was a long time ago and my Cantonese was never very good.

THE TEA

"Welcome to Chung's. Is this for here or to go?"

Armed with a smile and a red waiter's jacket with the perpetual plum-sauce stain. That's how my dad greeted any new face who entered the lobby of our popular Chinese restaurant in Detroit. Interestingly, my great-great-grandpa Gong Li had faced this same question in the late 1800s as he stood cold and alone on a rickety dock in Guangzhou, China, trying to decide his future and that of his young, impoverished family. *For here or to go?*

For here or to go? As I got older, it was a question I asked myself.

Starting in our restaurant's long and open back kitchen, where my family made some of our most popular items, including the tangiest barbecue pork and best-smelling almond cookies, my mom taught me my first lessons. Before diving into math, English, and geography, she began with a little American history, tales of elders and ancestors, our family as prologue.

Over endless cups of oolong (or orange pop, if my siblings and I behaved ourselves), I learned how drought, famine, and the Opium Wars—when the British Empire forced the addictive opioid on the Chinese—pushed Gong Li to pack and leave for America. I giggled whenever my mom repeated how he first traveled from Canton, China, to Canton, Ohio, expecting to find hordes of other Chinese immigrants but seeing few.

When he heard about jobs and a slightly larger community in Detroit, Gong trekked north. Auto factories were revving up, but due to his limited English, he could only find manual labor in one of the city's few hand laundries. After a decade of scrimping and sending money home to his wife and family, he saved enough to open a dry-goods store, selling to his fellow Chinese memories and links to home—clothes, medicine, and prayer beads.

Gong hoped to expand his business, but there were barriers. No one in Chinatown uttered the words *Chinese Exclusion Act*, but they all knew what it was and how it ended many of their dreams. With America limiting the number of Chinese who could enter the country, the Chinese American population remained small, even shrinking. Only after congressional legislation introduced an exception for merchants could Gong sponsor his oldest son, Joe, now a teenager, allowing him to join his father.

From the three or four black-and-white photos that survived, worn edges and all, I could tell that Joe had Motown swag. According to my mom, he was the one who opened the gambling den beneath the family store and, if the other rumors are true, made whiskey runs from Canada during Prohibition in the 1920s.

By the start of World War II, Joe's two children born in China, one of whom was my grandpa Tom, had immigrated to America too. Now, under increased pressure from its new Chinese ally, the United States further loosened its anti-Asian immigration policies, and Tom was able to bring over his own young wife and daughter. They could even apply for citizenship. This development coincided with another game-changer: Chinese restaurants. With plentiful high-wage factory jobs and women joining the workforce, Detroit's new middle class sought affordable dining options outside the home. Expanding beyond its original immigrant clientele, chop suey joints were suddenly all the rage. Chow mein and lo mein were now mainstream.

In 1940, Joe, with the help of his two oldest children, Tom and Tui, and their spouses, opened Chung's Cantonese Cuisine on Third Avenue, in the city's old Chinatown. With its ample portions and late-night hours, the restaurant was an instant smash. It was one of the rare places in the segregated city where everyone felt welcome. Black or white, rich or poor, Christian or Jewish—the restaurant took anyone's money.

Featuring Americanized versions of Cantonese dishes as well as new American fare like chop suey and egg foo yung, the menu appealed to Jewish customers, who appreciated the absence of dairy ingredients (mixing milk and meat isn't kosher) and the fact that we, as fellow non-Christians, were open on Christmas Day. Black customers, who faced discrimination elsewhere, could stay and enjoy dining-room service. The white customers admired the "exotic" dishes that whisked them far from the grime and sweat of the factory floor. Our cheap-cheap prices? That was for everyone.

After two successful decades, due to eminent domain and an incoming highway, Chung's relocated a few blocks north to an area known as the Cass Corridor. Squeezed between the skyscrapers on the riverfront and the world headquarters of General Motors in the New Center area, the neighborhood was a mix of poor Black and white residents, nicknamed Little Kentucky. The merge made sense since we were hillbillies too.

At the same time, my family, who had been living above the store, hoped to move out of the city and into a better-funded school district. They found a nice plot of land near Eight Mile Road, just beyond the city's northern edge, but the white developer wouldn't sell to them. My grandpa had to ask for help from one of his Jewish customers, who ended up buying the land and reselling it to my family at cost. They repaid the man's kindness with free egg rolls for years. Mazel tov!

The restaurant's move to 3177 Cass—its location when I was growing up—doubled its size, but Chinese workers were still hard to come by. My paternal grandma, or Ngin-Ngin, tried to solve two problems at once. She had already asked her third-born son—my dad, then a twenty-something playboy—to drop out of community college to join the business; now she sent him across the ocean to find a nice Chinese wife, one who would also fold dumplings for free. No surprise, Ngin-Ngin even had a specific girl in mind.

When my dad arrived in British Hong Kong in 1964, he discovered that Ngin-Ngin's draft pick had a secret boyfriend. Desperate not to disappoint his mom by returning home empty-handed, he hired a local matchmaker, who presented him with a binder full of pretty girls.

Enter my seventeen-year-old mom, whose picture, according to her, so captivated my dad, he agreed to marry her on the spot. She had big dreams of being a Canto-pop star or, if that failed, an accountant. But raised to be an obedient daughter like her two older sisters already in North America, she agreed to marry my father, and she dropped out of high school with one semester to go. The only thing she knew about her future home of Detroit was that it made great cars and even better music.

For generations of Detroiters, our ninety-four-seat dining room was the happiest place on earth. Chung's had it all: ferocious dragons flying across the walls, mosaic lanterns spinning from the rafters, the familiar sounds of Motown soothing the air. For sweets, there were tubs of fortune cookies, a display case full of Wrigley's gum, and a minifridge stocked with bottles of Coke and Faygo. It was like Disneyland Detroit. We even had a mouse or two.

But in the summer of 1967, as the Supremes prepared for the release of their greatest hits and the Supreme Court welcomed one of its greatest stars, Thurgood Marshall, racial tensions erupted across the country. On the morning of July 23, my parents were cooking in the back kitchen when customers burst in, alarmed. After another overnight altercation between the majority-white police force and the Black community, the city was on fire. Like many of the Chinese business owners, our family put a sign in the window—WE ARE YOUR BROTHERS—then shut down for five days, the longest Chung's had ever been closed.

My parents and my two older brothers sheltered in the tiny home they shared with my grandparents and my dad's younger siblings. Somehow, my American-born dad, nicknamed Big Al for his girth, and my immigrant mom, Shui Kuen, the prettiest girl in Chinatown, were able to, in the immortal words of Marvin Gaye, "get it on." Nine months later, I was born, the family's riot baby, otherwise known as "Number Three."

As the third child in a house filled with four brothers, a sister, two parents, two grandparents, and the occasional cousin, second cousin, and family of Vietnamese refugees who my dad took in, I often felt overlooked and overwhelmed. The 1980s in Detroit were tumultuous times. Trying to understand, accept, and establish my own identity by race, class, and sexuality was difficult, especially when these inter-sections contradicted and collided.

The important lessons that guided me through my childhood came served like a big Chinese banquet, from the highs of cooking with my mom and dad to the lows of waiting on some of the rudest customers: a chorus of sweet and sour, salty and savory, sugary and spicy flavors that counseled me toward a well-led, and well-fed, life.

With so much love, family, friends, and delicious Chinese food at our table, this time, I was glad we decided to stay.

APPETIZERS AND SOUPS

A-1.

"Mo-yung!" my short and pudgy grandma screamed at me.

In a Chinese restaurant, using your indoor voice meant yelling at the top of your lungs. Of all our voices, Ngin-Ngin's was by far the scariest. Her screech was so loud, it drowned out the clanging woks and rattling dishwasher. If I annoyed her too much, her standard scolding escalated from "Mo-yung" to "*Jin-hai* mo-yung." This time, she went all Chinese acrobat with a triple backflip: "*Jin-hai jin-hai jin-hai* mo-yung!"

But my grandma was wrong. I wasn't useless. I was six. I could barely tell the difference between sugar, salt, and MSG. I'd offered to help her bake her stupid almond cookies only because my two older brothers, Craig and Chris, had hogged the best seats in front of the busted-up color TV in our back kitchen. It was either baking, watching the timer on the industrial-size rice cooker, or taking a nap on the large stack of hundred-pound rice bags. Slim pickings.

Much of my childhood was spent simply looking for a good place to sit. My parents, who worked all the time, as much as eighty hours a week, didn't believe in babysitters (or child labor laws), so I was often stuck at the restaurant after school, on weekends, during the summer, and on holidays and birthdays. Finding a clean spot to plant my fat butt proved difficult. Hard surfaces ruled our back kitchen—the cast-iron stove, the metal meat grinder, the wooden mahjong table.

This morning, I'd sat at the prep table across from Ngin-Ngin. My grandma's cooking was her one redeeming quality. Her sweets were so tasty, they made me forget how sour she could be. As the warm nutty smell of her baked goods filled the toasty air, she'd told me to put a sliver of almond atop each of the round balls of golden batter, but she could've been a nicer teacher. All she did was shove the bowl of toppings in my face and grunt as she waddled off.

Of course, after seeing how the raw cookie dough resembled Play-Doh, I thought to myself: *Dough, play—duh.* Before long, the baking tray morphed into my new canvas. I used half the almond shards to turn the dough balls into an army of mangled faces and a fleet of ridiculous spaceships. The other half I used to transform the one-inch orbs of flour, butter, sugar, eggs, and Virginia Dare almond extract into baby porcupines.

When Ngin-Ngin returned for the next tray to put in the oven, I happily offered her my latest masterpiece. "Look. This one has fangs!"

My grandma pooh-poohed my artistry. A stern figure whose face resembled the good earth—craggy and dry—she kept a small Buddhist altar by the ever-churning rice cooker. The most devout member of our family, she would burn her joss stick every morning and pray to Guan Yin, the goddess of compassion. But whenever I interrupted her chanting to ask what she was praying for, she would threaten to throw her prayer book at me.

This time, Ngin-Ngin slapped my wrist, sending the tray of cookie dough flying; it went past the bent rabbit ears of the TV and splattered on the dirty green linoleum floor. Craig and Chris, who often ganged up on me, briefly shifted their attention away from their morning cartoons to shoot me one of their nasty *Quit it* glares.

The slap surprised me until I saw my grandma's grin. She loved criticizing me, saying I was fat and danced like a monkey. She must have known I wouldn't be able to resist the temptation to show off my artistic flair. I had given her the perfect excuse to go all Madame Mao. She pointed her fat little finger at the screen door. "Sow ne choot guy!"

My parents and siblings all spoke English, and the multiple dialects I heard at our restaurant confused me, so I rarely used my limited Chinese. But I knew enough of Ngin-Ngin's greatest hits to understand that she was throwing me out. It would've been fun to go and play with the other Asian kids in Chinatown, but my mom had Rapunzeled us thanks to Big Foot. Not the hairy yeti who stalked the Pacific Northwest but the serial killer with size 14 shoes who had raped and murdered seven prostitutes on our block.

As if on cue, my mom bounced in from the main kitchen carrying a stack of clean bowls. At the age of twenty-six, despite already having four rambunctious boys, she was often mistaken for an older sister. Most likely she was smiling because one of the cooks or waiters, all of whom were men, had again complimented her on her rosy cheeks or her colorful homemade dress. That day, she wore the pink one with purple and orange stripes.

My grandma sneered at my mom. "Kai doi."

Ngin-Ngin never referred to any of us kids by a name or even a number; if one of us did something wrong, she used the generic "bad boy." My parents were left to guess which boy she meant. Usually, it was me.

When my mom spotted my flattened artwork on the floor, she shook her head. I wanted to hide behind one of the umpteen refrigerators lined up against the far wall. "I'm sorry," I said. Wasting good food or even making my grandma mad never bothered me. Upsetting my mom did. She had warned me not to cause any trouble, but I'd messed up.

This wasn't the first time. A few weeks earlier, as my mom unpacked our weekly delivery of live lobsters, she'd warned me to stay away from the dry ice. But the swirling smoke looked too much like a witches' brew, so I smacked my big fat tongue on the cold block of tundra. By the time my mom noticed my eyes tearing up, my tongue had cracked and my taste buds were demolished.

Now my grandma looked at my mom in disgust. "Jin-hai mo-yung."

Ngin-Ngin may not have liked us kids, but she hated my mom. From the chatter in Chinatown, I learned that their rift had begun even before my mom arrived in town. Without calling his own mother to confirm, my dad had picked my mom to be his wife. This simple act of free will became my family's original sin. No matter how nice my mom was to her mother-in-law or how hard my dad tried to win back his mom's favor, their marriage would always be unforgivable. Ngin-Ngin withheld not only her love but my family's share of the restaurant's profits.

Seeing how my grandma retaliated against my dad—boycotting his wedding, shredding his photos, and buying gifts like Rolex watches and trailer parks for his siblings but not for him—I understood that a parent's feelings toward a child could be forfeited. If a mom or dad didn't approve of a son's or daughter's choice in life, the affection could be lost. I swore that I would never do anything to lose my parents' love.

My grandma stormed off, tray of rice in hand. I couldn't tell who she wanted to whip with her feather duster more, me or my mom. My mom put down the bowls and untied her apron. "Don't upset Ngin-Ngin. It's not worth it." With a cease-fire in place, my mom led me to the empty mahjong table. "Sit. I'll get you breakfast. You want cereal? Buns? Jook?"

According to my mom, every region in China possessed a specialty. Pretty girls came from Suzhou; silk dresses from Hangzhou. My family's ancestral roots were in Guangzhou, the southern port famous for its cuisine and dim sum. It's why the Chinese say "Sick ja Guang-zhou" ("Eat like you're in Guangzhou").

The restaurant had thirteen refrigerators spread over our main and back kitchens and a walk-in freezer in the basement, so my mom made sure our bellies were always full. Food was the one thing we had in abundance, so we never went hungry. The moment we arrived at the restaurant, a fork, spoon, or chopstick was stuck in my mouth. That's probably why I was such a fat kid.

"Let me make you something to eat," she said. (See?)

"But I'm not hungry," I replied. I had been snacking on almond cookies all morning. I could usually go for something, but I had my limits.

My mom pointed at my older brothers. "Then go watch TV."

"But I don't like Bugs Bunny. He's mean."

Craig, the oldest and the one with the shortest fuse, snapped, "Stop making so much noise."

Chris, number two but the bossy one, picked up the pliers and notched up the volume. "Yeah, and where are those cookies you were supposed to get?"

Hoping to avoid a fight, my mom grabbed my hand. Back then, her hands were still soft; this was before the years of lugging vinegar jugs and rice pots took their toll. She led me to the front of the back kitchen, far from the meat grinder, vegetable press, and other bodies.

Here, there were cases of canned bamboo shoots and baby corn, bottles of Coke, and the broken chairs and tables that my parents were too cheap to throw out. Instead of putting me in a typical naughty chair, my mom sat me on a naughty case of canned peaches. "Is this okay?"

I noticed my mom seemed tired and it wasn't even noon. She had recently given birth to number four, Calvin, and often looked for her own place to rest. I decided not to prolong her grief. I was no longer the youngest. I had to set a good example for my baby brother. "It's fine. I can sit here."

My mom smiled, relieved. She pointed out the window. "You can help watch the door."

My eyes surveyed the cityscape, the same view I had seen nearly every day my whole life. Burton Elementary, with metal bars on every window and door, a single beech tree in its front yard. The old auto-body shop across the street. The pair of ratty gym shoes hanging from the traffic light. The majestic James Scott Mansion, my version of a Barbie Dreamhouse, next to several run-down apartment buildings. The old Chinese bachelors walking and talking with the young and pretty Black and white girls.

"What am I looking for?" I asked.

"Whatever you see."

Throughout the afternoon, as I snacked on more of my grandma's cookies—like I said, she was a good cook—I watched the people come and go from our back kitchen: the waiters picking up a fresh case of Coke, our dishwasher emptying the trash, the ahoos stopping by to gossip with Ngin-Ngin. Every now and then, the slowness would be broken up by the sight and sound of a police car whizzing by, pursuing some fleeing criminal, maybe even a missing serial killer.

In the end, my new location suited me perfectly. Not only did it give me the best view of the goings-on inside and outside the restaurant, but I didn't have to deal with any stupid brothers hogging the TV or my grandma acting like Godzilla with my artwork. I realized everyone had a place in our kitchen—I just had to find mine.

A-2.

Before letting me get on the big yellow bus for the first time, my mom shared with me her mantra for school as well as life: "Work hard. Be quiet. Obey your elders."

She also gave me a little white takeaway bag from Chung's to give to my teacher. It contained some of our best treats: fortune cookies, oolong tea, a pair of pink chopsticks. My mom may have believed in meritocracy, but she wasn't above a little bribery too.

With gift bag in hand, I ran through the halls of Lederle, the elementary school closest to our home near Eight Mile Road. I had one goal in mind: making new friends. In Chinatown, where our restaurant was located, there were other kids to play with, but I was the youngest in that gang. I wanted friends my own size. In school, Craig and Chris had each made friends with a Cho brother. I wanted my own Cho brother.

By the time I found my homeroom, which was all the way at the very end of the hall, it was full. My eyes bounced around as I admired the blue-green globe, the American flag, and the hamster in the tank by the window. I took in the two dozen unfamiliar faces. I started to sweat. No one looked like a Cho. In fact, there weren't any Asians at all—no Chinese, no Filipinos, no Indians. Just Black and white bodies. This was definitely not Chinatown.

The other students were already seated in their own individual desks. After weighing my options, I took an open one by the door (just in case I needed the bathroom). A white boy with short sandy-brown hair, a sport in his green and white Adidas shirt, occupied the seat in front of me. When he turned around with a shining smile, his handsome face glowed like a silver dollar, the kind my grandpa collected. But then again, all the kids looked good to me. When he introduced himself—his name was Erik—I breathed a sigh of relief. School would be okay. In fact, it might even be fun.

Several days into our budding friendship—playing on the jungle gym, trading erasers, sharing our free lunches (strange delicacies like Tater Tots and fish sticks)—I grew attached to Erik. I even rested the bottoms of my gym shoes on the back legs of his chair, just to feel like we were connected. But then Erik leaned over my desk and asked, "Are you half white?"

I looked up from the circles and squares on my paper. "What?"

"Is your mom or dad white? My family's German and Italian."

I scrunched up my face. I had light brown hair, pale skin, and big eyes, the same features as my brothers. I had no idea where this question was coming from.

For once, no words escaped my chatty mouth. I was torn. I didn't want to disappoint Erik—I really wanted him to like me—but if I said I was half white, I would have to give up my mom or my dad, and I couldn't choose one. I liked them both.

Erik and I continued being friends, but the incident pointed to one of the defining aspects of my first year of school. In addition to learning the three basic Rs—reading, 'riting, and 'rithmetic—I would be learning a fourth: race.

I grew up around Detroit, a famously divided city, so the touchy subject came up often. During recess that first week, the Black girls liked to show off their double-Dutch skills. One day, as I cheered on their flashy moves, one of my classmates, Althea, took a break from her jumping. She and her three friends cornered me behind the big dumpster. "Touch that Oriental hair." "It's so smooth." "It's like silk. Is it silk?" Confused, I smiled back. "Thanks. My mom cuts my hair."

Another time at lunch, Wendy, a white girl with freckles and thick glasses, approached me with a special request. After praising everything about Chinese food—which I couldn't agree with more—she asked me if I could teach her how to use chopsticks. She had seen several people use them at a restaurant and wanted to try them. I said I could, but I didn't have any with me. Wendy held up two pencils. I obliged, even though I thought it was a serious health-code violation.

On the playground every day, the boys jockeyed for control of the courts, chanting, "Fight, fight between a Black and white." Unsure which side to choose and hoping we could all play together, I'd give a half-hearted "Go get 'em." Both sides considered my neutrality unacceptable; they taunted me with bars of "Ching-Chong Chinaman" and fake karate chops. Playing the role of Switzerland only turned me into Swiss cheese.

To avoid further conflicts, I sometimes stayed inside with my teacher, Mrs. Ringeiser. The curvy blonde with Farrah Fawcett hair made for pleasant company. After she called me "Mr. Chin," she officially became my first crush. Like a puppy dog, I ran around pushing in the chairs and watering the plants for her, the same chores I did at Chung's. I thought the love was mutual. But one day, things changed. I realized she had no use for me at all.

During class, Mrs. Ringeiser liked to toss out questions, then scan the room for responses. My mom's advice to "be quiet" stuck in my head. But my teacher lavished praise on the other students for correct answers, and I wanted to get in on the action too. I started raising my hand and shouting out the answers. I felt guilty for not listening to my mom, but the high of getting mad respect from my teacher and the other students was addictive. It was the kind of attention I didn't always get at home or at the restaurant.

At the end of the second or third week, Mrs. Ringeiser called my name. At first, my fingers tingled. I expected to be praised for my quick trigger hand, but then I noticed the other kids giving me strange looks. Mrs. Ringeiser pointed to a middle-aged redhead waiting by the door. "Please go with Mrs. Morrison."

My stomach dropped. There were thirty-odd students in the class; why was I being singled out? I knew from watching *Mutual of Omaha's Wild Kingdom* that certain doom followed for any stragglers separated from the pack. I thought to myself, *Don't get up*, as the other voice in my head—the one that sounded like my mom's— echoed even louder: *Obey your elders.*

Mrs. Morrison led me down the hall to a square room not much bigger than a broom closet. The air felt stale. No windows. No plants. Only a few posters were affixed to the wall, some of them illustrations of animals and others trumpeting the twenty-six letters of the alphabet. It felt like a punishment. Maybe I should've listened to my mom and stayed quiet.

Two Black boys, who must've been from the other first-grade

class, were already seated in the hard plastic chairs, their arms folded across the table. Mrs. Morrison looked at her clipboard. "Have a seat, Mr. Chin. Or may I call you Curtis?"

I shrugged and turned to my fellow captives. They seemed average to me except they were a bit quiet. It felt like *Invasion of the Body Snatchers* and they had already turned into pods. My body clenched up. "Do I really have to stay?"

Mrs. Morrison grinned, exposing her teeth. They were big and white, like the Big Bad Wolf's. "We just want to hear you say a few things."

My chin drew back. Was there something funny about the way I spoke? I knew my Chinese sucked, but no one had ever said anything bad about my English. In fact, the other kids in Chinatown—who came from all over Asia—were jealous of my perfect American accent. They said I sounded just like the kids on *The Brady Bunch*. I was practically Bobby!

For the next hour, I sat in the room acting like a circus seal with its snout angled in the air. As she pointed to the posters taped to the wall, I called out the answers: "Tractor!" "Rabbit!" "Carrots!"

After school, as usual, my mom brought me and my brothers down to the restaurant so she could help with the dinner rush. She'd never warmed to the restaurant life—for her, it was more of a means to an end—but her shift was only a few short hours, and if she was lucky, there might be enough players to get in a round or two of mahjong.

The adults ran around the restaurant, and my siblings and I worked just as hard on our homework. Studying was a group activity, so we converted one of the mahjong tables into a communal desk with all the supplies that my parents had picked up at the Teacher's Store:

Elmer's glue, Crayola crayons, and two dictionaries (so we could get a second opinion).

Before beginning our studies, we had to refuel. My mom considered food an essential study aid, and thanks to our well-stocked kitchen, we had over a hundred items to choose from. Since I was feeling a bit down, I needed a pick-me-up. That meant something sweet and sour. Red tomatoes, green peppers, yellow pineapple—a mix of the luckiest colors—surrounded the protein of my choice: chicken, pork, or shrimp.

This time, I picked all of the above.

White rice was the main staple in our house. We served it at nearly every meal, with the possible exception of our Chinese Christmas, which featured Little Caesars pizza and fried chicken. (That would have tasted weird.) Gripping my chopsticks, I shoveled the specks of grain straight from the blue-and-white ceramic bowl into my mouth. The chunks of pineapple sweetened my rough mood, its sugary juices coating my tongue. Every bite was like a therapy session.

When I was mid-snack, my mind drifted back to school. What flaw had my teacher detected? Was it the Hoiping accent from my grandparents, the Cantonese from our cooks, the Black slang from our delivery guy, the Hindi and Tagalog from the other kids in Chinatown, the Portuguese from our cook from Brazil, or even the French-Canadian from the CBC, the station across the river that broadcast Ernest *et* Bart?

When my mom caught me licking the last drops of gooey sauce off the tray, she grabbed the metal container. "What's wrong? Did something happen at school?"

"No. I'm fine." That was the first time I recall lying to my mom. It didn't feel good, but I had no choice. It had been so embarrassing to be pulled out of class like that. I couldn't tell her how I was really feeling. In my defense, my response wasn't completely fake; it was more like a half-truth—I chose what parts to leave out, a skill I became pretty good at as I got older.

"You need help with schoolwork?"

Without revealing too much, I nodded. "Yes, please."

Diplomas were rare in our house. My mom had dropped out of high school; my dad had gone to community college for only a few semesters; my grandpa stopped going to school after eighth grade, and my grandma got only as far as fifth. But as "ABCs"—Asian Buddhist Confucians, a culture where studying led to godliness— they pressured us kids to focus on our ABCs and 123s.

My mom began my extra studies with some positive reinforcement and a little bragging. Public education wasn't available in Hong Kong, but after she'd aced a citywide test, her name appeared in all the local papers, even the *World Journal,* and she—the middle child of seven—earned a full ride to Sacred Heart, an exclusive all-girls Catholic school, where she excelled to such a degree that her fellow students nicknamed her "Abacus."

My dad had promised that she could continue her education in America, but within a month of immigrating, she found herself pregnant with Craig, then Chris, then me. Except for parent-teacher conferences, she never saw the inside of a classroom again. Given that my mom had the brains to match her beauty, I knew that excelling at school had less to do with intelligence and more to do with opportunity.

My mom supplemented my schoolwork with extra lessons written on the back of our paper place mats, the ones with the twelve beasts of the Chinese zodiac. (I was a monkey—clever and creative.) After completing the problems, we'd go over the answers, correcting any mistakes. These study sessions are some of my best childhood memories. They represented a rare chance for mother and son to bond, our common language being math.

The next day in school, I returned to my quiet ways. I sat at my desk, hiding behind Erik's head. I felt like a spy, observing how the words fell from my teacher's mouth. Under my breath, I repeated her inflections and rhythms.

After a week of trips to the Island of Misfit Toys, my exile ended. When the time came for me to leave for my session on Friday, my teacher said I could stay with the class. But my victory felt hollow. The incident reinforced the isolation I'd encountered that first day, when I hadn't seen any faces that looked like mine.

Though I continued to be self-conscious about the way I spoke, slowing down to ensure I was pronouncing everything correctly, I felt relieved to be fitting in. Years later, I learned that what I was doing was called *code-switching*—consciously speaking and acting differently depending on the background of the people around me—but at that age, it was called *survival*.

Thanks to my mom's continuing-education program, and quite a few of my grandma's egg rolls, by the time I reached third grade, my confidence had been built back up, problem by problem, answer by answer. I started to speak up again. Knowing I could do the work, I raised my hand and shouted out the solutions even before being called on.

A few weeks into the new school year, my teacher, Mrs. Berney, an attractive white woman who wore too much blue eye shadow, summoned me to the front of the class. My heart pounded hard. What was wrong? Did my speech sound funny again?

I enunciated my words: "Yes? How may I help you, ma'am?"

Mrs. Berney called a few more names from the attendance roll—"Cheryl Peck, Sharon Johnson, Alan Thomas"—and sent us to several empty desks stationed in the front corner of the room. As the four of us inched over there, I wondered if I could talk my way out of this, offer some plausible explanation of how I spoke, until I realized that our quartet consisted of the students who turned in homework on time and scored highest on the exams. Unless my teacher supported the Cultural Revolution—where the intelligentsia was purged—I had no reason to sweat.

In fact, Mrs. Berney announced that the four of us were being put on an accelerated track. What an ego boost. Yes, it meant more homework, but to me, it wasn't a burden; it felt more like an honor. My mom never called me or my brothers gifted or talented. In fact, she would say we were no better than any other students. She wasn't trying to be mean—at least I hope not. I think what she was trying to say to us was that we could do whatever we wanted as long as we put in the effort.

I had put in the effort, and now victory was mine!

I couldn't wait to get home and brag to my mom. For the reward, which she always gave with good grades, I had a big choice to make: Jell-O or chocolate pudding. I couldn't decide.

As I'd suspected, the news made my mom beam. She patted me on the back for a job well done. "I told you math is better. Numbers don't lie. If you get the right answer, the teacher cannot tell you that you're wrong."

I nodded, acknowledging my mom's wisdom. We went inside, hand in hand. Chocolate pudding sounded great.

A-3.

Sometimes I hated being at the restaurant. Okay, a lot of times I despised being there. Nothing ever changed. Mondays, we made dumplings; Tuesdays, almond cookies; Wednesdays, plum sauce; and so on. Even weekends bored me. By Saturday, our main kitchen was running low on fresh produce for our most popular dishes. With the next delivery not due until Monday, our cooks would send my grandpa—Yeh-Yeh—on an emergency pickup run.

Saturday mornings for me and my siblings were all about our cartoons: *Super Friends, Scooby-Doo, The Jetsons.* Except we each had different favorites and we'd argue over the pliers. My grandma hated the noise, so my parents would send us off with our grandpa. While getting out of the restaurant might sound like fun, it wasn't like we went to the arcade. It was work.

Every national grocery chain had abandoned Detroit, so buying fresh vegetables meant going to Eastern Market, the forty-three acres of food stalls and warehouses across the freeway. Yeh-Yeh liked to get a good bargain, so he'd check out every single vendor and haggle over the price. Our job was to serve as his interpreters and, when that was done, to lug his bags of watercress and gai lan to his gold Cadillac.

Thankfully, one day when I was ten, our routine changed. My grandpa, whose generosity was the yin to my grandma's stingy yang, decided to swing by McDonald's after our run. He had a craving for French fries. While my siblings and I loved eating our Chinese food, we deserved a break today too.

When we returned to the restaurant, Yeh-Yeh helped the cooks unload his haul before sneaking off to his usual hiding place: the gambling den beneath Chung's. (He knew better than to be around when Ngin-Ngin found out about our detour.) Prior to scurrying off, he insisted we follow two rules. One was, after we were done eating, we had to bury the wrappers at the bottom of the trash. We couldn't let any of our customers see us eating American hamburgers. The other was to thank our grandma before we ate. So much for getting a free lunch.

Ngin-Ngin was hunkered down at her prep table. It was Saturday, so that meant making the filling for our egg rolls, which we called chun guen. This involved shredding a dozen cases of cabbage; mixing in the meat, a brown and orange blend of ground pork, chicken, and shrimp; and adding her secret ingredient, a whole tub of Jif peanut butter. Our egg rolls were so popular that we sold over four thousand every week. (This amounted to ten million over the restaurant's six decades.)

My siblings and I sucked in our guts and approached our grandma. "Thank you, Ngin-Ngin! We love you!" It might have been overkill, but we wanted to make sure there were more all-beef patties with special sauce in our future.

When my grandma looked up and saw the bright-colored boxes in our hands, though, she was definitely not happy with our meals. "Aiya, jom say ne ga how!" As she threatened to chop off our heads, she usually had a bloody knife in her hand.

Whatever. It wasn't my fault that my grandma was stuck in our back kitchen. She had only herself to blame. She'd failed her driving test seven times. My mom, who had passed her test on the first try, had taken Ngin-Ngin out driving every morning, but my grandma drove like a turtle, so all the other drivers would honk at her. With no license and limited English, my grandma couldn't go anywhere unless someone drove her.

As my siblings and I sat down for lunch, Chris turned on the TV. We'd gotten back in time to catch our favorite dance show, *Soul Train*. A good song was playing. Earth, Wind & Fire sang about "September," and I jumped up and waved my arms on "the twenty-first night." Unlike math, which relied on predictability, dancing freestyle expressed creativity and randomness, and I loved it.

Ngin-Ngin stormed over and turned off the TV. "Sai hak gwai goh!"

Again, she was wrong. It wasn't "stupid Black devil music." It was Motown, disco, and soul, and it was the soundtrack of my youth. Michael Jackson. Stevie Wonder. Martha Reeves. They were as much my cultural heritage as chicken chow mein and moo goo gai pan. I happened to be in the groove, so I turned it back on. "Come on, Ngin-Ngin, dance!"

"Aiya," my grandma said. She raised her hand to exact a punishment before realizing her fingers were covered in batter. Her head turned toward the main kitchen. "Ah-gin, Ah-gin!"

That was my dad's Chinese name, the one my grandma shouted whenever we were in trouble. Craig and Chris inched away from the TV. Once again, my brothers failed to have my back. They were the heir and the spare. I was just third in line. Dispensable. I turned to look for our mom, but she was busy in front, too far away to notice.

To my relief, Big Al, aka Dad, came sliding in from the other side of the restaurant. A Drew Carey look-alike with a crew cut and thick black glasses, he was a happy-go-lucky kind of guy who loved to chuckle at his own corny dad jokes. He smiled. "What's up?"

My dad and I might have been in the same building, but we rarely saw each other. The restaurant had two distinct halves. The women and children were stuck in the hot and sweaty back kitchen, but the men got to be in the air-conditioned dining room. I'm not sure why my grandma and mom didn't go over, but my brothers and I were banned because of our age. My grandma said it looked unprofessional to have kids running around, so we weren't allowed to go in the dining room, at least not during business hours. But I always had hope. My face brightened up. "Hey, Dad."

Ngin-Ngin pointed at the TV while jabbering in Cantonese. I could usually pick up enough words to understand, but this time, she was talking so fast that I was lost.

My dad turned to us. "Who wants to help in the dining room?"

Oh my God. This was it. This was the day. I raised my hand. "I do. I do."

Craig and Chris, the freeloaders, joined the conversation. "We wanna go too." Finally, some cooperation. Was that so hard?

My dad placed his hand on my shoulder. "You guys promise to behave yourselves?" He was obviously referring to me.

I nodded. "I promise. I won't move at all." As proof, I stood as straight as a pair of newly cleaned chopsticks. "See?"

My grandma shook her head. "Jiu mut?"

"I'll be in the kitchen," my dad said. "I need someone to watch the front door."

Great. Security. That was my specialty. I later learned that my dad wanted us to sit in the dining room because he reasoned that no one would rob a place with small children in it. His rationale didn't make me feel comfortable, but I wasn't arguing. We were being invited over.

Technically, my grandma never gave us permission. It was not her style to give us a yes. Instead, she just stopped saying no.

We quickly dashed toward the short hallway that separated the two halves. As we reached the entryway, I knew I was leaving behind the world of the women and children: my mom; my younger siblings, Calvin and, now, Cindy; and Ngin-Ngin. I couldn't run fast enough.

Our dining room was a bright spot in the grime of Chinatown. Roughly equal in size to the back kitchen but shaped like a square, it felt bigger and more elegant. The floor was fully carpeted, and antique artwork hung on the walls. On his trip to Hong Kong, the one where he went shopping for a new wife, my dad had picked up all the decorations, wooden paintings of the Chinese countryside: rice paddies, mountains, a rickety dock.

On the right wall, a bank of six red booths with high seat backs stretched from end to end. The red vinyl seats were the most comfortable in the whole place. During winters, whenever our cars were stuck under feet of snow and we had to wait for the overnight plows, we slept in here. The seats were so soft. Who cared if our customers had farted on them?

My brothers and I each snatched our own booths, right under the flow of the blasting air conditioner. As the cool breeze blew across my face, I imagined being on a landspeeder cruising across the deserts of Tatooine, trying to avoid the evil Tusken Raiders, aka Craig and Chris.

"Nice try," Big Al said, pointing to the other side of the room. "Over there."

We looked to the left of the water and tea station. That other corner was cluttered with a small table, an old metal coatrack, a stack of plastic booster seats, and two wooden high chairs. "But that side's gross," I said.

"You wanna go back to your mom?"

I shut right up, and my brothers and I sprinted to the opposite side. Chris took the better seat at the table, the one closest to the ice machine and facing the front door. Craig grabbed the other seat, next to the wooden folding screen. With both seats taken, I was left to sit by myself at the next table, the one off the lobby. Once again, I was the odd man out.

Before heading to the kitchen, my dad looked at me. "Sit and behave. You promised."

I tried to make the best of my situation—parked at my own table, staring at the yellow-papered walls—but after fifteen minutes, boredom hit. I kept peeking over at my brothers. Whenever one of them said something to the other, I tried to lean in to hear what they were saying. Occasionally, I'd get up and walk over, which would make Chris yell, "Sit down or you're gonna get us kicked out!"

Eventually, I resigned myself to finding things to do on my own, cool projects to make my brothers jealous. My creativity had to kick in: Twirling the ashtray in circles. Flipping through the phone book to find all the Chinese names. Replacing the boring fortunes in the cookies with my own wisdom, like "Craig and Chris suck."

Mostly, I dove into the stack of newspapers left behind by our customers. The comics that the editors considered funny—*Blondie, Hagar, Family Circle*—I didn't, which forced me to move on to the word puzzles: Jumble, Scrabble, Find-a-Word. It was fun juggling the different combinations of letters in my head. I even tried my hand at the crossword puzzle. I think I might have gotten two right answers that first time, but it was the start of an obsession with words that would only grow over the years.

My dad treated the three of us as human guinea pigs. He popped in several times to make us sample his latest offerings. Thanks to changes in the U.S. immigration laws in 1965, the Chinese community in America had diversified and now included immigrants from other regions of China, such as Sichuan and Hunan. With customers curious about these new cuisines, my dad looked for novel ways to satisfy their palates.

This day, he was trying something called kung pao chicken, a dish with so many ingredients I couldn't identify them all, but they included diced chicken, red and green bell peppers, Sichuan peppercorns, and dried chilies.

As non-Christians, we never said grace, but we always had a moment of silence for the food set before us. Our gods were our chefs. Craig, the most adventurous, gobbled up everything my dad put in front of him, while Chris, the pickiest, sampled only the smallest bite. Craig also liked to eat spicier fare; Chris preferred everything bland. I was in the middle, eating some, but not too much, and spicy, but not too spicy.

As the dinner hour approached, the chairs in our dining room began to fill up. Every time the front door opened, I looked up in anticipation, wondering who would be the next lucky soul to enjoy our pork fried rice and pan-fried noodles. My brothers and I were too young to handle money, so each time the front door opened, I ran into the kitchen and called to my dad, "Customer!"

My dad would come out to help the guests. The most coveted seats were up front, where five huge windows gave diners a full view of Detroit's bustling Cass Avenue. At first, I thought these diners were picking those seats for the beautiful scenery. But then I realized they were watching their cars to make sure they weren't stolen.

Dressed in his polyester waiter's uniform—a red jacket with black trim and pockets deep enough to hold his order pad, pens, and spare chopsticks—my dad looked so professional. In our family, every day was Take Your Kid to Work Day, but I had never seen him performing his magic with our customers. You could tell from the gleam on his face that he loved his job. His voice sang: "Welcome to Chung's. Is this for here or to go?"

Seeing my dad talking so confidently with the different customers surprised me. Here was a man who had spent his entire life in Chinatown, yet he found something in common with everyone who walked into our lobby. Other parents may have warned their kids not to talk to strangers, but my dad encouraged it. Thanks to him, I learned not to be afraid of people who were different from me.

That night, the last customers in the dining room were a young couple in the front booth by the window, under the towering corn plant. It had recently sprouted a fragrant flower, a sign of good luck. My dad called us, and I ran straight over. By now, I had a routine of checking out what was on the table before looking at the actual customers. I wanted to see what they had ordered and how much was left on their plates. These two had done a good job, leaving only a few scraps of bok choy and some brown sauce. I don't know why, but the sight of their empty plates filled me with pride.

I turned to the couple, both in their late twenties. The guy, dressed in a tracksuit, looked white; the girl, who had big hair, looked Mexican. They introduced themselves. He worked as a bus driver, she in some downtown office. They'd both gotten off late and were craving Chinese food. There wasn't anything particularly unique about them, but my dad made them feel special. I think that's why all the customers loved him.

As I stood there, I noticed my dad staying quiet. He just sat there, listening to his friends. I realized that Big Al hadn't brought us into the dining room to give Grandma a break or even to protect the restaurant; he had really brought us there to discover the outside world, which was sitting right at our tables. All we had to do was listen.

A-4.

The U-Haul van was a frequent sight on the residential street behind our restaurant. Every month, an orange-and-gray vehicle would show up in front of one of the dozen or so apartment buildings. My siblings and I would run to see which family was the next to be moving away. If it was one of our friends, our hearts would sink. We'd barrage them with so many questions: *Why are you leaving? Where are you going? Can I have your bike?*

Our sadness would give way to MacArthur-like proclamations of triumphant returns that never came to pass. Once our friends left Chinatown, they disappeared for good. Gone were the late evenings and weekends of playing flag football, Ultimate Frisbee, and Chinese jump rope. It was like another chapter of *Halloween* or *Friday the 13th* and some crazed camper was picking us off, one by one. At this rate, the only kids left in Chinatown would be me and my siblings. If so, that would be a real horror.

The exodus from Chinatown had begun in the mid-1970s. Technically, the area was "New Chinatown." An older, larger community once existed on Third Avenue, but when white flight emptied Detroit in the 1950s and '60s, city officials decided to build a freeway to connect the runaway residents to their white-collar jobs downtown. Despite the protests of its remaining citizens—mainly poor and working class—the city of Detroit declared that Chinatown and Paradise Valley, a Black neighborhood, were slums, and it demolished both.

As compensation, city officials promised to develop a tourist-friendly area called the International District. My great-grandpa Joe—the most successful entrepreneur in the community; he was so wealthy the other men joked that he had more money than Henry Ford—felt an obligation to his customers to keep his empire in the city. Along with a handful of businesses and some residents who were too old, too poor, or too stubborn to head out to the suburbs, he stayed and moved the restaurant to the corner of Cass and Peterboro.

With the area's rising crime rate, thanks to the popularity of a new drug called crack cocaine, which was cheap and easy to produce, New Chinatown was in danger of being wiped out too.

It started with the disappearance of one of our best cooks.

During the day shift, four men worked in our restaurant's main kitchen. The crew hailed mostly from Sze Yup, the four counties in southern China that produced the first wah kius, or overseas travelers. Though we were all Chinese, the cooks and I had little in common. I was friendly, with an open-door policy, but they were like the Great Wall, cold and uninviting. They were foreign. I was domestic. They spoke little English. I spoke even less Chinese.

As one of the few American-born kids in Chinatown—my siblings being the only others—I wanted these immigrants to appreciate my hometown as much as I did. I wasn't rude enough to say, "Go back to where you came from," but I did feel they should've tried harder to blend in. I'm more sensitive now to the alienation that immigrants face, but back then, I thought playing cultural ambassador to help them assimilate would be most helpful.

I tried to give these men a crash course on American culture, or at least Detroit culture. Sadly, my efforts to expose them to the local traditions always fell flat. I couldn't explain to them the difference between a Temptation and a Four Top or why hockey fans threw perfectly good edible octopuses on the ice (an octopus signified the eight wins necessary to secure the Stanley Cup).

Heng Sook was different. He came from another part of the globe, South America, and he was nice to me. As he cooked up some of our most popular dishes—sweet-and-sour pork, breaded fried shrimp, and egg foo yung—he whistled songs from his hometown of São Paulo. Before he told me about Brazil, I was interested in only three countries: the United States, where we lived; China, where our ancestors came from; and Canada, where we got dim sum. Now I realized, like Heng Sook, I could go anywhere.

The fry station, with its boiling vegetable oil next to giant bowls of chicken and pork nuggets and trays of breaded chicken and duck fillets, could get hot, so it sat at the end of the row of woks by the open back door. Whenever I approached Heng Sook to request a snack, he hummed his usual opening number, the first bars of "The Girl from Ipanema."

One afternoon, Heng Sook wasn't singing but talking. Everyone had gathered around the prep table in the kitchen for story time. After elbowing my way to the middle, I heard him recount his cigarette break. Bent at the knees, he demonstrated his squatting position behind one of the outside planters. After taking one last drag, he said that he heard a loud bang. (He slammed the table for effect.) Heng said he stood up to see a man running out of Bow Wah, the restaurant across the street. For once, the kitchen quieted down.

My parents tried to shield us from the dangers of the neighborhood, but they could hide only so much. Our restaurant served as gossip central, and the area surrounding Chinatown, the Cass Corridor, was the most crime- and drug-ridden section of the city. (Yes, Detroit had a bad part.) The majority of businesses in the area were seedy bars, hotels that charged by the hour, and bookstores labeled ADULTS ONLY. (I used to think that was so unfair. Kids liked to read too.)

Over the next few hours, as more ahoos stopped by, additional details emerged. The gunshot had capped the end of a botched robbery. The man darting into the alley was the prime suspect. The yellow police tape meant the place was an official crime scene. What our fry cook didn't realize then was that the restaurant's owner, Tommy Lee, was now dead.

Even though I was young, I don't recall the late-breaking news scaring or upsetting me. Throughout my childhood, I heard sirens whiz by our restaurant every few hours, the vehicles bypassing Chinatown on their way to some other part of the city. Maybe it was time that they stopped by us. Every night on the news, the anchors flashed the sad picture of another victim. Maybe it was time it was someone I knew.

If anything, I approached the murder like an episode of *Hart to Hart*. I wanted to get to the bottom of the crime. Were there any witnesses? Did the police have the weapon? Was the victim's body already cold? I wanted to talk to Heng Sook and hear what he would say to the cops, but I never got the chance. According to my dad, Heng Sook was afraid of testifying in court, so he did a runner. I was upset at my friend. I didn't understand why he didn't want to help catch the killer. He could be the hero. Didn't he believe in fighting for justice? Or had I just seen one too many TV detective shows?

After Tommy Lee's death, Chinatown seemed DOA too. Families began vanishing, as did businesses and community events. The medicine shop and kung fu studio were the first to go, followed by the festive gatherings—Hong Kong movie nights, the Miss Chinatown pageant, and the Autumn Moon Festival. The scant selection of dining options—Golden Dragon, Forbidden City, and the only Indian establishment, the Maharaj—shuttered. Then Shanghai Café closed its doors, and Chung's became the last restaurant standing.

Thankfully, our kitchen remained a bright spot, one still ripe with adventure. In addition to the five refrigerators in the back kitchen, we had eight in our main kitchen; there was also a long service station that featured several prepared soups. It was like a choose-your-own-adventure meal. I was the Soup God, combining the different options into new creations: hot-and-sour soup with wonton dumplings, vegetable soup mixed with yee mein noodles, egg drop soup sprinkled with chashu bits.

Not only was it fun creating my own soups, but I learned some fundamental truths about cooking, like the importance of trying unusual combinations and how adding a single ingredient could change a bowl's taste and that size didn't matter—sometimes, the smallest ingredient, like a dash of salt or pepper, could pack the biggest punch.

One day in the summer before fifth grade, I was scarfing down my latest creation—chicken noodle soup with mushrooms; I'd overdone the noodles, so I'd had to add more fungi—when my dad came in with a glow on his face. "Who wants to go for a ride?"

Usually that meant sitting in the van so he could double-park as he dropped off a delivery at the hospital or police station. Back then, wearing seat belts wasn't mandatory, which was good, since our van didn't have any actual seats in the cabin, just cases of canned vegetables to sit on. The roads were often broken and bumpy, full of potholes, and the only windows to look out from were the two in back. It wasn't exactly a joyride.

My soup of the day tasted pretty good so I decided to pass. "Try what I made, Dad. If you put this on the menu, I bet you'd sell a billion." Every few months, I'd propose a new entrée for our menu, even if it was just a concept and I hadn't actually tasted my idea.

As usual, my dad ignored my suggestion. He grabbed my bowl from me and put it down. "Come on. Everyone else is waiting."

I looked around the room. My uncle Phil, a co-owner with my

parents and grandparents, was reading the paper while our waiters were peeling peapods. But where was my immediate family? Yet again, I'd been so into my own world that I was left out of the loop.

Once my mom, siblings, and I were packed in our faithful maroon Ford E-Series, my dad headed north on the freeway. The city and northern suburbs were laid out in a grid, with the riverfront being ground zero and Eight Mile Road serving as the legal and psychological border between the two. While most people stayed on one side or the other, my family crossed this divide every day, going between home and work.

As our trusty workhorse approached Sixteen Mile Road, I saw a sign at the off-ramp that read TROY, THE CITY OF TOMORROW... TODAY. I had never been this far from Chinatown before. The greenery was new to me. There were barns and farms and even a golf course. From the road, I saw horses and sheep. The only livestock in Detroit were stray cats and even bigger giant rats.

Our final destination appeared to be a new housing development called Sylvan Glen. The project was nothing like the projects in Detroit. The paved streets, so much better than the ones in the city, were clean and smooth. Nearly a hundred homes—Colonials and ranches in various stages of completion—lined the route. We drove past a two-story house with a two-car garage and pulled into its empty driveway on the side.

From the back of the van, I leaned forward. "Who are we seeing?"

My dad, whose smile hadn't left his face during the twenty-minute ride, turned off the engine. "No one. This house is ours."

After picking my jaw off my chest, I asked, "Really? Are you sure?"

My dad nodded yes, sending my siblings and me into a frenzy. We all screamed until the van shook. My dad loved surprising us, but this was a whopper. I couldn't believe this was *our* new home.

Compared to our place in Southfield, this house looked like a mansion with its second floor, olive-green siding, and double-paned windows. We felt like we were George and Weezy Jefferson and we were movin' on up.

My dad clicked open the garage door. My siblings and I swarmed up the driveway like a boatload of pilgrims landing on Plymouth Rock. "I get the big room!" "Not if I see it first!"

When I reached the garage, I turned back to thank my dad. (We had been taught to show our appreciation.) From the clear bliss on his face, I could tell this day meant a lot to him. In his mid-thirties with a beautiful wife and five kids (so far), he had lived his entire life under Ngin-Ngin and Yeh-Yeh's roof. This was his first real home.

I turned to my mom. Her reaction was fuzzy to me. I couldn't always figure her out, which frustrated me. She often complained about her life and about not having the chance to make any choices. Yet whenever she did have the opportunity to decide something, she deferred to my dad. It was as if she were scared of making a mistake. She didn't even feel comfortable picking out new clothes, so my dad bought everything for her. Thank God he had good taste.

When my dad reached my mom on the other side of the van, he threw one big arm around her small shoulders. They looked each other in the eye. Any time my parents showed any public displays of affection, it was always fleeting, as if love were something to be kept a secret between the two parties. This time, the pair lingered. I watched as they looked at each other, still saying nothing. No words were necessary to express their love.

After slipping off our gym shoes, my siblings and I ran through the first and second floors and the basement, opening every window and door. We even had an attic. I was so excited. For the first time in my life, I felt rich. Craig, Chris, Calvin, and I would no longer have to share one bedroom. The four of us could now split up into two rooms. My dad said we'd even get our own beds, though we all still had to share one bathroom.

I wanted to check the outside. I ran through the darkened foyer and whipped open the double doors, which had been painted lucky red, like the ones at our house in Southfield. Sunlight flooded in. The trees and bushes outside resembled an enchanted forest. I stepped onto the porch to get a better view, and beneath my tube sock, I felt a smooth groove on the ground. I looked down to see, carved into the clean concrete, the letters JAP.

I instantly recognized the word. That was what the American soldiers called those sneaky enemies in those war movies on TV. I knew it was a slur, but I laughed it off. Not only had I heard worse things at school, but these idiots couldn't even get their name-calling right. We weren't Japs—we were Chinks. I couldn't wait to show my siblings so they could laugh too. "Hey, guys. Come see this!"

My dad, who was going around the house putting together a list of the repairs needed, happened to be in the foyer making a note of a broken fixture. He poked his head out. "What's up?"

I pointed to my feet. "Isn't that funny?" My dad glanced down. Before I could explain, he yanked me back inside. He pulled so hard, I got whiplash. "What is it?" I asked. "Did you see a spider? Was it a daddy longlegs?"

His nostrils flared as he shut the double doors. "Stay inside."

"Why? What's wrong?"

My dad was generally a happy-go-lucky guy, but there were two things that were guaranteed to set him off: a Tigers loss and anyone saying anything bad about Ngin-Ngin, which none of us were allowed to do, not even my mom. But this was worse. My dad's eyes were beady. His nostrils kept flaring. He looked ready to blow. Whatever it was, I felt like this was my fault. I should've just stayed quiet. If I hadn't opened my big mouth, he would still have been smiling.

On the van ride back to Chinatown, my siblings were still jumping around in back. Chris took charge and handed out our room assignments. He announced that he would be sharing with Calvin, who was still too young to have a say. That left me with Craig. That sort of made sense, since we both liked watching sports, but Craig was upset that Chris had claimed the nicer room—the one with the built-in bookshelf—for himself and Calvin. Cindy, as the only girl, would get her own room. I was too distracted by what I'd seen to make a fuss. Whatever they decided, I would just learn to deal.

As we pulled onto the freeway, Craig directed his frustration at me. "So why were you being such an idiot? What was that yelling about?"

I looked at my dad in the driver's seat. His joy had yet to return, so I said nothing. In the past, when I'd told my parents about kids at school who were teasing me, my mom would say, "Sticks and stones may break your bones, but names can never hurt you." Clearly, she was wrong. The damage caused by words could be even worse. It took longer to heal, if it ever did. I turned to my brother. "Forget it."

Craig said, "You better not act that way in our room or you're sleeping in the hall."

I just looked out the window, waiting for the scenery to become familiar again.

Two months later, our family migrated to our new house. To my chagrin, that included Ngin-Ngin, Yeh-Yeh, and my cousin Patty, who had to share Cindy's room. (She lived with us until my youngest sibling, Clifford, was born a year later.) The developers smoothed over the concrete on the porch, but a long list of other projects remained—finish the bathrooms and basement, build the deck, landscape the backyard, install the railings for the stairs. From the tense conversations between my parents, often late at night, I could tell this was their stretch home.

I was excited about my fresh surroundings. After the house across the street from us in Southfield, where my classmate Leonard lived, was raided by the police as a suspected drug den, my mom never let us go on playdates, so I had no friends. Hopefully, my mom would ease her rules in Troy.

On my first day at my new school, Martell, I looked around for friendly faces. The other kids looked nice enough, but I couldn't help but think, *Where are all the Black kids?* Unlike my old school, this one was 95 percent white. If there had been a "fight, fight" between the Blacks and the whites, I knew which side had won.

Fitting in seemed to be more of a challenge for me in a school where there was one clear majority. In a more diverse school, there was less pressure to conform to a particular side. In Southfield, I could hop around to the different groups, depending on my mood. Martell had one main highway, and we were all expected to merge onto it without getting hit by the speeding traffic.

Despite this obstacle, I managed to make friends. Unlike at my old school, where I was pulled into the corner as part of an accelerated math track, in Troy, all the kids worked at the same pace. Thanks to my mom's extra problem sets, I was a few steps ahead of everyone else. Because I finished so fast, I was able to help the other kids with their homework. Some may have thought I was showing off, but I wasn't going to not play my best hand.

At the new house, the summer's graffiti turned out to be a sneak preview. Each time my parents made a home improvement, it triggered another incident. When we planted flowers, our mailbox was smashed. When we installed a basketball hoop, skid marks appeared across our lawn. When we seeded a vegetable garden, our back windows were shot with a BB gun. I wondered why this was happening. I kept thinking: *If only these people—whoever is doing this—gave us a chance, maybe I could even help them with their math homework.*

Even more hurtfully, slipped under our front door was a letter from a group of neighbors complaining about the delivery van parked in our driveway, which, the note said, was "below community standards." Granted, with its dirt and dents, the van could've used a good wash, but did twenty families need to sign the letter? Couldn't one of them just drop off some soap?

Despite the hostility, my parents chose to stay. The Troy school district had one of the best reputations in the state. According to the real estate agent and my aunt and uncle, who'd moved to this area first, the schools had high test scores, plenty of advanced placement courses, and a strong alumni network. My parents weighed their kids' future against the present. To get a good public school education, we just had to put up with a little discrimination.

With the extra eight minutes it took to get to Chinatown, my mom preferred to stay home. Since she adhered to the belief that friends are temporary, but family is for life, she didn't let us go out and make friends in Troy either. My siblings and I had to stay home and play with one another. It wasn't so bad, since we had a large basement, and if we pooled our action figures together, our reenactments of the Death Star scene were epic.

Chris, the science geek in the house, got to explore his interest in botany. He potted and watered shelves of jade plants, African violets, and Boston ferns that he placed in every room in the house, even Grandma and Grandpa's. Outdoors, he grew pink and red roses. Yeh-Yeh was happy that he had free cut flowers to brighten Chung's lobby.

In the spring, Chris's scientific interests expanded to include zoology. One afternoon, he mentioned the small creek behind his middle school where his classmates collected minnows and snails. He convinced Craig to accompany him on his expedition by offering to let him ride shotgun the next time we went to the restaurant. I decided to stay home since I didn't want to deal with either Chris's bossiness or Craig's sharp attitude.

Our house resembled a northern outpost of the restaurant. Usually, it was a big mess, with unopened bills littering the kitchen counter, dirty aprons and napkins in the laundry room, boxes of paper supplies cluttering the halls. In Southfield, my grandma had forced my mom to scrub the floors until her hands bled. Now that my parents were paying the mortgage, my mom resolved not to clean up after anyone else ever again.

The one chore my mom did keep up with was cooking. She enjoyed hearing all the accolades from her kids that we raced to shower on her, and it reminded her of one of the happiest times in her life. After she dropped out of high school and married my dad, the newlyweds moved into their first home, a small room in a crowded three-bedroom flat in Kowloon that my dad had been renting from a family with five daughters; the father was living in Vegas, working as a cook.

Every morning for three months, as they waited for my mom's immigration papers to clear, they walked to the local markets on Gay Leung Gai. With a strong U.S. dollar, they shopped like kings, buying fresh produce and meat. Back in the shared kitchen, my dad taught my mom how to cook all the recipes from Chung's. She'd never heard of chop suey, but she loved the new flavor. If this represented a taste of America, she was all in.

As my brothers were off exploring the creek, my mom made her tasty Italian spaghetti and meatballs. After arriving in Detroit, she had expanded her repertoire to include more American fare. (Since Marco Polo had "discovered" noodles in China, I'd always considered spaghetti to be honorary Chinese food.) I offered to stay around to help, and by *help*, I meant dip my spoon into the pot every five minutes to ask if the sauce was ready yet.

While my dad cooked like a dog, my mom was a cat. With him, it was an adventure, with no written recipes. He relied on gut and tongue. My mom was more methodical, following the prescribed measurements printed in her *Better Homes and Gardens* cookbook. Both methods produced great dishes, but my mom's had the advantage of consistency. I always knew exactly how things would taste.

I was seated at the big red circular table that dominated our kitchen. As the garlicky sauce simmered on the stove top, my mom handed me her red-and-white-checkered cookbook. "Memorize the ingredients. I will ask you to repeat them later." (Everything was a test with her.) She then headed off to help Cindy with some geography puzzles.

Reviewing the recipe, I tried to follow my mom's lead and commit the ingredients to memory: oregano, basil, onions, tomatoes, ground beef, sugar, and, of course, garlic. I read through the instructions step by step to make sure I understood the whole process.

An hour later, Chris and Craig returned home with mud on their jeans. Their five-gallon bucket, which once contained Kikkoman soy sauce, was now full of dirty creek water and black dots with squiggly tails. I took a closer look. They were tadpoles! Other than the box of turtles gifted to us by a customer—which my grandma had turned into turtle soup—and the alley cats that waited by the back of Chung's door meowing for scraps, these were our first pets.

Unfortunately, my mom was, like the Stevie Wonder song, very superstitious. If I shook my hands or legs, that meant I would be poor. If I didn't finish all the rice on my plate, I would marry a girl with freckles. If I ate the eyeballs from fishes, I would see better. In this case, tadpoles, with their wiggly motion, brought bad luck. She refused to let them in the house.

My mom gave us ten minutes to play with our new pets before we had to come inside for dinner. With the clock ticking, my siblings and I lugged the bucket back to the driveway. Mr. Dudley, our cheerful neighbor from across the street, waved to say hello. He and my dad often stood outside discussing the day's news. The Dudleys happened to be Black. As the only two minority families in Sylvan Glen, we felt an unspoken kinship. Though they saw our dirty van more than anyone, they hadn't signed the letter.

Chris played quarterback, directing Calvin to stand back and sending me and Craig to grab the hose coiled against the wall. "You better not hit my roses!"

Craig was the strongest, so he got the fun part—aiming the water—while I was left to turn on the spigot. As the water in the bucket began to clear, a black-and-white cruiser pulled into our driveway, its siren off. I was confused and excited. I thought maybe they had caught the culprit who had vandalized our porch and wasted all those good eggs. I was about to invite them in for my mom's spaghetti—they'd be our first official guests since we'd moved in—but then I remembered that our house was probably a mess. Would I have time to go in and clean it up?

No metaphorical welcome mat was needed. The two cops, both

white and older, had frowns on their faces. The one from the driver's side tipped his cap. "Your mom or dad home?"

Chris jumped in front of me, probably to stop me from opening my big mouth. My mom, who had left the garage door ajar so she could hear us playing, appeared at the doorway. She looked at the cops, then me and my siblings, then back at the cops. The two men advanced toward her, a thin Asian woman half their size. "We had a complaint about some kids climbing onto the school roof and throwing rocks. The caller said they saw those kids come back here."

I turned to look at my brothers' school, which was only two houses away. Chinese belief held that the businesses closest to a family's home dictated the children's future careers, so my parents tried to live as close as possible to our schools. Heck, my mom would've had us live on the fifty-yard line of the football field if that were possible.

As I surveyed the school's plain tan brick facade, my first thought was *Dang, how did my brothers get on the roof?* Then: *Why didn't I go along with them?*

My mom, the smallest of the three adults standing in the garage, had a different response. Without even turning to ask Craig and Chris if they were guilty, she shook her head. "Not my sons. It wasn't them."

The cops shifted, surprised at my mom's quick defense. "Are you sure?"

"They don't like us here," she said. "It's because we're Chinese, isn't it?"

The cops took a few steps back. "Well, we—"

My mom advanced on them. She must have been holding in a lot of shit as she pointed to the beautiful homes around us, making sure to skip the Dudleys'. "Why don't you go ask those people? Their kids don't get straight As like my kids." (My mom always checked the honor roll to determine whom we were allowed to associate with.) "Did you go to their homes too? Those kids get Cs and Ds."

My mom had clearly broken one of her own rules—be quiet—and it made me so happy. This was her home. She wasn't going to let anyone, not even the police, come in and accuse her kids of causing trouble. My brothers and I all had smiles on our faces. We couldn't wait to see if Mom was going to headbutt them.

The cops surveyed us again. With zero proof, they admonished us with their fingers: "Well, don't go up there. It's off-limits."

As the cop car drove off, my siblings and I chattered away. *How exciting was that? Let's see if they dare come back here!* This was better than *CHiPs!*

My mom exhaled, wiping the sweat from her brow. Watching her not cede a single inch, I learned an important lesson. Just because you're accused of a crime does not mean you're guilty. It was important to stand your ground.

I grabbed my mom's hand. "Good job, Mom."

She looked me in the eye before pointing at the tadpoles. They were still squiggling about. She yelled, "Get rid of them now!" She was right—those little suckers were bad luck.

The visit by the cops hurt bad. For the past year, my family had tried so hard to fit in. If we saw a neighbor at Kroger's, we waved and said hello. At Halloween, instead of trick-or-treating in Chinatown with our cousins, we stayed home and passed out Kit Kat and Twix bars. On Christmas, which wasn't even our holiday, we put up the most strands of lights!

Maybe that day, we realized that nothing we did would ever be good enough.

For the next several weeks, my mom brought us down to Chung's more often. Once again, as the adults ran around the restaurant, my siblings and I had our afternoon egg rolls while doing the extra homework from my mom.

Unlike the others who'd left Chinatown and never returned, our family had found our way back.

A-5.

It was Craig's idea to do the smut run. Two years older than me, he reached puberty first, and he decided to take advantage of our restaurant's proximity to a pornucopia of porn in the Corridor. To cover our disappearance from the dining room, the plan was for him to go out the back door first and for me to follow a few minutes later. Of course, Chris wasn't going to tarnish his image as the golden boy, so he decided to stay behind and practice his Cantonese.

The two of us targeted the big party store a block away on Second Avenue. Unlike the ones in the suburbs, which carried Mylar balloons and colorful confetti, the party stores in Detroit sold cigarettes, lottery tickets, adult magazines, and Mad Dog 20/20 wine. Here we could explore our budding sexuality as well as pick up a large bag of Better Made chips.

After scooching by the Black kids hanging out by the front door, we slowly made our way to the back of the store and the giant shelf of magazines. To throw off suspicion, Craig flipped through the latest issues of *Ebony* and *Jet* before shifting to the good stuff. On the bottom row were all the popular titles: *Penthouse, Penthouse Letters, Penthouse Forum*. In a nod to diversity, they also carried *Big Black Juggs* and *Oriental Teens*.

Craig, a brand-name snob who favored fancy things, went for *Playboy*. As he flipped to the centerfold, a middle-aged clerk who looked to be Chaldean passed by. Thankfully, this was the Cass Corridor. My brother and I were clearly underage—he was fourteen and I was twelve—but no one ever got carded for anything here. The clerk winked before continuing on with his case of beer.

My brother zipped through the rest of the pages. Judging from his bulging eyeballs, he was super-happy. Craig couldn't stop beaming, but when I looked over his shoulder and took in the view, pages of naked white girls in stretched-out poses, I wondered what the big deal was. In fact, I didn't feel anything at all—no excitement, no guilt, nothing—until I spotted another title for sale, *Playgirl*. The cover alone, with the cute white guy, made me want to sign up for a lifetime subscription.

As early as first grade, I had noticed that some boys were better-looking than others—the ones with clean hair, smooth faces, stylish clothes. I didn't think much of it. All kids were unique in some way. Some were athletic, a few artistic, others were math geniuses. These boys just happened to be attractive. I thought I was acting like my dad, noticing the good in everyone.

By the time I hit fourth grade, these observations had grown into fascination. I wanted to spend more time with these pretty boys. Again, I brushed off the significance. I wasn't the only one trying to make friends with them. Everyone was. Boys and girls. My efforts to get closer to kids like Josh and Jamaal, feeding them answers to homework or giving them free mints from Chung's, just seemed to be a typical strategy to become more popular.

This described my situation with Rudy, the cutest boy in Chinatown. A year older than me, the Filipino Fonzie had slicked-back hair and a cute dimple, but his most captivating feature was his mouth, his crooked smile formed with his imperfect lips. I couldn't take my eyes off him. The sight of him made me think, *Halo-halo.*

Rudy brightened every trip to Chinatown. Whether our gang was sitting on one of the apartment stoops trying to win butterscotch candy from the old Chinese bachelors or walking up and down Cass collecting empty bottles to pay for cherry Kool-Aid at the party store, his presence turned me into mush.

When my cousin Wai-mon told me Rudy had moved away, I couldn't control myself. I shouted, *"What? No! Not Rudy! Why Rudy?"*

My swift outburst caused my brothers and cousins to laugh, but I couldn't help it. It was my first real sense of loss, even worse than the death of Mr. Lee, and it hurt.

My cousin gave me a funny look. "What's so big about Rudy? You in love with him or something?"

Duh, of course. Isn't everybody? He's so cute. That's the thought that popped into my head, but from the way my cousin posed the question, I knew she expected a different answer. I instantly connected her response to the words I sometimes heard on the playground, directed not at me but at some weaker boy, things like *faggot* and *That's so gay.* Some innate sense told me that my attraction wasn't just different—it was bad, and I needed to hide it.

Thus, I left the *Playgirl* untouched.

After that first outing, which we both considered a success, Craig suggested we go back again. However, so as not to annoy the owner, he thought we should wait a few weeks, at least until the next month's issue came out. I agreed, hoping that my indifference was due to my younger age. Maybe by then, my hormones would have bloomed and I would be excited too.

Sadly, we never got the chance to go back. Soon after, the owner of the party store was shot and killed in a robbery. A few months after that, another employee—I recall hearing that it was the dead owner's brother—was shot in a second incident. In a neighborhood where going down the wrong street could mean the difference between life and death, my mom forbade us to head to Second Avenue, which my grandma had christened "hak gwai how," or Black devil neighborhood. I didn't know who the actual killers were, but I didn't think to argue.

To protect ourselves from the crime wave hitting the neighborhood and to bring some good feng shui, lucky charms filled our dining room: laughing Buddhas, corn plants with red ribbons, a red-and-gold piece of paper with the Chinese character for "fortune" written upside down. An aquarium—with its flowing water and gold-colored fish—was the most advantageous item. Chris, who had a couple of tanks at home, decided to set one up at Chung's. I offered to help.

The Birdtown pet shop was located a couple of blocks north on Cass Avenue. With cages of parakeets, mice, and hamsters, the tightly packed store brought some feral wildlife to the Corridor. Using money we got for our report cards—twenty dollars per A—we bought guppies, a ten-pound bag of blue and green gravel, some fake seaweed, and a plastic pagoda to make it look Chinese. We set up the tank next to the display case in our lobby and it looked so peaceful. Unfortunately, we'd run out of money and couldn't pay for a water pump, so the next day, we came back to the great guppy massacre.

One afternoon, I went with Chris to the store so he could pick up some more fish for the tanks he kept on the shelf in his bedroom. He was in the back with Pat, the white twenty-something co-owner with the bushy brown mustache. To get the best value, Chris picked the fattest, most pregnant breeders on sale. If he was lucky, by the time he got back to the restaurant, the females would have given birth, producing a bag full of twenty or thirty babies.

As Chris patiently stalked the tanks, I moved on in search of my own exotic animal: Gary, the other twenty-something co-owner, who wore tight tank tops and even tighter denim jeans. On TV, people with blond hair graced every channel, especially among the younger, sexier characters. In real life in the Corridor, though, residents were Asian, Black, Arab, and Jewish. Gary's golden locks and pale white skin made him a unicorn.

I checked both aisles of the store, but my favorite pet-shop boy was nowhere to be seen. Hoping to catch a glimpse of his firm body at work, I tiptoed past the diamond-studded leashes and plush scratching posts. As I went by the counter, the fluorescent lighting reflected off a shiny surface. I leaned in to look. Sitting atop a stack of mail was a catalog whose cover featured an island paradise with a blue sky, white sandy beaches, and a pair of male tourists with Hawaiian shirts unbuttoned enough to expose some nipple.

My feet shuffled past the counter over and over; each time, I pretended to check out the canisters of TetraFin fish food on the back shelf. On my fifth pass, I caught the title: *International Male.* I thought, *Cool, a publication for guys like me who yearned to travel.* This was way better than the *Pots and Pans Weekly* junk mail we got.

My brother's voice drew closer, and I turned to see him approaching with a bag of orange swordtails. Thankfully, his eyes were glued to the swimmers. My heart began beating hard. A mad dog barking in back set off my whole body. I didn't know if it was the monkey or the Taurus in me, but I grabbed the catalog, stuffed it down my pants, and bolted out the door.

Thank God I could run fast. My little legs kept churning, pounding the crooked, weed-covered pavement. The coins and mints in my pocket jostled along with my red Velcro wallet. With each slamming step I took, the catalog's corners poked into my thigh. It hurt so much that my hands had to cover my crotch to protect the family jewels.

Ignoring every DON'T WALK sign, I booked the two blocks to Chung's, passing the welfare center, the pawnshop, then Bow Wah's now empty storefront. Soon, our red awning came into view. I had to slow down. Our cooks were outside on another cigarette break. When they saw me waddling like an injured duck, they cupped their own privates. "Ne yow tze saw?"

"I'm gonna pee on you if you don't move it!" I screamed. They moved right away.

Inside, I searched for a place to hide and sit, but all my usual spots were taken. Craig was in my grandpa's office organizing his collection of Topps baseball cards. Calvin was by the canned peaches reading a book—probably something from the Mr. Men and Little Miss series that my dad bought him—while my mom was at the mahjong table making Cindy show off her world-geography skills to some ahoo. By the age of two, she could assemble a map of America.

I needed more privacy to view my own Mr. Men, preferably a place that wasn't a hundred degrees. I had the perfect spot in mind. I ran downstairs to our walk-in freezer. It was where we kept our bags of bean sprouts, baskets of live lobsters, and bushels of green vegetables. It was also the best place to hide when we were playing hide-and-seek.

The enclosure, about the size of the back of our van, felt damp. Condensation coated every surface, but I didn't care if my butt got wet. I sat atop the stack of peapods and pulled out the catalog. I took a deep breath before plunging in. Bon voyage.

Inside the pages, an array of men—all white and in their twenties or thirties—modeled sexy swimwear. Their tanned and muscled bodies glimmered, but my eyes zeroed in on one feature: the massive bulge between each man's perfect thighs. The mounds were so huge, it looked as if they had stuffed their trunks. By the fifth or sixth page, I felt some tingling in my gray corduroys. I looked down at my flat, prepubescent groin. It wasn't as big as theirs. How many socks would I need to fill out my pants? Did I even own enough pairs?

I don't recall how long I stayed in the freezer, but it must've been a while. I had gone through the catalog enough times for some of the colored ink to rub off on my fingertips. My session ended only when our head cook, Kin Sook, came in for some gai lan. I didn't want him or anyone else to see the excitement on my face or in my pants, so I made some excuse about playing Attack of the Sea Creatures with the lobsters and ran out.

One night, after finishing some more extra math problems, I was snacking on a plate of chicken chow mein. Noodles were a sign of health and longevity, so I tried to eat them at least two or three times a week: lop chow mein, Singapore noodles, yee mein with shrimp and eggs, Cantonese-style. I could usually finish a whole entrée by myself, but when our front door opened and Gary the god walked in, I nearly choked.

He was with Pat and two other guys I recognized from their store. Every week or so, one of them came in for a large carryout. But there weren't any bags on the back table to be picked up. I figured they must be dining in. Or maybe it was something else. My mind jumped to the stolen goods still in my schoolbag. Did they know I'd taken the catalog? Had the four of them come to retrieve it? If they knew it was in my possession, would they tell my mom or dad?

Looking down at my remaining plate of noodles, I felt ready to hurl.

The quartet, who all looked hip and happy, were dressed in vests and Jordache jeans. My dad greeted them with a nod. As fellow business owners, my dad and the guys were part chamber of commerce, part neighborhood watch, part survivors' support group. Given the size of their party, my dad skipped his usual greeting and led them straight to the front booth.

I focused on Gary. He sat facing in my direction. I smiled and he smiled back, or at least I like to think he did. He looked so handsome sitting in our booth. Cute face. Nice hair. Fit body. A thrill zipped through me as I admired him. In that instant, a realization hit me.

I had always thought that my attraction to guys was due to my friendly nature, an inheritance from my dad, or simply a desire to hang out with the older boys. But now I saw it as something real. Something more. Something possibly sexual.

I suddenly understood what Craig saw in those spreads from *Playboy* and *Penthouse*. It was a physical attraction of pure joy and lust, a carnal knowledge. The pictures in my head had advanced from G to PG and were well on their way to R or even triple X.

I was scared that our guests might discover my secret—my sexual attraction to other boys and men—and my survival instincts kicked in, so I did the only reasonable thing I could do: I fled to our lobby and slipped the catalog into our lost and found.

As the weeks went by, the photos of the gorgeous men from the catalog kept revisiting my head. Their toned bodies and twenty-dollar trunks may have been out of my reach, but I didn't care. The images of the sandy beach and warm sun looked so enchanting that I needed to believe that that life was possible. Sure, the clothes were too expensive and the men were all white, but maybe there would be a sale, and didn't those guys need a cute Asian friend?

The mail-order catalog gave me my first extended glimpse of a life very different from the one I had in Detroit. Who these people were or where this place might be, I hadn't a clue. But the excitement it generated in me told me that, one day, I would need to find it. I just hoped I'd have my passport.

A-6.

In Detroit, the Motown sound was everywhere, and in my mind, the one and only Diana Ross reigned supreme. Her sweet, youthful voice combined with her radiant smile served as an inspiration to me. In addition to sharing Chinese zodiac signs—the year of the monkey—we were from the same area; the international superstar had grown up blocks from our restaurant in the Brewster-Douglass Housing Projects, the largest government-subsidized housing in Michigan. Though Ross's label, Motown Records, had abandoned the city a decade ago, I used to fantasize that one day the singer would make a splashy return and we'd share a dinner for two in our front booth.

When I reached seventh grade, Diana's hit "I'm Coming Out" came bursting onto the airwaves. I was twelve, and the term *coming out* was new to me. I had never heard it before. I thought it was cool, but I didn't think it had anything to do with being gay or lesbian. The lyrics were more universal. The song championed personal freedom and independence. I could definitely relate, as there were four adults in our house with a thousand heavenly mandates (that is, annoying rules).

Whenever the song came on the radio, I cranked up the volume and channeled my inner diva. Unfortunately, one morning before we opened, as I sang along in the dining room, I had an unexpected audience: Derrick, one of our younger waiters. A member of the old kung fu club, the John Travolta wannabe had a ripped chest that he liked to show off by leaving a button or two undone. As I shook my booty and stretched my lips, pink chopstick in hand, he snuck up behind me, and when I turned, he swished his hand from side to side. His limp wrist may not have been a motion in American Sign

Language, but the gesture was so well known that even a Chinese waiter from Hong Kong understood its meaning: *fag*.

Thankfully, no one else was in the room, and Derrick had the memory of a goldfish; he never brought up my dancing again. But his accusation put fear in me. No one in my family ever said anything anti-gay, not even Ngin-Ngin, who could spout some pretty offensive things about race and gender, but no one said anything positive about being gay either. That left a big question mark in my mind. How would they react if it turned out to be true, that I was like that?

Back in the early 1980s, the perception of gays and lesbians outside the major cities on the two coasts, pre-AIDS and pre–pride parades, was much harsher, more toxic, than it is today. There were no positive role models in music, television, or film. Homosexuals were lumped in with drug users, alcoholics, and pedophiles. There was no guarantee that things would get better.

But despite my resistance and denial and the many cold showers I took, I couldn't ignore my growing attraction to boys. It happened too often to be a fluke or a one-off. Until I could figure out what this all meant, I needed space to sort through it. To buy myself time, I tried my best to blend in.

After the close call with Derrick, I paid more attention to the way my body moved in the world, how I walked and talked, ate and laughed. I started to notice how others were perceiving me too. While I didn't think I had any effeminate habits, I still tried to butch things up. No more silly dancing to the Queen of Motown. I needed to find a strong, respectable male role model, one who was straight.

First, I thought back to images from TV. Actor Benson Fong—who happened to be a relative; he'd married my grandpa's younger half sister Gloria—was one of the most recognizable Asian American stars of the 1960s and '70s. Playing a series of honorable, family-oriented father figures, he most famously appeared as "Number Three Son" in the Charlie Chan detective films and as a wise neighbor on the sitcom *My Three Sons*. Whenever he came on TV, our entire family gathered around the set as if we were about to discover who'd shot J.R.

According to my mom, Benson Fong was as kind and trustworthy in real life as the characters he played on TV. She often recounted for us the story of her first and only visit with the star. After my parents' rushed wedding in Hong Kong, the newlyweds swung through Los Angeles for a three-day honeymoon. Following a trip to Disneyland, my parents were invited to eat at one of Benson's Ah Fong restaurants. He had several locations throughout Southern California serving such A-list celebrities as Frank Sinatra and Gregory Peck.

When my mom first mentioned that Benson had what seemed to me like a second job, I was surprised. "He's a big TV star. Why is he making Chinese food?"

"Benson has five kids. They have to eat." Her answer left me more confused. I knew all my family members wore multiple hats, but did Hollywood celebrities do that too? Were Erik Estrada and Alan Alda selling tacos and pizza on the weekends?

My next potential role model came from the big screen. My parents were always busy with work, so I recall them taking us to the movies only once, when I was around this age. My siblings and I were in the back kitchen annoying Ngin-Ngin just by breathing. After my grandma complained to my dad, he suggested we go catch a show. I had to clean the wax out of my ears to be sure I'd heard that one.

My mom looked up from her bowl of filling. "No. We can stay here."

It wasn't that she hated movies. My mom loved them, especially the American ones she had watched with her siblings in Hong Kong. In fact, she'd named me after an actor in one of her favorite movies, the

American drag comedy *Some Like It Hot*. The movie starred square-jawed he-man Tony Curtis eluding an angry group of gangsters by disguising himself in an ill-fitting wig and a frumpy sundress. Basically, she'd named me after the worst drag queen ever.

But as finance director of the family, my mom set the budget. Her priority was education, not entertainment. She never hesitated to take us to the Teacher's Store, but we rarely set foot in Toys"R"Us or Harmony House. Movie theaters were a mystery too. All the first-run houses were in the suburbs, and even the ticket prices for the second-run theaters in the city were too high for a family of, at the time, seven. Besides, we had TV and that was free.

My dad stacked up our schoolbooks. "It's a weekend matinee. Tickets are half off."

My siblings and I turned up the pressure: "Please. We promise to be good."

My mom turned to Chris as if he had a say. He was her sounding board on any potential social activity; he assessed its educational value. My brother, who wasn't a total dweeb, shrugged his shoulders in approval. My mom put down her bowl. "When we come back, you all have to do extra math problems."

We cheered. I even patted Chris on the back.

"*Star Wars*," I screamed. That was a no-brainer for me. The international blockbuster had been out for months, but the kids at school were still raving about Han Solo this, Luke Skywalker that. I might have been late to the party, but I still wanted to join the rebellion.

My dad had his own movie in mind. His face lit up. "Let's see *Return of the Dragon*. It's got Bruce Lee."

Bruce Lee? No friggin' way, I thought. That guy was the worst. I hadn't heard his name in years, but at my old elementary school, the Black and white boys used it as the punch line to every joke.

Whenever they taunted me with their pseudo karate chops, they invoked his name. "Show us your kung fu, Bruce." "How high can you kick, Bruce?" "Crack this pencil with your flat face, Bruce!"

Unfortunately, everyone else was just happy to get out. Overruled, I grudgingly joined my siblings in the back of our van.

The film was playing at the Fox Theatre on Woodward Avenue. Built in the 1920s, the movie palace that had once hosted live stage shows with stars like Shirley Temple, Frank Sinatra, and my mom's favorite, Elvis Presley, now survived on a rotation of *Shaft* and *Superfly*. We entered the cavernous interior, which had a strangely Oriental motif; the design was amazing, even more ornate than the artwork we had at Chung's. But there was little time to appreciate its grandeur before the lights dimmed. We grabbed the only open seats, which happened to be in the back row. I got a whiff of buttered popcorn, which smelled way better than the bag of dried chow mein noodles that my mom had taken out of her purse.

The movie began, and I slowly became a believer. Every time Bruce creamed one of his opponents, I slapped my knee hard. The whole audience must've agreed, as the refreshments went flying. The final bout pitted Bruce's character against his archrival, played by Chuck Norris. When he snapped his nemesis's neck, the theater burst into cheers: "Get 'em!" "Slam 'em!" "Honky!"

I wasn't used to such loud reactions. I looked around and realized that, except for us, everyone in the theater was Black. I figured I should just follow the crowd. I jumped up and down. "You show 'em, Bruce! Teach him who's boss!"

My mom yanked on my shirt. "Sit down or we're not coming back!"

I tried to stay seated, but I couldn't stop myself. The release of these pent-up emotions felt so liberating. Bruce wasn't like Arnold, the wacky Japanese American diner owner on *Happy Days*, or Hop Sing from the reruns of *Bonanza*, or the clueless husband in the Calgon commercials. He was the big dog, and he got to kick ass.

I made my family stay through the end credits, then it was time to head back to study. The sidewalk was packed with moviegoers as we waited for my dad to get the van. I mimicked some of Bruce's best moves—a chop there, a kick here. Some other fans outside the theater pointed at me and giggled. It felt like déjà vu, the start of another playground putdown. I turned to my family for cover, but they were climbing into our metal carriage. I closed my eyes, bracing for the barrage of fake *hai-ya*s.

But the hits never came. I opened one eye and saw the expression of one of the boys, who was about my age. He was smiling. The tension in my shoulders dissolved as he and his friends pumped their fists in the air. "Aw, man, that movie was sick! You done killed it!"

Okay, it was kind of racist for them to assume I had anything to do with the movie—that would have been like me complimenting them for Diana Ross's excellent *Theme from Mahogany*—but it hit me that they were admiring Bruce, not mocking him. He was my man, but he was their man too. In a world with so few brown, black, or yellow stars, maybe it was okay to share our heroes.

Sadly, we never saw another performance. My siblings loved seeing Bruce as much as I did, and we pleaded for a repeat outing, even Chris, but since my dad had slept through most of the film, even snoring for a stretch, my mom didn't see the value of having Bruce in our lives. "Why waste our time sitting in the dark when we could be studying in the light?"

She wouldn't bend. Not even on Jewish Christmas—when our biggest demographic of customers engaged in their annual ritual of Chinese food and a movie—would she take us to the theater. We had to settle for eating leftovers and watching *It's a Wonderful Life* on free TV.

In my ongoing quest to find a straight male role model, I turned to musical theater. If I couldn't have a queen as my muse, then I would have a king.

One night, a delectable aroma, a mix of ginger, garlic, scallions, and star anise, infused the air of our back kitchen. Kin Sook, dressed in his white apron, was preparing the evening's group meal. As at most Chinese restaurants, the staff ate together once the customers had been served. Often called our "secret menu," these dishes tended to be the more traditional fare that my grandma didn't think our non-Chinese customers would appreciate, so they never appeared on our printed menu. Not surprisingly, these were some of our tastiest dishes.

Tonight, it was one of my favorites, see yao gai. (Yes, I had a lot of favorite dishes.) The easy-to-cook entrée was made by simmering two whole birds, including their heads and feet, in a giant pot of the aforementioned ingredients along with lots of light soy sauce. In order to nab one of the four drumsticks, I had to kiss our head chef Kin Sook's ass.

As I paced the hall between the two kitchens, rehearsing one of the few compliments I knew in Cantonese—"Gum ho sick"—my dad trundled by. He went straight to Ngin-Ngin, who was standing in front of the open refrigerator.

"Guess who just called."

Ngin-Ngin, who was clutching her Tsingtao beer, crinkled her face. In a family of teetotalers—or "tea-totalers"—my grandma was the only one who drank alcohol. At the end of a long day, she liked to unwind with a tall cold brew. We knew not to interrupt her during her moment of Zen. My dad must've had big news. He couldn't control himself. "*The King and I!*"

The King and I was the hit Broadway musical about the king of Siam and the English tutor he hires to teach his young children. Its revival, featuring Hollywood star Yul Brynner, was touring and soon would be opening at the largest theater in Detroit, the Masonic Temple. During weeks of preproduction and rehearsals, the cast and crew had been ordering takeout.

"They want us to host a private cast party," my dad said.

I had no idea what that meant, except that it was private, it involved the cast, and it was a party. The only parties I had ever been to were for weddings and anniversaries. I was in.

My dad was psyched. Big Al had a lot of pride. Like me, he'd grown up in the family business, so he had heard all the jokes about Chinese restaurants being dirty and greasy, about people getting headaches from MSG. It bothered him that our tasty cuisine didn't get the same respect as others, like French and Italian. To him, this reservation from people working with a big-time Hollywood star was confirmation that the meals we made were worthy of royalty.

When the big day arrived, my dad brought his A game. He pushed together eight tables to form one long seating area in the center of the dining room. He put out brand-new tablecloths with matching plates and silverware. He scrubbed all the teapots and filled the ice bin to the brim. He even bought ice cream, the fancy Neapolitan kind.

For backup, my dad asked my older brothers and me to work as busboys. We had been helping out our whole lives, doing random side work and trying to be sous-chefs, but this was our first official job. Though we were still unpaid, it was nice to have a title. My dad even gave Craig and Chris red jackets to wear. (I was still too small for the smallest size.)

Around five p.m., several members of the show's team arrived, lugging huge floral arrangements, rainbow gift bags, and a case of wine. The production hadn't been able to guarantee there'd be enough people to fill the whole dining room, so my grandma let them have the front half only. As a security measure, they conducted a formal sweep, checking the bathrooms and fire exits. I wondered if they did that for restaurants in every city or just the ones in Detroit.

An hour or so later, I waited at the back table for the show to begin. The place was already half full, good for a Monday night. Though the production people had warned us about contacting the press, my dad might have secretly tipped off a few of our best regulars. When the star and his well-dressed entourage finally entered our lobby, every head in the room turned toward them. Jaws dropped. Eyes popped. Hollywood had come to Chung's.

The pictures I'd seen in the papers made Yul Brynner appear to be a giant, but he was no taller than Ngin-Ngin standing on one of her overturned Coke crates. Hoping to catch his attention, I grinned so widely my cheeks hurt. I expected him to pass by my chair en route to our coatrack. Instead, he handed his fancy outerwear to an assistant. It was okay. He had only just arrived. There would be plenty of time for us to bond.

Yul occupied the center of the table, and the party orbited him. After a few rounds of egg rolls and fatty chashu, they placed several orders for their favorite dish: worr dipp harr. The elegant presentation featured six large butterfly shrimp, each layered with a strip of bacon, dipped in egg batter, pan-fried on a hot skillet, then set on a bed of raw onions and topped with a delicious orange sauce, green onions, and crushed peanuts. Because of the different steps involved, it was the dish that took the longest to make.

Throughout the night, Yul and his guests threw out a million requests—they wanted extra sauces, more tea, the lighting adjusted, the curtains opened, six feet separation from other diners. My dad was happy to provide them with five-star service.

The other customers lined up at our pay phone, eager to call their friends and families and give them the play-by-play. The waiters shuttled through the black doors, alternating between full and empty plates. The cooks took turns popping in to catch a glimpse of the star savoring their dishes. Even Ngin-Ngin checked in, though she pretended she was only there to refresh her tea.

With Craig and Chris doing most of the cleanup, I stayed in my seat, jotting down tips from the king of Siam. He was a man's man and he was giving me a master class in strut. His posture and hand gestures were so regal. He commanded everyone's attention, even people sitting two tables away. If only I could be his young prince, arms akimbo, my chest puffed out.

As I quietly mimicked his machismo, I formulated a plan to meet him one-on-one. Our men's bathroom offered the best privacy. That's when I could corner him and ask for some private tips. Every time his glass got close to empty, I offered to fill it again, but my brothers stepped in to do the work. I kept sending Yul telepathic messages: *Go pee, go pee, go pee.*

But it never happened. Either he loved being the center of attention so much that he couldn't pull himself away or he had the bladder of a camel.

Three or four hours later, the partiers had finished their desserts and post-meal chitchat. After settling their bill, they got up to go. This was my last chance to introduce myself, maybe get in some good face time. I took a deep breath and strutted toward his table.

Interrupting my approach, my dad appeared, holding his Polaroid. I was surprised. We had few pictures in the house or restaurant. Not only were the adults too busy working to take snapshots, but my grandma had thrown away most of our family photos, especially the ones with me and my siblings in them, after she'd used our pictures as dustpans. Judging from my dad's smile, he must have really wanted to savor this moment.

I stepped back to give him space. I wished I could jump right in, but if anyone deserved to meet Yul, it was Big Al. He had spent all week staying late and given up every spare hour to make sure everything went smoothly. This was his big night more than anyone else's. I couldn't take that away from him. My dad held up his camera to Yul. "Do you mind?"

"Oh, I can take it," I said. I reached for the camera. My dad smiled and gave it to me. Finally, a job for me to do. I was the evening's official photographer. I looked through the eyepiece for the best shot, but it wasn't necessary. The star raised his hand. "No photos."

My dad was taken aback. "Oh."

Yul motioned to the big bodyguard who had been sitting at a small table off to the side. "Give him your address. We will mail a photo to you."

Yul's terse response confused me. He was standing right there with my dad. Saying yes would be so easy, easier than saying no. He could've even saved himself a stamp. My disappointment and anger began to grow. If I'd been one of the citizens of Thailand, I would have overthrown this king. His head would be on a stake.

My dad, however, lived by the old adage "The customer is always right." He clasped his hands and bowed like a good Chinese waiter. "Hope you enjoyed everything."

I waved at my dad, wanting to get his attention and tell him to ask again. But he wouldn't turn to me. He kept backing off as Yul headed in the opposite direction.

I watched my dad watching Yul exit our front door. I handed him his camera and thought this was one lesson that I would not be learning. If a customer was ungrateful or rude, I would respond in kind. I much preferred the advice of Detroit's own daughter Aretha Franklin: "R-E-S-P-E-C-T. Find out what it means to me."

After getting our family's information from my dad, the bodyguard asked if anyone else wanted to receive a photo in the mail. Chris, who had earned his souvenir by putting in a hard day's work, noticed that I wasn't in line. "You better get your own. I'm not sharing mine."

"It's okay," I said. "I don't even care if he is Asian."

My brother rolled his eyes as he took off his jacket. "He's not Asian."

I threw up my arms. "Yes, he is. He's the king of Siam." Everyone within earshot started laughing. I acted as if I were in on the joke.

My dad leaned in. "That's the role he plays."

It never occurred to me that Yul Brynner wasn't Asian. I assumed Asian actors played Asian characters, the way Black actors played Black characters and Mexican actors played Mexican ones. I never saw Benson Fong play anyone non-Chinese. A few of the waiters tried to guess Yul's ethnicity—Indian, Russian, Portuguese—but I didn't care anymore. Whatever he was, he was no role model for me. A jerk was a jerk, no matter his race.

My dad went into the kitchen to help Kin Sook prepare the group dinner, and I couldn't wait to clear the bad taste in my mouth. I did, however, learn a big lesson that night: There were lots of different ways to be a man. If the values that were important to me included compassion and kindness, then I didn't need to look very far to find the best role model. There was one standing in front of me wearing a red waiter's jacket.

A-7.

On a Sunday morning, the one day we got to sleep in, my parents woke me and my siblings up early. I wasn't a happy camper, but I couldn't argue. It was Qingming, or Tomb-Sweeping Day.

After my brothers and I got dressed in black slacks and button-downs, we swung by Chung's to pick up a large tray of crispy roast pork, thick and doughy deep-fried hom sui gok, and another of my favorites, bak chit gai, poached chicken with scallions, ginger, oil, and salt. The food looked and smelled great, but it wasn't for us. It was for the dead.

Michigan in May was always gray and cold, the last month with a good chance of snow. After caravanning to the Evergreen Cemetery, we gathered in the small Chinese section with several branches of our extended family. In preparation for an afterlife bash, they lit three joss sticks and burned a thick wad of paper money before pouring shots of whiskey over the muddy dirt. They then took turns stepping forward to pay their respects to our ancestors, the ones who had fought so hard to be buried in this American soil.

When it came time for my family to approach my great-grandpa's tombstone, my parents bowed three times—first to heaven, then to earth, then to humankind. My dad then pointed at me and my siblings, signaling we were next on deck. Still sleepy and dreaming of hash browns and pancakes, I dragged my feet up to the grave's edge. Etched in marble was one of the few Chinese characters that I could read and write. It was our family surname, Chin.

Recognizing the simple brushstrokes, I was reminded of my own name, Chin Kwok Toy. In contrast to my legal name—Curtis Wing Chin—the three parts were reversed. Here, family came first, then generation, and finally the individual. While it was cool to know that my great-grandpa, the one who named me, had predicted I would be "the creative talent of the country," I was more struck by the ordering. It was a not-so-subtle hint that the individual came last.

Before everyone scattered to the suburbs, the family formed a tight circle. It was time to reflect as the adults reminded the younger generation of our family history. (This was where my mom learned most of her stories.) I wanted to wait in the car, where I could at least wake up to some MJ, but my parents said we had to listen to this instead, as if someday there would be a test.

Our family's journey began in Boh Yuen Fong, one of the poorest villages in the city of Hoiping, located in one of the poorest counties, Taishan, in the poorest province, Guangdong, in all of the Middle Kingdom. Did I mention my ancestors were poor? Like, the no-shoes, no-education, no-toilet-paper kind of poor.

As the eldest son of an eldest son, my great-great-grandpa Gong Li had no choice but to go out and ensure the health and longevity of the family tree. He arrived in Detroit but found that the welcome mat in America was not as wide as he had hoped. Fearing competition and depressed wages, the white autoworkers, recent immigrants from Europe themselves, protested the hiring of the even newer Chinese. With no chance to join the automotive revolution, Gong Li took whatever work he could find, mostly in domestic and household affairs.

If my ancestor was disappointed or angry about this, no one ever said. The family never discussed his hardships, only the joy of what he did with the cash he earned—like send money back to China and buy his fancy Model T. Did it ever occur to him that he could have demanded better, fairer treatment? Or maybe, as an immigrant, he just accepted that discrimination was part of the price of living in a new country.

I harbored no such appreciation for second-class citizenship. My parents always told me that the United States was not our *new* home, it was our *only* home. This was our soil. Their reminders reinforced my love for America, not so much because of the opportunities the country had given us, but because of our contributions to this work in progress. Yes, my family succeeded because of America, but America also succeeded because of us.

In late November, our extended clan gathered once more. Originally, the celebration was for my great-great-grandpa's birthday, but after his passing, it switched to being about Thanksgiving. Our restaurant was open 364 days a year. That was the one day we closed. All of our customers were home celebrating with their relatives, so my grandpa, who was the oldest of all the siblings and thus responsible for keeping the family together, threw a giant party for us.

Our restaurant was packed. China may have enacted a one-child policy, but my family more than made up the difference. Joe had been married three times, producing ten children and forty grandchildren. There were Chins, Chungs, Wongs, and Moys everywhere. My dad also invited a few longtime customers, so the party included some Greenbergs and Weinsteins too.

In reality, there weren't any *real* Chungs in the house. My great-grandpa had opened the business with his oldest daughter, Tui, and her husband, Harry. They used Harry's surname because he spoke the most English. But like most of the other Chinese in Detroit, Harry was a paper son: To work around the Exclusion Act, some boys and young men in China bought identity papers from Chinese Americans that "proved" they were the children of U.S. citizens. Harry, born a Yee, had purchased the name Chung. So in reality, our family restaurant bore the name of some stranger.

But Joe was proud to be a real Chin. In addition to being the name of the first emperor of China, Qin Shi Huang-ti, it was the name he had been given by his ancestors, one of the few things he carried with him from China. Though Yee was the most common Chinese surname in Detroit and there were only a handful of families with our last name, he founded the local chapter of the Chin Family Association, Gee How Oak Tin.

While Christmas was about the presents, Thanksgiving was about food and family. For our big meal, which happened at lunchtime, the men in the family battled for bragging rights for the best entrée. Because so many of them had gone into the restaurant business, there were always too many cooks in the kitchen, but my dad's Chinese roast chicken easily bested the rest. The day before, he had begun his preparation by slathering over twenty birds with his homemade marinade and hanging them to dry in the back hall in front of a giant whirring fan. After roasting them in the morning, he applied more sauce and scallions. Without fail, the two dozen platters would be gone almost as soon as they hit the table.

My mom's side dishes—which she made only for this day—were popular too, especially her sweet yams drenched in honey, butter, and melted marshmallows. A pair of honey-baked hams, bowls of buttered corn, stuffed tofu, gai lan with oyster sauce, green beans, pumpkin pie, and steamed rice completed the menu. The only thing missing was turkey, as we considered it to be the other white meat— as in, only white people ate it.

After stuffing our bellies—and dodging the one Christian cousin who kept asking us if we had heard "the good news"—the members of the extended family piled into their minivans and headed back north of Eight Mile. The Chinatown side stayed behind to clean up. The adults did a rush job, as they were eager to move on to the highlight of their day: a marathon session of mahjong. Between my family, our workers, and the handful of ahoos, there were enough players to seat four tables.

Meanwhile, my siblings and I, along with our second cousins—Wai-mon, Wai-kit, and Wayne—finally had the chance to rule the dining room. As we babysat one-year-old Clifford, we rearranged the chairs and tables into a circle and wheeled in the TV. For the next few hours, we raced to see who could finish the Rubik's Cube first and played Uno and Atari, though we only had two games: Asteroids and Space Invaders.

Around eight p.m., our stomachs began to growl. The adults were still gambling, so it was up to us kids to assemble dinner from the leftovers. It wasn't too hard. We just had to put the food on plates. Our restaurant didn't even have a microwave to reheat them. That's because Ngin-Ngin thought the new device would make our kitchen look unprofessional. On this point, I had to agree with her. There are no shortcuts to making good food.

We worked in an assembly line, and the job went smoothly. Chris took charge, directing us to put out enough plates for the adults and kids. We removed the Saran Wrap from the meats and vegetables, put a dollop of each dish on a plate, and delivered dinner to the adults in the back kitchen. Mimicking our waiters, we served everyone with a napkin and a smile. The players thanked us. We even earned a few tips.

As we handed out the final plates, a trio of last-minute guests appeared at the back door. The three men, in their late fifties and dressed in shabby suits, looked like the same clientele that hung out in the gambling den in our basement. They all had gray hair. One had glasses. Another had a thin mustache. None of the three men appeared to be holy or wise.

My family valued hospitality. We never turned anyone away, not the customers who came knocking on our door with one minute left before closing or the family of Vietnamese refugees that one customer's church was helping to resettle in the area. We took everyone in and tried to make them feel at home. There was always room at our table.

My grandpa greeted the men with a smile. As the current head of our Chin family association, he often received visiting dignitaries. I'm not sure where these men came from or why they were there or even if they were biologically related to us, but now they were our guests. Yeh-Yeh turned to me and my siblings and held up three fingers. "Hoo som ga won."

As requested, we ran back to the main kitchen. The place was quiet and dark. Unfortunately, the only scraps of food left were slivers of ham clinging to the bone and some orphaned strands of green vegetables. Everything had been eaten.

Chris picked at the ham. "There's a bit more here."

We all looked at the bone. There was barely enough to make half a sandwich.

My mind flashed back to the morning, when I'd watched all the adults cooking and roasting in the kitchen, running around with their pots and pans, their bags of ingredients in hand. It was like a factory floor. It looked like so much fun. It was time for us to show what we could do. "I can make something."

Craig folded his arms and sneered. "You can't cook."

Of course I could. I mean, it was in my DNA, right? I came from a family of great chefs. For decades, we had been feeding Detroit. Our fans included celebrities like Smokey Robinson and Joni Mitchell, the Earl of Snowdon and Senator Eugene McCarthy. We were all good at something: Ngin-Ngin specialized in dumplings and sweets. Yeh-Yeh excelled at barbecue pork and homemade tofu. In a cross-cultural twist, my immigrant mom made the best American fare, while my native-born dad cooked wonderful dishes from Hong Kong. Even my older brothers could make simple desserts with an Easy-Bake Oven.

I just hadn't had the chance to show off my skills. Lately, my dad had been trying to pass on his knowledge. For me, the lessons began as something to kill time. My dad, though, took my request seriously. He was happy when his kids showed an interest in the restaurant. He never said it out loud, but we all knew that he would love it if one of his kids wanted to take over. So he always tried to do things that made the job look fun, like balancing plates and saucers on his arm or folding napkins into origami jet planes.

My dad liked to cook at our oldest wok, which, after decades of use, had developed a very distinct and flavorful "wok meh." At first, he did all the heavy lifting during our lessons; I more or less stood by and watched. After a few sessions, he let me dip my toe in the water, asking me to hand him a spoon or throw in a dash of MSG. Each time, we tackled a different dish: pepper steak, shrimp subgum, emperor's delight. My dad's enthusiasm was clear. The pride he took in making a good dish rubbed off on me. The more we worked together, the more included I felt.

But what began with so much hope never ended with glory. My vegetables were soggy. My meat cuts were uneven. My sauces looked plain weird. I'd panic, searching for a quick fix: Higher heat. More spices—the yellow one, some of the black one, more of the white one. Nothing worked. Who knew there were so many different ways to ruin a good dish?

With each failure, I grew more frustrated. I got angry at myself for screwing up even the simplest things. I couldn't understand what

I was doing wrong. Nothing made sense. All I could do was wait for my dad to swoop in and salvage the dish.

After I mangled an order of gai kow, an age-old Cantonese dish of chicken, ginger, sesame oil, oyster sauce, water chestnuts, snow peas, bamboo shoots, and bok choy in a white sauce, Big Al put his hand on my shoulder. "Stop thinking so much."

That made zero sense to me. My dad's advice was the polar opposite of what my mom always said. She told me to use my brains and follow the written recipes. Now my dad was telling me to go with my heart. I didn't know which way was right. *What's wrong with thinking?*

My dad grabbed my wrist. "Hold your hands up to the flames. Inhale the heat." He pointed. "Use your eyes and ears. Watch and listen. Use your nose to smell and the tip of your tongue to taste. Feel what you're doing."

As much as I tried to adopt my dad's Zen approach to cooking, using all my senses, it never felt natural. My body couldn't relax. My shoulders stayed stiff. I craved specific written directions. After he realized I couldn't adjust, he gave up. Maybe it was his impatience or maybe it was my grandma's constant wailing about the wasted food, but either way, he rejected every request I made for more lessons. "It's almost time for dinner. I'm sure Kin Sook is making something great," he'd say. Or "Not now. We're running low on chicken." Never mind that the delivery guy had just dropped off a case of dead birds.

I felt like an outcast, the pink sheep of the family.

But that was in the past. There were three hungry men waiting to be fed and this was my chance to prove myself. "This'll be fun," I told my brothers. "We'll make something up."

Chris walked over to a side shelf and shifted a stack of dishes to reveal a covered tray. He pulled off the silver top. It was one of my dad's roast chickens. From past years' experience, we had been smart enough to put aside the extra bird for our dinner. "We'll just share some of this."

I yanked the chicken from his hand. Heck no. Chris was always a giant suck-up. He could kiss ass as much as he wanted. I was not giving up that last chicken. "No one touches this bird. It's for us."

Craig, who also liked the drumstick, took the secret stash from me. When it came to food, he never messed around. "We're eating this ourselves." Calvin, Cindy, and my three cousins all nodded in agreement. They were hungry too. Chris wasn't used to being challenged, but there wasn't anything he could do. He was outnumbered, seven to one. Even baby Clifford gave him a look. The others picked up their food and marched into the dining room.

Chris looked down at the extra plates. "Fine. Whatever."

With his approval, I took on the role of top chef. I zipped through the refrigerators pulling out a bunch of ingredients: roast pork, beef, button mushrooms, straw mushrooms, two more kinds of mushrooms I couldn't name. I turned on the flame and threw the pile into the wok along with a handful of spices. At first glance, the dish didn't resemble anything on our menu. It was more like the pot roast they served at school. In other words, it looked like the work of a professional. I could already picture the bouquets of flowers tossed at my feet: *Bravo! Bravo!*

Once again, the dish was coming along great... until it wasn't. Somehow, the look and taste were slightly off. Bumps and craters appeared. I swear it was making a noise. This was not good. I tried to balance things out, but nothing worked. At that point, I needed to try a Hail Mary.

During our lessons, my dad had said that every dish needed a secret ingredient. So I grabbed my most trusted condiment: ketchup. It wasn't an obvious choice, but like my dad, I liked to surprise my audience. I tapped a few globs into the bubbling contents in the wok. I dipped my finger in for a taste, then added a bit more. After I made a few more adjustments, the dish didn't taste half bad. In fact, I might even have used the word *good*.

Chris, who'd been cleaning up and washing dishes, looked at my creation. "Did you try it?"

"Yeah, it's good. Let's go. We don't want it to get cold."

Chris shrugged okay. The two of us assembled three plates, then ran back to serve our guests. Since I had made plenty, I shared some with the other adults, starting with my dad. He looked surprised. I winked at him. "Don't worry. It's got a secret ingredient."

My dad smiled as I continued making the rounds. After I'd emptied my entire tray, I looked around the room for snap reviews. One by one, the adults had stopped chewing. My heart started beating fast. What was going on? Why wasn't anyone saying anything?

Finally, Ngin-Ngin held up her napkin. She looked at me, then spat out everything in her mouth. I thought her dentures were gonna fall out. "Aiya, mo-yung!"

The three guests looked at one another and began conferring in Cantonese. No interpreters were necessary. Before I could explain myself or my dish, which I had even given a catchy name—Joe's Jumbo Jumble—they were putting on their coats.

As my grandpa walked them out, Ngin-Ngin glared at me. Any time I or one of my siblings failed, her face lit up. It was proof that she was right, that my parents weren't meant for each other. She snorted in delight.

I viewed my grandma's criticism in a new light. She had dismissed me my whole life, but this time, she had a legitimate reason. My dish was a mess. Maybe she had been right all along. Of everyone in the family, she saw the real me. She knew I was truly useless.

I hung my head in shame, ready to accept the damage I had done to our family's stellar reputation. After a few seconds, I peeked up to see my mom and dad still consuming my dish. Given how much they loved to eat and cook, this must have been torture for them. But there they were, forcing bits into their mouths. I didn't want them to have to suffer any longer. "That's okay. You don't have to finish it."

Neither of them said a word. They kept chewing.

I don't know why I did what I did next, but I bowed to them three times. I'm sure it must've looked funny and out of place, but it felt right.

A sudden calm came over me. I was growing up, coming into my own, but no matter how things were changing, it was nice to know there were constants in my life, that my mom and dad would have my back, that the Chin family name meant something.

A-8.

At night in our back kitchen, the clamor of crashing plates and chopsticks was often replaced by the clacking of mahjong tiles. Two or three nights a week, a rotating pool of players—my parents, grandparents, aunts and uncles, waiters, cooks, and ahoos—filled the table's four heavenly winds. No matter how many hours the adults worked that day, they were always up for a round or two...or six.

After finishing my homework, I liked to study the gamblers as they arranged their hands. The different styles of play—like gin rummy—mirrored the players' personalities. My dad, the optimist, went for the big wins; my grandpa, sunny and warm, smiled with every draw. My grandma's strategy was pure chaos theory. But the best player in Chinatown was my mom. She ruled as the Joe Louis of pungs and serngs, once winning twelve hands in a row.

Hoping to emulate her success, I picked up a lot of Chinese philosophy (or superstition, some might say) watching my mom. She warned me never to brush hands with another player, especially the ones who were losing, as their bad luck would rub off on me. And never to shake my legs, as that would cause the money in my pocket to slide out. The most important lesson, though, was purely fact-based: Pay attention to everything going on at the table. It wasn't good enough for my mom to know what was in her own hand; she was constantly assessing the other players' needs and desires.

Few things brought joy to my mom's face, but winning at mahjong was one of them. Her eyes lit up every time she won a hand, which made me smile too. My mom never hid the fact that she felt she'd been cheated out of a lot in life. After every tangle with my grandma or dad, she would mutter, "Aiya, I must've killed someone in my previous life to deserve this." I felt bad for my mom. Sitting next to her, I hoped these small victories would change her mind about Detroit.

I remained my mom's biggest cheerleader, but my attention was wandering by the time I hit thirteen. Our restaurant needed a new fry cook, and after mounting another worldwide search—a large pool of Cantonese-speaking workers in Detroit didn't exist—my dad hired a guy from San Francisco, the city our ancestors called "dai fou," or big city.

A cute twenty-something with thick hair and a glorious tan, Mr. Mah was a welcome sight in Chinatown, especially to the ahoos. Most of the men preferred to play mahjong in the musty den hidden beneath our restaurant, where they could smoke, drink, curse, and get a head start in any police raids, but Mr. Mah was happy to stay upstairs with the women. He just had to ignore their distracting attempts to pair him off with one of their unwed daughters.

I liked him too. Not only did he smell fresh—he was the only cook who seemed to own cologne—but his body was beautiful. Whenever he leaned forward to draw a tile from the other side of the table, his T-shirt slid up his back, offering a glimpse of his fine brown skin. More thrilling, his red underwear would ride up to say hello. Definitely not boxers—bikini briefs, something you'd order from an International Male catalog.

I struggled to avert my eyes. By now I understood what my clear attraction to other boys meant: a lifetime of ridicule and rejection, possibly even jail. The state highway patrol had begun entrapping gay men who cruised public restrooms. The high-profile arrests, part of a program later dubbed "bag a fag," were meant to send a message: Civilized society would not tolerate these sexual deviants. Stay straight or be shunned. After seeing the shame in the eyes of the offenders pictured in the newspapers, I was afraid that if I did anything gay, my photo might end up plastered in the papers too.

Worse than my fear of jail was my fear of a fiery underworld. I was a Buddhist, so when the kids at school yelled, "Go to hell," I gave them a blank stare. *Where's that?* But when our dishwasher Mae—who was older and Black—invoked the place, it scared the hell out of me. When I was younger, she loved to read to me about Noah's Ark. I liked that story. But now that I was getting older, she thrilled in sharing Bible passages about the fornicators and adulterers stoned to death and lustful civilizations burned to ashes. As I thought about the Corridor and its large cast of sinners, I wondered if she was right about purgatory and if we were already there.

Still, my greatest fear about being outed was that I might be banished from my own family. It wasn't that my life was perfect. I struggled. I was growing up in a multigenerational house of limited means, so most of my clothes were hand-me-downs and all my toys were time-shares. I rarely got to choose what shows we watched on

TV or what we ate for dessert. But loud and crowded or not, my house was mine. I loved everyone in it, even Ngin-Ngin—at least, when she made her delish pineapple buns.

In eighth grade, I made my first New Year's resolution. Lunar New Year—the most popular and last remaining community celebration—was my favorite Chinese holiday, and not just because we kids got red envelopes stuffed with twenty-dollar bills. It felt great to be a part of something bigger than me and my family. It made me feel safe and loved. Popping firecrackers and prancing lions filled the streets of Chinatown. As everyone else promised to lose those extra pounds or get better grades, I resolved not to be gay.

The term *conversion therapy* was not widely known, but the concept was in the ether. I wanted to de-gay myself. I believed I could do it. I just had to follow my mom's advice and work hard. For starters, I took long cold showers while chanting my own mantra: "Don't be gay. Don't be gay. Don't be gay." At the restaurant, I wrapped a thick rubber band around my wrist and flicked it any time a hot guy walked through our front door. The sharp pinch was meant to connect gay thoughts with pain. Instead, it piqued my interest in S and M.

As much as I tried, my efforts fizzled upon the arrival of Mr. Mah. Now I was sitting inches from him at the mahjong table, and my heart fluttered with excitement. I did everything I could to stymie my lust. I tried watching TV, but my brothers' fat heads got in the way. The few times I stood up to get an almond cookie, my mom complained that the sudden motion scared off her good luck. I tried reciting my mantra, but the words kept morphing into the lyrics of my own sad attempt at Motown: *He's so fine. He's so nice. Tastier than a plate of pork fried rice.*

It was a tug-of-war for my soul, and I was doing worse than the hapless Lions.

After a few more hands, it was Mr. Mah's turn to roll the dice. He turned to me and held up three fingers. "Dai sam."

Normally, I bristled when anyone referred to me as "Number Three"—like I was a combo plate off our menu—but with Mr. Mah, I would've thrown in a free drink. The guy had started working for us a few weeks earlier, but we had yet to talk. The fact that he knew where I stood in our birth order made me more infatuated. Not that I thought he was gay—despite high hopes, I didn't dare think that far ahead. I was just glad he noticed something about me. I blushed and batted my eyes. "Yeah?"

Mr. Mah held the dice to my face. I looked around the table. All eyes were on me. The pressure to perform was great. I knew what Mr. Mah was asking for, but I was afraid that the other players might figure out my real wish: some physical connection. I tried to stall, hoping to come up with a clever excuse, but my mouth stumbled ahead. "You want me to . . . blow for you?"

Mr. Mah chuckled and motioned toward my mom. "Ho che nay goh ma."

He was asking me to transfer some of my mom's good luck to him, but his request felt bigger than that. He was asking me to reveal a secret part of me, something I wasn't ready to do. I panicked. As my mom looked at me, I wondered if she had figured out my desires too.

I hemmed and hawed. Mr. Mah chuckled again. "Mama's boy!"

My folded arms registered my protest, but I knew he wasn't wrong. So did everyone else at the table. My devotion to my mom was obvious, but I didn't care. It was mutual. I cast an evil eye at all of them, wishing the other players bad tiles for the rest of the night. My grandma must have sensed my curse because she narrowed her eyes. "Mo-yung."

My mom nodded at me, signaling that I shouldn't worry. I didn't. How could I be mad at Mr. Mah? He was so cute, and cute people could get away with murder. I closed my eyes and blew.

For weeks, I struggled to quash these burgeoning feelings, but it kept getting harder and harder. Literally. I was an eighth grader now, and my body had discovered a new trick, one that was even more fun than getting past the first board in Pac-Man. Hiding in our men's bathroom, I spent long stretches of time doing my own "wakka-wakka-wakka."

I couldn't deny my body's reaction to seeing hot guys, but I hoped that it was just a phase or that it might happen with girls too. Maybe, like the character of Jodie on *Soap*, I was bisexual. I tried to explore this option. Whenever I saw a cute couple, I made sure to admire both his chest and her breasts. But that didn't work. I could intellectually tell if a girl was pretty, but although I attempted to direct all my thoughts and energies onto my penis to help it grow, grow, grow, it never did. Little Curtis disobeyed big Curtis.

It didn't help that Mr. Mah was playing Mr. Congeniality. Life would have been so much easier if he had been a jerk like the other cooks. Instead, he laughed at my silly puns and tipped me a dollar every time he won a big hand. This led to an even bigger prize one night: Mr. Mah was on a hot streak when he ran out of cigarettes (okay, so he wasn't perfect), and, not wanting to disrupt his luck, he asked me to go to his apartment and pick up a pack. He didn't have to ask twice. I grabbed his keys and ran.

Across the narrow back alley, an aging Victorian in sore need of a good paint job served as a boardinghouse for the shrinking pool of Chinese bachelors in Chinatown. Once owned by Lewis Cass, who governed Michigan when it was still a territory, the three-story home had been the centerpiece of a large country estate. Now it stood as a reminder of the street's former glory.

I bolted up the creaky stairs. On the second floor, I fumbled open the heavy wooden door. The room was bare and Zen, more spartan than I'd imagined. In addition to the queen-size bed, expertly made with hospital corners, there was a nightstand, a dresser, and a red vinyl chair that clearly came from our restaurant's dining room.

Spotting the Marlboro Lights by the alarm clock, I took one last chance to breathe in the sandalwood scent. I sat down on his bed and ran my hand across the bumpy surface. I wanted to throw off the cover and roll under the sheets, but I knew that would not be a winning move. Instead, I gently placed my head on his pillow and inhaled the faint smell of hair gel. I hoped someday to be a regular visitor to his room, but in case I was never invited back, I wanted to remember every detail.

After that night, I engineered different ways to build my bridge to Mr. Mah. I ordered all my meals from the fry station. I scarfed up his dishes: shrimp egg foo yung, breaded fried shrimp, sweet-and-sour pork, almond pressed duck, even the fried gizzards, which weren't half bad. The cavalcade of entrées tasted great, but the extra grease caused an acne eruption. Any spare cash I had went straight to Clearasil.

A new plan was needed.

One afternoon, the kitchen sat empty except for Mr. Mah and Mae. Mae was taking her sweet time stacking the teacups. When she finally picked up her mop and bucket and left to clean the bathrooms, I couldn't wait to pounce. My plan was to ask the guy for private cooking lessons. Hopefully, things would go better than they had with my dad.

I sucked in my gut, arched my back, and combed my short black hair, dabbed with a bit of my grandpa's Brylcreem. In addition to my deeper voice and a dozen or so pubic hairs, puberty had melted away the bouncy girth around my stomach. I now had a firm jawline and sharp cheekbones. I thought I looked pretty good. I could even imagine the ahoos pinching my cheek and praising me as a "lang jai."

The growing pile of eggshells overflowed the garbage can, as Mr. Mah was cracking eggs for another vat of golden batter. The metal bowl tinged with each hit. As I strode over, my eyes fixed on his back—the slow slope of his spine, his even shoulders, the thin apron strings dangling over his perky butt.

Like Icarus closing in on the sun, I could feel the heat. My confidence suddenly vanished, and I pushed out a tepid "Hi." My mouth dried up. Water—where could I get water? Asking for lessons was far more complicated than ordering lunch. My words were so awkward, I've since blocked out what I said, but I know my English came out as bad as my Cantonese. Now I was an idiot in two languages.

Mr. Mah finished another tray and gave me a once-over. "Ju mut."

I flapped my wings to get closer. "Can you show me how to make your almond boneless chicken?"

Almond boneless chicken, or wah sui gai, was Chung's bestselling entrée, nearly as popular as my grandma's egg rolls. It was one of our signature dishes and, according to Ngin-Ngin, a Chung's original. It was our Friday lunch special, and customers would come in and order that dish every week. Mr. Mah turned up the flame on his wok. "Ne im jung yee ngoi ga wah sui gai?"

I shook my head. "I like your chicken fine. I just want to learn how to do it myself."

Mr. Mah flipped his spatula. "Dim guy?"

The aborted lessons with my dad popped into my head. I still wanted to get it right. "Everyone else in my family knows how to cook. I should too."

Mr. Mah stared straight at me. His eyes were the color of Kona coffee with a blend of milky cream. I could tell from his indifference that Mr. Mah wasn't keen to play Julia Child. But I didn't care. I was going to make it happen even if I had to get on my knees and beg. To my relief, it didn't come to that.

The door to the dining room swung open. It was Alfred, one of our surly waiters. He shouted, *"Two ABCs,"* which was often short-hand for "American-born Chinese" but in this case meant "almond boneless chicken."

I couldn't believe my luck. I clasped my hands together. "Please."

Mr. Mah grabbed four pieces of fillet, all lightly breaded. "Tie je ngo."

Yes. That was my green light, and I was going. I stepped in closer. My eyes stayed glued to his sinewy forearms as he slipped the meat into the hot oil. The sizzling pops and Vesuvian heat raised my temperature. A thin layer of sweat glistened on Mr. Mah's skin. I could practically taste that chicken.

A minute later, he scooped out the pieces and dropped them onto the wooden chopping board, which he kept immaculately clean. I watched in admiration as his cleaver came down in a series of crisp chops.

The anticipation built as the warm familiar smell wafted in the air. He slid the pieces onto the bed of finely shredded lettuce on the first tray. The arrangement looked perfect, full and fetching. The first bite was always with the eyes. He held out his knife. Thoughts of my past kitchen disasters flashed through my head. What if I messed up like I had with my dad? Would Mr. Mah ever speak to me again? I gave him my best puppy face. "Me?"

Mr. Mah nodded and again offered me the knife, hilt first.

We traded places. He wasn't much taller than me, so our bodies were evenly matched. Feeling confident, I lifted the knife above my head. Suddenly, a hand cradled mine. It was small and rough. I froze. Outside of wrestling in gym class with a sweet, dimpled boy named Steve Kramer, this was my first not-so-innocent physical contact. But this time, there were no giggling classmates making innuendos about me being gay that I had to pretend not to hear.

As my body stayed frozen, my eyes spotted a scar on his wrist. I recognized it as the result of splashing oil. I knew because I had one like that too, from when I was younger and threw a half-eaten Snickers into the deep fryer. I wanted to tell him about our connection, but I was too smitten to speak. Mr. Mah tightened his grip. His voice tickled my neck. "Go."

I closed my eyes and brought the knife down. I waited for the clash of elements—metal on wood—but the sound never came. My blow was too soft, too weak. Mr. Mah released his grip, but I didn't want him to let go. I wanted him to hold me, to stay exactly where he was, to never move. I considered screwing up so he could swoop in to rescue me, but I chose to show him that I was strong and mature, that I could handle myself.

I brought the knife down again, this time with purpose. The fowl split perfectly. Several more chops, and the meat was quartered. I felt manly, on the verge of adulthood. My persistence had paid off. All it took was a bit more confidence and clarity.

After I ladled on the perfect amount of gravy and sprinkled on the slivers of snow peas, water chestnuts, and the eponymous crushed almonds, I showed my masterpiece to Mr. Mah. He gave the dish a once-over before winking his approval. I was desperate for a kiss on the lips or at least a pat on the back, but all I got was a nod of his head. Still, although Mr. Mah called me Number Three, I felt like his Number One.

A final lesson I'd learned from the mahjong table was the importance of building momentum, or good karma. My mom liked to win a bunch of smaller "chicken" hands to generate enough good luck to pursue the big wins of complete runs. I had to be patient. Today was my first small bite.

Over the next few months, Mr. Mah continued to give me lessons. I never figured out why he was so attentive to me or if he ever suspected what was really going through my head, but our friendship blossomed. I would watch him work, stealing glances at his lithe body—which remained surprisingly tanned—but more often, I sat with him and we talked about nothing. He practiced his English with me. I made a sad attempt at speaking Cantonese. It was our daily dance to find some common language.

By the spring, though, Mr. Mah had had enough—not of me, but of Detroit. Like most of the out-of-towners who relocated to work at Chung's, he found the challenges of the Rust Belt too great. After a few months, most workers would return to the East or West Coast. They complained about the city's never-ending snow and cold, the expense of owning a car here, and, most frequently, and ironically, the lack of good Chinese food.

I didn't remember most of the cooks who came and went—there was a parade of them—but I often thought of Mr. Mah and our brief connection. Those afternoons and weekends were formative for me. While I might have fantasized that our relationship was more intimate than it truly was, it felt fertile and thrilling, and, more important, it felt natural. I knew it would be risky, but I had no choice but to try. I prayed that the odds were on my side, that I could find another guy someday who considered those feelings to be normal for him too.

RICE AND NOODLES

R-1.

One Sunday morning in the summer of 1982, as I was preparing to enter high school, the four adults were in my grandparents' room, whispering about a fellow member of our family association. Vincent's wedding was set for the following week, but the night before, the twenty-seven-year-old draftsman had been in some sort of accident or altercation at a bar. No one was quite sure. But now, we were stunned to find out that he was in the hospital in a coma, fighting for his life.

Vincent was twice my age, so it's not as if we hung out, but I knew who he was. He was one of the cool Asian guys who were buddies with some of our younger waiters and managers. They liked to hang around the back of our restaurant. As my parents discussed which flowers brought the best luck and who would visit him first, I wandered into our kitchen to scrounge for some Apple Jacks. There on the counter was the red-and-gold wedding invitation from Vincent and his fiancée, Vikki. The date was just a week away. I wondered if he would get better in time.

That night, we waited for any coverage on the news, but we didn't see a thing. In the early 1980s, the local stations had one lead story: the city's ongoing economic plight. Domestic car sales were down. Factories were shuttered. Union members were losing their homes. At 17 percent unemployment, Detroit, the birthplace of the American middle class, led the nation in joblessness. Detroit had fallen and it couldn't get up.

In Chinatown, though, we followed our own headlines. It was all about our Vincent. Our workers were beside themselves, as they felt such guilt for not being there to defend their friend. A stream of ahoos and members of the On Leong Chinese Merchants Association dropped by with updates from the hospital. Emotions ping-ponged by the hour, from hope to dread and then back to hope. It was scary and comforting to see so many faces I hadn't seen in years. This time, the elders didn't even bring up my grades or report cards.

After four long, tense days, word came back that Vincent had suffered too much brain damage to survive, and his family had decided to pull the plug. The news surprised me. Vincent was young and healthy. Why couldn't his body fight back? What about the doctors? They had all this education and medical expertise. Why couldn't they save him?

Over the next few months, details of the night emerged: Vincent had been at his bachelor party at a strip club when two white men—who we later learned were stepfather and stepson—came in. After some drinks, words were exchanged between the groups. All of them were tossed out. Soon after, the white men spotted Vincent and a friend sitting outside a McDonald's, waiting for their ride. The stepson grabbed Vincent and pinned him down while the stepfather bashed Vincent's head multiple times with a baseball bat. Vincent's last words were "It's not fair."

As a shocked Chinatown coped with the untimely loss of one of our own, my mind kept returning to Vincent's mom, Lily. Her face always had a natural smile, and I had seen her slurping my mom's pork-bone soup at the kitchen table in our home. But when I saw her on television, her eyes and mouth read only despair. It was rare to see any Asians on TV, much less in public, exposing their hurt, but Lily epitomized the most universal figure in history: the grieving mother. How could anyone hear her anguish and not think of their own mom? I know I thought of mine.

Vincent wasn't the first person I knew who was murdered, nor would he be the last. But his death had the most impact on me. Before his killing, I had felt secure as an Asian American. Sure, we encountered some discrimination, but for the most part, I thought we had been accepted by both our white and Black neighbors. My great-grandpa Joe's naturalization papers had even labeled him as "white." But the incident clarified any misunderstandings. We were outsiders.

As the start of high school loomed ever closer, I began to experience new-kid jitters. Troy was a northern suburb of middle- to upper-middle-class haves and have-mores. The population was almost all white, Christian, conservative, and, on the surface at least, straight. Being none of the above, I worried about fitting in. At this new, larger school, would I be able to relate to these other kids? Would they be able to relate to me? In order to be accepted, I knew I had to find some common ground with them. The easiest route was through politics.

In Troy, that meant being a Republican.

Two years earlier, the GOP had piqued my interest after holding its 1980 nominating convention in Detroit. The party, still trying to redefine itself post-Watergate, went nationalistic, targeting a newly identified voting bloc: white working-class citizens who were traditionally Democrats but who would vote for Reagan. Neither my parents nor my older brothers had ever expressed any party affiliation, but one of our customers offered us comp tickets to the event, and my family never turned down free stuff.

Cobo Hall, the sprawling arena down the street and the center of the renovated waterfront—part of Detroit's new "Renaissance City" campaign—had been covered in red, white, and blue banners. The endless vendors, both sanctioned and bootleg, sold everything from buttons to T-shirts to flags to Honest Abe bobbleheads. They were selling America the Beautiful, and I wanted to buy it all.

My favorite subject in school had always been social studies. I loved learning about our nation's history—the *Mayflower*, the Revolutionary War, Manifest Destiny. By embracing our Founding Fathers, I wanted to show that I was as apple pie as anyone in my school. Though my age prevented me from voting yet, in the words of the party's presidential nominee and resident cowboy, Ronald Reagan, I was going to help "make America great again."

In hindsight, as much as I would like to say that my conservatism was just a desperate ploy to fit in, I don't think I could have been as gung ho as I was unless I truly held some of those beliefs. The party's call for less government spending and more family values did resonate with me. A welfare center operated several doors down from our restaurant, and at lunchtime, dozens of men and women queued up outside it for free meals. The line was so long, it seemed busier than we were. That ticked me off. Why did these people expect handouts? Did my immigrant mom have to go over and explain to them the American dream?

The welfare recipients—both Black and white—received giant blocks of American cheese. Some of them would appear at our back door and try to get cash for the wholesome Midwestern product. This made me mad too. These people were supposed to eat the cheese, not sell it. As at most Chinese restaurants, our menu had no dairy items. But that didn't stop my dad; he couldn't pass up a bargain. Whenever my mom complained about the golden bricks piling up in our refrigerator, he would hold up his fingers and beam. "Three bucks."

While I now understand the importance of generational wealth and the effects of systemic racism on poverty (and also that my dad was just trying to show some compassion), back then, I thought these people were lazy. My family members all had multiple jobs. Couldn't they get just one? It was the same type of sentiment espoused by the lead character of my new must-see sitcom, *Family Ties*.

The Thursday-night show centered on a wholesome Midwestern family with clashing political beliefs. Expertly played by Michael J. Fox, the oldest child was adorable and clever and got all the best jokes. His railings against Big Brother and the welfare state made perfect sense to me. Dressed in preppy pastel polo shirts, button-downs, and the occasional bow tie, I became the Asian Alex P. Keaton.

When I ran for student council, I pushed for shutting down the student smoking lounge. This aligned with First Lady Nancy Reagan's Just Say No campaign, but it's something I had thought of on my own. I hated the way smoking customers stunk up our dining room; I couldn't smell our delicious Chinese food. Plus, our cooks and waiters were always taking cigarette breaks. Shouldn't they be working? To bring home my point, I passed out dinner mints from Chung's at school: "Fresh breath from a fresh face." The election results were posted by the main office, and strangers patted me on the back—I couldn't believe I had won. America truly was, as the Chinese called it, mei gwok, the beautiful country.

Everything was going great and high school was exceeding my

expectations until one day in freshman English. I raised my hand to answer a question about whichever John Steinbeck novel we were reading, and the teacher, who happened to be white, pointed to me and said, "Yes, Vincent."

The other kids looked confused. A couple of them giggled. The teacher apologized for the faux pas, but it still stung. It was annoying when any teacher called me by one of my older brothers' names—which happened more times than I care to remember—but this was worse. Vincent and I weren't related. We didn't even look alike. He had a mustache. Didn't any of them know it was bad luck in Chinese culture to call someone by the name of a dead man?

History class was no better. The teacher brought up what he perceived to be the bigger picture: the economic downturn in the area. For once, the might of American manufacturing was in question. Japan—which had surpassed America as the world's largest auto producer—became an easy scapegoat. The teacher focused on the laid-off workers but never discussed Vincent or his family. I wondered why we weren't talking about the TV ads of white and Black Americans bashing the hell out of Toyotas with sledgehammers and the connection to the baseball bat beating of Vincent's head!

As the court case against Vincent's killers crawled through the fall and winter, the mood in our dining room shifted. Our customers still chatted and laughed, but their joy seemed to be tinged with an unspoken sadness. Some would whisper their thoughts and prayers, trying to ask if we had any insight from the victim's family. I wanted everyone in our dining room to be happy, so I faked the best smile I could. No need to worry our guests.

In truth, I was confident. After years of watching TV detective shows, including the latest hit, *Magnum P.I.*, starring Detroit native Tom Selleck sporting a baseball cap with the Old English–style *D*, I expected American justice to prevail. The police had charged Vincent's killers with second-degree murder. The investigators had the weapon, and there were plenty of witnesses, even an off-duty cop who'd been sitting inside the McDonald's. For me, it wasn't a question of *if* the killers would go to jail but for how long.

One day the following March, I was in the kitchen, preparing myself a bowl of wonton soup. A regular order included two of the pork and shrimp dumplings, but I was hungry, so I treated myself to four of the bundles of joy. One of the Chinatown leaders called with an update on the case. My dad gripped the phone as he relayed the verdict.

The charges had been reduced to manslaughter, and the judge sentenced both killers to three years of probation and fined them three thousand dollars each. There would be no jail time.

Chinatown was stunned. Even my mom, the one least confident in government, couldn't believe just how bad it was. I couldn't, or didn't want to, believe it either. I figured there must be some mistake. Before reacting too strongly, I thought, I had to get the full story.

That evening, the news confirmed the worst. The authorities excused Vincent's death as the result of an out-of-control bar fight and said race had nothing to do with it. The judge would later say, "These weren't the kind of men you send to jail." I wanted to believe Vincent's death was all an unfortunate accident, an isolated incident that got out of hand, but I knew that wasn't true. His death was related to all the slurs and hateful acts I had learned to live with, accept, and, yes, excuse over the years. It was even connected to naive compliments like "Your English is so good" and loaded inquiries like "Where are you from?" followed by the even more irritating "No, where are you *really* from?"

A month or so later, a familiar smell of goodness filled our back kitchen. My grandma was frying up a batch of kok chai, a tasty treat made of ground peanuts, white sugar, sesame seeds, and salt stuffed into a wonton skin and deep-fried. Her gifts, shaped like triangles, were meant to distract us from the lingering pain. She didn't even fuss when I grabbed a few from the pile before the grease had a chance to cool.

I joined my siblings gathered around the TV. From the teasers, a big story was coming. That morning, while we were in school, hundreds of Asian Americans of different ethnicities had gathered downtown to protest the results of the trial. Except for the Far Eastern Food Festival, this solidarity rarely happened. Due to the horrible atrocities committed in Asia during World War II, many of the older Chinese Americans wanted nothing to do with any Japanese Americans. Thankfully, this seemed to be a generational thing. The different Asian kids in Chinatown hung out together. I was glad to see the adults doing the same.

Craig in particular seemed captivated. He insisted on controlling the channels, turning to Channel 7. As local legend Bill Bonds reported on the rally, I was comforted to see such a diverse group of attendees. In addition to other Asians, there were visible allies from the Black, Jewish, and white communities. Over the past few months, our community had seemed to be alone in this fight. It felt good to know that wasn't true.

As the reporter prattled on, my dad came in from the main kitchen with one of his snacks—an order of chicken chow mein—and a fistful of clean silverware. "Who needs a fork?" My dad loved feeding his family, but he stopped in his tracks when he noticed the image on the screen. He put down the plate and pulled up a chair. "I was there today, you know."

I spun around. My dad hadn't said much these past few months. He was always more of a listener than a talker. I hadn't known what he thought about the whole incident or if he missed his dead friend. "Why'd you go?" I wanted to know.

"On Leong asked, so we went," he said. "We closed for lunch."

Whoa. Except for Thanksgiving and the occasional race riot, we never shut our doors. This revelation framed my dad in a new light. The only civil rights activists I had seen before were the ones we read about in school: Rosa Parks, the Freedom Riders, bra burners. Now I could add my dad, a Chinese waiter, to the list. I turned back to the TV, excited to see if I could catch a glimpse of him holding a sign or going on a hunger strike!

My dad went on to describe the crowd. His friends from Chinatown took center stage along with a whole bunch of faces none of us had ever seen before. My father's voice was firm, yet soft; his heavy arms were draped over the back of the wooden chair. By now, my mom had drifted over to join our circle. She stood behind my dad as he looked each of us in the eye. Shifting the conversation a bit, with emphasis, he said, "You guys need to be careful out there."

Since we'd been old enough to play outside, my parents had cautioned us about the dangers of the street. The Corridor was filled with drug dealers, thieves, and prostitutes. Those warnings had seemed obvious to me, so why repeat them now? "What are you saying?"

"Keep an eye out. That's all."

My dad's vagueness frustrated me. Big Al was never one for big words or long sentences, so I was used to his cryptic answers. But this time, I couldn't read between the lines. I wanted clear answers. What were we looking out for? What was he not telling us? Maybe I understood more than I cared to admit, but I had to hear him say it.

My dad confessed that he and my mom couldn't guarantee our safety, nor could we count on the police to take our side if anything bad should happen to us. It didn't matter that we were model citizens or that our restaurant was on all the "Best of Detroit" lists. We were vulnerable. But if that was the case, what was the point of following the rules?

Before I could ask another question, Craig jumped in. He had been extra-grumpy for the past few months, complaining about the pace of the investigation. I knew he had issues with being teased at school, but he never talked about it, and I never asked. Craig kicked the front leg of his chair. "If someone comes after me, I'll kill them first."

His words puzzled me. "Who's 'them'?"

My dad scrunched up his face. "C'mon, Craig."

As the two most physically dominating men in the house, my brother and dad clashed a lot. Whenever they fought—usually over something simple like what game to watch on TV—words, and sometimes even kitchen utensils, would go flying through the air. As a kid who hated conflict, I always ran to the other room to avoid getting caught in the cross fire. No such luck here. Craig told me, "Dad's talking about white people."

I turned to my dad for his next move. He stood up and shook his head. "That's not what I'm saying." He pushed aside his chair. "There are bad people of all kinds."

"Yeah, but white people get away with it," my brother said.

Chris and I giggled. I'm not sure if Calvin and Cindy understood what was going on. Clifford was just a baby.

Big Al picked up his plate of chow mein, now too cold to eat, and walked back to the kitchen. "Just look out for each other. That's all I'm saying."

I shrugged, unsure of what to make of our family meeting. I didn't know what was going on. Like most people in Chinatown, my parents wanted to forget the tragedy and move on. I'm not sure if it was a Chinese cultural thing or just my family's attitude, but we never liked to discuss our miseries. It was as if the mention of any misfortune willed more bad things to happen.

As I stood up, I caught my mom's eye. During most of the discussion, she hadn't moved, but now she was rocking her head. She didn't say a word, but I knew what she was thinking: *This is why I wouldn't let you go outside to play. This is what I was trying to protect you from.*

That night, as the thoughts in my mind continued to swirl, I looked around my bedroom. Craig's half was a neatly organized shrine to his beloved Red Wings and Tigers—some baseball cards, a hockey puck—while mine glorified the Republican Party; I even had a statue of Lincoln and a jar of jelly beans. I held my stuffed elephant as I considered the Stars and Stripes hanging above my bed. How many nights had the red, white, and blue been the last colors I saw before closing my eyes?

I thought of taking down the American flag but stopped when I remembered that my family had been in Detroit for nearly a century, long before there was a Motown Records or even a Ford Motor Company. My ancestors believed in America, even when the country excluded them, cut off their ponytails, and demolished their homes and businesses to build a damn freeway.

I still wanted to believe in our beautiful country. But I was beginning to have my doubts.

As I reached to turn out the lights, I noticed the Polaroid on my nightstand. It was our family—my parents, Craig, Chris, Calvin, Cindy, Clifford, and me. My dad's words from earlier that night rang in my ears. These were the people I needed to keep watch over.

This, my family, was where I was really from.

R-2.

Buddhists, even lazy ones like me and my family, are taught to study and meditate after any tragedy. Vincent's death and the subsequent trial provided a chance to seek wisdom and compassion. Everyone in our house seemed a little more pensive. For me, it sparked a greater interest in civil rights for all Americans.

My parents had bought our olive-and-cream-colored *World Book Encyclopedia* set—the precursor to Wikipedia—for us kids even before any of us were born, and every day, I lugged a different volume to the restaurant. I scoured the pages for anyone who looked like me, but other than the gold rush and the transcontinental railroad, there was little to find. The Chinese Exclusion Act, it seemed, applied to our place in history and literature too.

As I plowed through the alphabet looking for relatable stories, I stumbled on several entries about the fight for civil rights in America. Most of them centered on the Black struggle. While I couldn't relate 100 percent—and certainly not when it came to slavery—my mom and dad had mentioned how our ancestors had suffered similar experiences in housing, employment, and education. That made those entries about discrimination feel personal to me.

Detroit, it turned out, was a hotbed of social-justice activism. I learned about the 1967 riot or, as some now call it, the rebellion, the late-night arrest of almost a hundred partygoers that led to large-scale protests. I read about the underlying racial tensions between Black and white Detroiters that had simmered for decades, driven by deep disparities in employment and economic opportunities, housing segregation, the city's inadequate public schools, and the Black community's dissatisfaction with a virtually all-white police force.

I was proud of Detroit. It was the birthplace of Motown Records, the country's most successful Black-owned business, and home to the largest chapter of the National Association for the Advancement of Colored People (NAACP); it was where C. L. Franklin had preached, where Malcolm X had spent his formative years, and where Martin Luther King Jr.—whose birthday had just been named a federal holiday—had given his "I Have a Dream" speech, two months before he delivered the same iconic words at the Lincoln Memorial. We were first.

Two women in particular filled me with hometown pride: Rosa Parks, who was welcomed to the city after being blacklisted in her state for leading the Montgomery bus boycott, and Viola Liuzzo, a white mother of five who'd traveled to the South to help register Black voters and was murdered by the KKK. I grew up surrounded by strong women. Their struggles always spoke to me.

After the unjust verdict in Vincent's trial, my mom became even more protective of her children. She urged me to avoid politics, even questioning my role on student council. It wasn't that she thought discrimination didn't exist; it was that she didn't think anything would change. She had grown up in Communist China and colonial British Hong Kong. Racial equality was not high on either government's agenda. Why would America be any different? Rather than worrying about the Great Society, my mom calculated it was better to focus on her family's own great leap forward.

My dad, on the other hand, encouraged my civic activities. Big Al was nonpartisan. He wasn't political, but he was optimistic. He believed in miracles—not the kind who sang backup for Smokey Robinson, but the kind where the Lions won the Super Bowl or the Big Four automakers staged an economic comeback. Winning the lottery was not a question of if, but when. It was the type of magical thinking necessary, he believed, to survive in Detroit.

After Vincent's death, my grandparents changed their habits too. My grandpa gambled less, and my grandma prayed more. They decided to shorten Chung's hours, closing before midnight. Ngin-Ngin made my dad install a buzzer by the front door. Now we would decide whom to let in and whom to keep out.

For my part, as a big consumer of the news and a budding logophile, I picked up a new hobby: penning letters to the editors of the local papers, a convenient destination for my ever-growing list of conservative opinions. My dad had a habit of buying fancy office equipment (I think it made him feel more educated), but he rarely got past the instruction manuals. One item was an IBM Selectric typewriter with built-in white-out tape. When I lugged the heavy machine into the dining room in hopes of raising my political voice, I think my mom assumed it was to make my homework look more professional. No need to autocorrect that one.

Organizing my thoughts into sentences and then paragraphs renewed my faith in the American political process. I went from being a passive victim to an active participant. I could address any issue, but I tried to stay local. One big battle involved the first assembly plant to be built in the city in decades. Claiming that the plant would be an economic spark plug, Detroit and General Motors used eminent domain to reclaim a section of Poletown, one of the few white neighborhoods left below Eight Mile. Of course, the working-class residents protested the seizing of their property. In my heart, I felt bad for them, but it also nagged at me; I wondered if they had felt the same way when, decades earlier, the city had appropriated the old Chinatown and Paradise Valley and demolished both.

A few days after mailing off these missives, I would scan the front sections of the papers and the editorial columns, looking for my name. Though not a single one of my letters had been published, I remained optimistic. I figured the odds were on my side. It might take a month or two, or even a year, but I was going to get something in, even if it meant chopping down all the trees in the state's Upper Peninsula.

One spring afternoon, I typed my latest attempt, arguing that, thanks to a permissive pop culture, America was in a state of moral decay. I blamed Madonna. The sex-crazed pop singer with local roots was a degenerate influence with her skimpy outfits and gyrating pelvis. Hoping to stem this slouch toward Gomorrah, I warned my peers not to be seduced by the Material Girl. This was not a holiday. There would be no time to celebrate.

As I tapped away, one of our most powerful regulars came into the restaurant. Dressed in a three-piece suit and beaming his thousand-watt smile, Mayor Coleman Young—or, as he called himself, the "Motherfucker in Charge"—led his entourage of aides and bodyguards to a table in the center of the dining room. Detroit's population was over two-thirds Black, and Young was the city's first Black mayor. Depending on whom you asked, the former union organizer was either a legend or the devil.

The mayor and the residents of the suburbs clashed daily. Those residents, who were mostly white, claimed that Young fanned racial tensions and mismanaged the city. It was as if they wanted him to fail. Some of the papers even accused him of outright hating white people. Mayor Young responded that the press—the same one that glossed over the Vincent Chin case—sensationalized any bad news because they didn't like seeing a strong Black man succeed.

My reasons for not trusting the mayor were more personal. When

I was in second grade, my parents used my cousins' address in Chinatown to enroll us at Burton, the public school across the street from Chung's. It was easier to drop us off before work. Being in class with our cousins and friends from Chinatown made school more engaging and fun. With so many familiar faces, I didn't feel so alone. When the holidays rolled around, all the school-age kids were invited to a big soiree at the mayor's mansion. With promises of McDonald's and free gifts, I couldn't wait. Finally, I'd have a toy to play with that I wouldn't have to share!

The mayor's home, located on the Detroit River, was enormous, with a driveway that seemed to stretch longer than Chinatown. Colorful Christmas lights and oversize ornaments provided a burst of holiday cheer. Unfortunately, the party was super dumb. The Happy Meals were late, and Santa kept yelling at the kids to shut up. Most important, the one toy in my swag bag—a wind-up plastic Model T—wouldn't start. The mayor's party was my first impression of city government and it sucked.

Sadly, our stay at Burton didn't last long either, as my parents realized the lack of rigor and resources, and the excessive fire drills, were not worth the price of convenience. They enrolled us in our suburban school, where the promise of public schools still prevailed.

That day at the restaurant, the mayor ordered his usual egg foo yung. The deep-fried omelet was made with eggs, bean sprouts, white onions, and a choice of minced meat—the mayor always chose lobster—smothered in a thick brown gravy and sprinkled with chopped green onions. At $12.95, the lobster egg foo yung also happened to be the most expensive item on our menu. We made so much bank off the mayor that my grandpa changed the spelling from "egg foo yung" to "egg foo Young."

As the mayor ate, I turned back to my latest belles lettres, hoping to finish before the afternoon mail arrived. My fingers hunted and pecked so fast, I got cramps. But I was in the zone. As an oft-forgotten middle child, I had become adept at drifting off into my own world. It was a skill developed out of spite: *If you're gonna ignore me, I'll do my own thing.*

On his way to the kitchen, my dad tapped my paper. "You should go say hi."

It wasn't a bad suggestion. I might even have thought of it myself, but like any teen, I hated being told what to do, especially by a parent. I sipped my orange Faygo. "We'll see."

Big Al winked. "You can hand-deliver one of your complaints."

Of course that was how my dad would characterize my efforts. It would never occur to him to write a letter to the editor. He didn't like to say anything negative, especially in writing. I pushed back. "They're not 'complaints.' They're suggestions. And don't you say anything."

That was a clear warning, but to my dad, it sounded like an invitation. He loved seeing us squirm when he bragged about us to the customers. How could he pass up telling the longtime liberal that I was our family's token Republican? I was sure my dad was eager to remind us all that Mayor Young had called my idol Reagan "prune face."

Somehow I had to change the subject. Given how persistent my dad could be sometimes, especially when it came to needling his kids, I thought the best way to deal with any awkward situation was to get it over with as quickly as possible. "I'll say hi when he's done."

Our customers preferred to chat after they were done eating. This gave me time to come up with a good topic. I scanned the room and noticed the new buzzer system my dad had installed. It would have been a great opportunity to bring up the skyrocketing crime problem. A decade earlier, as part of a beautification project, the city had installed concrete benches on Peterboro. With most of the old Chinese bachelors dying off, those same seats were now being occupied by crack dealers who treated them as their storefronts. But I didn't want the mayor to feel he was unsafe in our dining room, so I skipped the police report.

I looked out our window and noticed my former school. The broken blacktop with the bent hoop was a genuine hazard. The kids at Burton often suffered minor injuries. The difference between my school in Troy and this school was Black-and-white. I figured it might light a fire in the mayor's belly if I told him that the schools in the suburbs were way better than the ones in the city. I started jotting down all the disparities. I began with the poor lunch options before moving on to the even worse textbooks.

Thirty minutes later, as his staffers split open their last fortune cookies, I got up to talk, but before I could challenge the mayor, my mom beat me to his table. Tired of being stuck in the back kitchen with Ngin-Ngin and taking a cue from her kids, who had successfully transitioned to the front of house, my mom had started helping out in the dining room, where she could bask in the air-conditioning too.

As she charged ahead, I knew what was on her mind; she had been complaining about it for the past week. The city had recently extended the bus lanes on Cass Avenue, removing the free parking in front of our restaurant. Now our customers had to park in our private lot across the street, and en route to Chung's, many of them were mugged at gunpoint. Standing at the mayor's table holding a replenished plate of fortune cookies, my mom batted her large brown eyes and explained our predicament. She was concerned about the safety of our customers. She didn't want them getting robbed or killed. The mayor listened intently, ready to perform a little constituency service.

After finishing her story, my mom passed by my seat and winked. I began to have second thoughts. There was no way I could follow her act. I wanted to run into the kitchen and hide, but my dad called my name. I could've strangled him right then and there, but I wouldn't do it in front of the mayor. It would have to wait until we got home.

As I dragged my feet over, my dad held up three fingers. "This one is Curtis. He's number three."

The mayor leaned back in his chair. "What you typing back there?"

As I'd expected he would, Big Al opened his big mouth. "He's writing these letters to the editor." *Letters to the editor* sounded as if it were in air quotes.

The mayor perked up. "Yeah? What you got to say?"

I didn't want to "What you" anything. I was outnumbered, and his bodyguards had guns. I wanted to end his meal on a high note by saying something pleasant, but before I could respond, my dad interjected, "Who knows? He's always complaining about something."

My dad thought he was being funny. He wasn't.

The mayor chuckled, then asked why I was so angry. I wanted to say, *Because my dad has no filter,* but I remembered my mom's mantra: *Be quiet.*

The mayor leaned forward. His voice turned serious when he asked again, "What the hell you angry about?"

I looked at my dad, wondering how I would get back at him, then shrugged. "Nothing."

"You're a kid. You gotta be mad about something," the mayor continued. "You mad at your parents for making you work here? You mad at your brothers for getting something you wanted? You mad at your teachers for giving you so much goddamn homework?"

I wanted to say, *Yes, all of that and more.* I was angry. No, I was pissed. I wanted to complain about being a middle child in a big crowded family in a messy home, about being called Bruce Lee on the playground, about being attracted to boys and not knowing what to do with that. I even wanted to tell him about the broken toy at his stupid Christmas party.

But my lips wouldn't, or couldn't, form the words. Thanks to the Buddhist side of my upbringing, anger was not an emotion I was comfortable with. I'd always been told to let go, find compassion, and preach nonviolence.

At the same time, over the years, I had come to associate anger with Black people, and never in a good light. I'm not sure where I picked this up—TV shows, movies, my Republican club meetings. Some stereotypes—the most destructive ones—are so pervasive, you don't know where they come from. This was one of them.

Like any budding politician, I puffed out my cheeks and lied. "No, I'm fine."

Mayor Young wasn't convinced. He picked up the bill and looked me straight in the eye. "Well, you think about what makes you angry. And then you think about how you gonna fix it."

I turned to my dad, who looked so proud that he had engineered this ambush. I rolled my eyes. The mayor left with his entourage, including the extra bodyguards outside who'd been watching his limousine. I returned to the back table to stare at my typewriter. I was no longer in the mood to write. Madonna would get a pass today.

According to my parents, the next morning, before they arrived to open up, the city removed the signs about the extended bus lanes. By lunchtime, every parking spot in front of our restaurant was filled. Our customers had returned to sitting by our windows, keeping an eye on their cars. My mom had gotten over her initial anger and figured out how to fix the problem. Once again, she had proven she was the real motherfucker in charge.

R-3.

"Be a part of the heart. Be a part of the heart of Detroit." Motown superstars Levi Stubbs and the Four Tops sang these lyrics in the city's latest attempt to rehabilitate its battered image. From "Tell 'Em You're from Detroit" to "Say Nice Things About Detroit," the city was always launching high-profile campaigns to get the suburban crowds to come back downtown. Good luck. My friends in high school—the ones who never ventured below Eight Mile—mocked each song and slogan. And with all the continuing bad news, could I blame them?

In the spring of 1984, after I turned sixteen, some suburbanites finally had a change of heart. In Detroit, as in most blue-collar towns, the people's mood depended on the success of the local sports teams. Detroit had been in a championship drought; despite fielding teams in every major sport from baseball to football to hockey to basketball, the city had not won a national crown since 1968, the year I was born! Now, with the Tigers blasting off to a sizzling 35-5 record, the city and the suburbs found a way to come together. Reunited, and it felt so good.

Even my family regained some of our lost Motown spirit. Craig, who had been the most loyal of Detroit sports fans, watching every game even when the Tigers were mired in the bottom half of the American League East and supporting the Red Wings when they were called the "Dead Wings," wheeled our battered color TV into the dining room so our customers could watch while they chowed down on their fried rice. When the fans on the TV screen performed a new stadium trick called the wave, all of us in our dining room followed suit, raising our arms in the air and chanting, "Bless you, boys."

To my surprise, of all the fans, my mom cheered the loudest. In the past, she'd preferred pro football games over baseball. And she didn't root for the perennially losing Detroit Lions; she rooted for the 49ers, since her parents lived in San Francisco. But now she was a bona fide Detroit baseball fan too. Every time home-run hero Kirk Gibson stepped up to the plate, her body would tense up and she'd scream, "Go, go, go!" Judging from the fervor in her voice, I knew she didn't completely hate her life in Detroit.

In the fall, Tiger mania reached its peak. Led by the infield duo of Alan Trammell and Lou Whitaker, the team powered their way to the World Series. In game five, the Tigers defeated the San Diego Padres 8–4 to clinch the championship, and the city's years of pent-up frustration exploded onto the streets. Our family couldn't wait to join the mayhem too.

For the previous seven months, all of us in the restaurant had begged, prayed, and crossed our fingers until they were red. This was as much our victory as it was the team's. My mom was in such a great mood that she skipped as she refilled the pot of white rice and said we could join the impromptu celebration outside the stadium. We just had to finish refilling the soy sauce bottles on every table.

Tiger Stadium sat on the corner of Michigan and Trumbull, a twenty-minute walk from Chung's. We had to hurry or we'd miss the World Series celebration. As I urged my brothers to pour the soy sauce faster, the TV newscasters reported that intoxicated fans were flooding the streets, flipping over cars, and setting them on fire. We all knew the consequence of that: there was no way my mom would let us join the celebration.

The next morning, the national press, instead of cheering Detroit's victory, reported on the city's destruction. Relatives from California and New York called us, repeating their concerns for our safety and that of the restaurant. We were okay, but once again, we found ourselves defending our hometown. Nothing we said, no slogan or catchy tune, could repair this damage. The irony was that most of the rioters were from the suburbs, not Detroit proper.

Two weeks later, our city was set ablaze once more. In Detroit, Halloween eve had morphed into what was known as Devil's Night. What began in the 1950s as childish pranks—toilet-paper tepees, dog poop in burning paper bags—had turned violent; people set fire to hundreds of abandoned homes and businesses. Mayor Young blamed the mass destruction on institutional racism and the lack of economic opportunities for the city's Black youth, but my mom called it insurance fraud.

Chung's was open, but we lay low that night; our diners stayed home to defend their cars and properties. After experiencing the riots of 1943 and 1967 in the city as well as the everyday troubles, my family had grown used to the carnage and violence. To us, it was just another Tuesday night.

We all did our own thing at the restaurant. The three youngest siblings played with their Halloween costumes from Kmart. As kids, Craig, Chris, and I weren't allowed to go trick-or-treating in the Corridor—it was too dangerous to be walking around in masks and knocking on the doors of strangers. Now that we were in Troy, Calvin, Cindy, and Clifford got to experience a more suburban childhood.

My dad took advantage of the quiet to tidy up the place. It was important to him that the restaurant pass every health inspection with straight As. In the back kitchen, he had one whole refrigerator devoted to his leftovers, half-eaten dishes that he promised to finish but never got to. He'd save bowls of winter melon soup, trays of pepper steak with black bean sauce, and little plates of chicken curry and rice. At the end of the month, he would conduct a giant cleanse, looking sad at all the missed opportunities.

Meanwhile, I focused my attention on the evening news. A big election was coming up the following week. Throughout the fall, any spare hour I had, I spent volunteering at the county headquarters of the Republican Party. My dad dropped me off so I could make phone calls and stuff envelopes for Reagan. Despite Detroit's continued hardships, it was "Morning in America," as the country's economy had recently shown some signs of recovery. I was hopeful that the trickle-down economics that the president first promised four years ago would finally reach our restaurant.

Despite my optimism, though, the regularly scheduled bad news stayed the course. Bill Bonds and Mort Crim reported on the mounting hellfire on the streets. Like staffers at a Jerry Lewis telethon, the TV anchors kept a tally of the estimated financial damages. Forget coming to see the Renaissance Center or a long-awaited Motown museum; the fireworks around Devil's Night were so popular, travel agencies were selling tour packages to out-of-towners. Like spectators at the Circus Maximus in Rome, visitors came from all over the world to watch our city burn.

When my dad caught wind that an abandoned storage facility on Grand River was on fire, he jumped at the chance to see it, almost as if it were a rite of passage. "Who wants to go for a ride?"

Except for Chris, who seemed more annoyed by the damage than scared, my siblings and I raised our hands. "I do!"

Coincidentally, I had recently written another op-ed on Detroit's history with fire. The first time the city went up in flames, in 1805, it was still a French settlement. That's when the inhabitants penned the city's official motto: *Speramus meliora; resurget cineribus*—"We hope for better things; it will rise from the ashes." With so much drug use, crime, and murder in the city, I suggested maybe it was time for it to burn again. Perhaps then, like the phoenix, Detroit could rise and start anew. None of the editors liked my take, apparently, since my letter once again went unpublished.

This seemed like a good chance to see my theory through. I grabbed my plum-colored Members Only jacket. "Let's go!"

"Hurry," my dad said. "I want to get a good spot!"

"Ready," I said as I zipped up.

Just then, my mom entered from the kitchen carrying a tray of peapods. After Chris ratted us out, she straightened her back. "No one's going anywhere. That's the law."

And she was right. Thanks to the previous year's tally—over six hundred homes and businesses lost to the flames—Mayor Young had instituted an eight p.m. curfew for anyone under eighteen. My mom used the new ordinance as a convenient excuse to enact her own stay-at-home rule. "It's not my decision. It's the mayor's." Given her past interactions with Coleman Young, I wasn't sure she hadn't suggested the policy to him.

Craig, who was working as a part-time dishwasher, went back into the kitchen. I was not so easily convinced. For some reason, I felt compelled to follow the action. I had been conceived in the summer of 1967, when the burning, looting, and bloodshed in the city had led to the deaths of forty-three people and the injury of another three hundred and forty-two. Maybe it was inevitable that I would be drawn to fire. Maybe rebellion, as well as my interest in the issues of economic inequality and racism, was my birthright. It was in my riot baby DNA.

I headed to the door. "Nothing bad will happen to us."

My mom shook her head. "You don't know that."

"Yes, I do." I pointed. "We'll be with Dad."

My mom turned to Big Al. I had accidentally thrown him under the bus.

Concerning the raising of kids, my parents had competing philosophies, a chasm they didn't fully recognize until they'd had their first child. I'm not sure it's as simple as saying it was a cultural difference—one parent born and raised in China, the other in the United States—but my dad was clearly more lenient than my mom. Yet to our chagrin, when it came to these domestic decisions, he always deferred to my mom and her default no.

My mom couldn't stop my dad from taking off—he did what he wanted—but she could control us. Through the window, I watched as our van pulled away. I turned to give my mom the stink eye, but she was gone by then.

My dad had asked Chris to cover for him, and the rest of my siblings followed my mom to the back kitchen. I stayed in the dining room. Stubborn like my mom, I was not going to give her the pleasure of my company.

With my homework done, the only thing left for me to do was eat. I ordered another one of my favorites, beef and mushrooms with a smooth-tasting brown sauce. Normally, I would use a bowl and chopsticks. But whenever I was angry, I replaced these gentle utensils with a fork and knife—tools the Chinese considered weapons—and jabbed and cut my food. Not only did it allow me to get out my aggression, but it was also a blatant rejection of my family's culture.

As the evening ticked by, the live coverage on the news continued. Each report increased my curiosity and desire to go out. I grew more and more restless. Every time a cop car passed by, I ran to look, like a dog with its tongue hanging out. I had assumed that the older I got, the more freedoms my parents would give me, but it seemed to have had the opposite effect, as my mom was even more controlling.

With some extra time on her hands, my mom decided to make a time-consuming Chinese delicacy: zhu yook bang. The most comforting of comfort food and another of our tastiest off-menu dishes, it featured a steamed pork patty with diced water chestnuts and a cracked egg, the yolk of which blended perfectly with the juices from the pig. She knew how much I loved the dish. I considered that her apology for making me stay in.

Around eight p.m., with no word from my dad, my mom asked me to wheel out the lazy Susan. That meant a family meal. I placed the circular stand in the middle of the table and spun it around to test its balance. A giant boom rattled our windows. "What the hell was that?"

I turned to Frank, our new security guard. My dad had recently hired the three-hundred-pound ex–military man to work nights. Due to the shrinking tax base, city services were being cut, and the police substation up the block had been shut down. With the growing number of crimes in the city, the timing couldn't have been worse. The police were overstretched. Our customers, as well as their cars— even the ones parked right in front—became easy prey.

Dressed in dark blue slacks and a matching shirt, Frank, one of the last white residents on the street, did his best impression of a vigilante mall cop. Given his trigger-happy finger, I don't know if I felt safer or more scared.

Frank sprang into action. "Wait here." He poked his head out the front door. Nothing. He ran through the dining room and into the kitchen, passing the prep table and deep fryer. I followed. I might see some action after all.

He ran to the back hallway, his belly jostling up and down as he pulled up his oversize pants. I was right behind him. Chris was standing by the woks, snooping around the kitchen. He looked over. "What are you doing?"

"We're checking out the noise!" I screamed.

"What noise?"

"The one outside."

"You better not be going out there!" he yelled. I knew his next stop would be updating our mom about the situation, but I pretended not to hear him. I'd learned long ago that it was better to ask for forgiveness than permission.

At the end of the passage, where we hang-dried our chickens and stored extra bags of bean sprouts, Frank whipped open the metal gate. The rusty barrier banged against the cinder-block wall. I pulled up behind Frank and peered around his round, fleshy body. As usual, the back alley smelled funky, a mix of garbage, crushed beer cans, and dead rats.

Frank shouted, "Who's out here?"

The dusk had turned the sky a burnt orange, and the lights shining from the apartments above flickered against the broken glass below. The alley was empty. The prostitutes and johns in their parked cars were nowhere in sight. Nor did I see any patrons sneaking in the Gold Dollar's back door or any vermin scurrying under the abandoned couches. I looked over at Frank. "See anything?"

He surveyed the grounds around the gate. My mind took a quick step back in time. Gone were the days when our Chinatown gang would walk up and down the alley, looking for anything salvageable to take to the pawnshop: An old blanket. A worn pair of boots. A busted lamp without a shade. We never found anything of value, but we always had high hopes.

Curfew be damned. I followed Frank as he stepped out farther.

The arsonists often targeted trash bins. Our big blue dumpster had been pushed against the brick wall, so Frank wanted to check on it. He hoisted the heavy plastic lid and poked in his head. The rotting smell, whatever it was, caused him to jerk back.

In the few minutes of our escapade, the sky had gotten noticeably darker. I looked up at the roof. Given Frank's extra weight, we both knew there was no way he could make it up there. A burst of bravado overtook me. I pointed up. "We should check."

Frank shrugged. He looked up and down the alley once more before clasping his hands to make a cradle and bending his knees. "Ready?"

I planted my right foot in his palms, and he hoisted me atop the dumpster. From there, I hopped onto a narrow ledge and poked my head over the soot-filled edge. I could see the whirling heating vents, a pair of abandoned milk crates, and a graveyard of empty beer bottles. Any troublemakers were long gone.

Disappointed, I shouted down, "All clear."

Frank raised his hand. "Let's get out of here."

But I was halfway up, so I decided to finish the job and jump onto the roof. If I was lucky, I might see a fire or two in the distance.

Chung's rooftop offered one of the best spots to take in Chinatown. Thanks to so many abandoned lots, it had a full 360-degree view of the surrounding area.

Across the street, the Bow Wah storefront had sat empty for the past decade, ever since Tommy Lee's murder. The landlords, On Leong, wanted to rent out the space, but according to Chinese superstition, the storefront was cursed and needed to be left untouched for ninety-nine years. The ghosts must have overruled the gangsters.

Beyond Chinatown, fields of zebra grass, six feet tall, had replaced the playground of my youth—stores and restaurants were gone, homes and apartments shuttered. With drugs flooding into the city from warmer climes, violent gangs with names that sounded like boy bands—Young Boys Incorporated, the Chambers Brothers, the Errol Flynns—patrolled the streets.

From the safety of my secluded perch, I tallied the losses of property, of life, of hopes and dreams. It must be sad to grow up in a city that had always been poor. It was even sadder to grow up in one that was formerly rich. Detroit's past glory was evident in its landscape—the deserted mansions, vacant lots, and boarded-up hotels with empty windows on the top floors.

As I took one last look at my hometown, a random term popped into my head: *cause and effect.* I knew karma affected people, but did cities have karma too? Detroit had a complicated history, at least when it came to issues of race and class—and sexuality. Were the sins of Motown's past catching up with it? Was the city getting what it deserved? I had forgiven Detroit for its past transgressions against me and my community, but had the universe?

I looked across the way to the bigger street of Woodward. Another cop car whizzed by.

With all the distractions of the past year and a half, I had been able to push off dealing with my sexuality. More pressing issues of race and class had catapulted to the forefront. But inevitably, these gay thoughts would creep back in. A handsome anchor on TV (Rich Fisher). A sexy new dishwasher (Greg). A cute rookie on one of Detroit's sports teams (Steve Yzerman—although, really, take your pick). These small fires were growing. And where there was smoke, there was a young gay Asian boy itching to, in the words of Miss Diana Ross, come out.

These feelings could no longer be avoided.

A few minutes later, our van came rumbling down Cass Avenue. My dad was coming home, hopefully with some good stories to tell over dinner. As sirens—the new Motown sound—screamed in the distance, another slogan popped into my head, one that appeared on T-shirts as part of a guerrilla campaign:

Detroit, would the last one out please turn out the lights?

R-4.

The model minority. Thanks to *Time* magazine and its shiny cover story, an old stereotype came roaring back during my junior year of high school. The cover photo featured children clustered in front of a chalkboard with the caption "Those Asian-American Whiz Kids." According to the article, we were the perfect students—obedient and academically gifted. My mom loved the piece so much, she kept a copy in her Gucci knockoff purse.

Chris would have been an ideal subject for the story. After a customer advised my mom that we needed to list nonacademic accomplishments on our college applications, she started to let us join school clubs. Chris went nuts. Not only was he on track to be class valedictorian, but he was also class president and head of the school's chapter of the National Honor Society. He founded the science club and the Science Olympiad team, volunteered at the local children's hospital, and raised money for public television and the Humane Society. I think he might even have cured cancer.

My brother's reputation went global—or at least as far as Canada. Every week, my grandpa crossed the border to buy Chinese goods not sold in America—baked baos, fresh lychees, rare green vegetables that he had to hide under the front seat on the return trip. According to my grandpa, on one of his pickup runs, the border guard looked at the name and address on his license and asked, "Are you related to that Chris Chin at Troy High?" It turned out that the guy had a son who went to our school. My grandpa was so giddy that when he returned to Chung's, he treated us all to McDonald's. (Thank you. We love you, Grandma.)

Back then, when I still thought some stereotypes could be good, I had no problem with my brother perpetuating this unicorn myth.

To me, it was payback; after decades of Asians being thought of as dirty and disloyal and sneaky, it was nice to hear some positive words about us in this country. It made up for some of the unfair past treatment. I also think the stereotype might have helped me in my classes, encouraging my teachers to give me the benefit of the doubt: *He's Asian. He must be smart.*

With my brother dominating the sciences, I tried to find my own turf at school. Building on my interest in politics, I continued to serve on the student council. It was fun hanging out with the popular kids, even if I wasn't completely sure that they knew my name. But given my growing acceptance that I was gay and a recent sex scandal in Congress involving a Massachusetts representative and his male page, I realized there might be a ceiling to my success. As backup, I knew I had to pursue other interests.

Over the summer, I had joined the country's ongoing fitness craze, led by celebrities like Olivia Newton-John and Jane Fonda, building up my upper body and losing the rest of my baby fat. Our back kitchen became my own personal gym, the place where I did push-ups, pull-ups, and sit-ups. Looking good and feeling fine, I explored the idea of being a jock.

First, I tried wrestling. On school trips to the Detroit Institute of Arts, in addition to my favorite piece of artwork, Diego Rivera's Ford factory murals, I'd seen Greek statues of naked men that made that sport attractive. But after attending the first team meeting, where the coach explained all the rules and regulations, and seeing all the cute guys grabbing each other on the mat, I knew there was no way I wouldn't get too excited and be disqualified.

Track and field came next. If you grew up on the streets of Detroit, fast feet were essential. In school, as part of the Presidential Fitness Test—the national program meant to encourage physical fitness in

America's kids—every student had to run a mile around the track. After clocking the fastest time of the four hundred students in my grade, I waited for my invitation to join the track team. When that didn't happen, I approached the coach, but he was too busy trying to woo the more popular, but bigger and slower, football players. I was furious. I had proven myself—why wasn't I getting my just reward? The whole idea of meritocracy was starting to smell like bullshit.

Still in search of the right clique, one that would look good on a college application and meet with my mom's approval, I resigned myself to joining my brother's nerd herd, the science club. The thought of being around my brother in a club he'd founded grossed me out. I didn't want the constant comparisons. But the logistics made too much sense. With our matching schedules, my mom could pick us up at the same time.

Most of the other kids at school exhibited the usual anti-intellectualism, but on a larger scale, nerd culture was becoming more mainstream. *Jeopardy!* had returned to the air after a long absence. Many of the hottest toys and games—from Trivial Pursuit to Rubik's Cubes—required some brainpower. Video games were big. Super-hero and sci-fi movies were no longer fringe—they were summer blockbusters. It was like *Revenge of the Nerds*. I could live with that. So what if Asian guys were seen as stereotypical geeks? I had a brain, and I was going to use it.

In pre-calc, my teacher decided to administer an IQ test. The other kids groaned at the thought of another standardized test, but I perked up. I was one of those oddball students who got excited about taking big tests. For years, I had been in the back of the dining room doing every word puzzle in the papers. I had gotten to be pretty good at them, even the Sunday crosswords. Some kids had their spring con-cert or Friday-night football game, but this was my Super Bowl.

The exam contained a hundred questions on math, logic, and verbal analogies. To kick off the challenge, my teacher revealed her own results: 115. I ended up scoring 120—the top in the class. The teacher tried to make excuses for herself, blaming her poor testing conditions and allergies, but the other kids in class snickered and gave me the thumbs-up.

I signed up for more classes in biology, physics, and chemistry, as well as the Science Olympiad team and Students Against Smoking. The school's second floor—with its science labs and greenhouse—housed all the (meager) diversity our school had to offer; the student body was 96 percent white, but the science club was a third Asian American. We never discussed our experience of being minorities at Troy High, but there must have been a reason that we gravitated to the same club. Or maybe it was simply that we all had the same Asian moms.

Though my new friends included kids who looked like me, I never mentioned my life in Chinatown. These other Asian Americans had parents with professional backgrounds, the kind favored by U.S. immigration after changes in the laws in 1965. They were the off-spring of doctors and academics, engineers and researchers at the auto companies. Due to my own insecurities about money and class and Chinatown's reputation of being too *hood*, too *ghetto*, I didn't think my new friends could appreciate or relate to my life, so I never mentioned Chung's, not even our delicious egg rolls.

Instead, I focused on the things we had in common. We all liked to study—or at least understood the importance of getting good grades. We all planned to go to college—or at least wanted to keep that option open. We all enjoyed talking to our teachers after class—or at least hoped they would remember our names when it came time to pass out grades. In short, we all followed my mom's mantra of obeying our elders, being quiet, and working hard.

One of my closest friends was Scott, a sandy blond with big hair that qualified as mullet-adjacent. He belonged to our school's small Scandinavian American clique. The two of us sat next to each other in physics. When he invited me to his house to prep for a big test, I was excited. My mom had started to let us have friends come over to our house, where she could keep an eye on us, but homework was the only reason she would let us go to a friend's house.

I prepared for our study date as if it were a real one, picking a clean shirt and splashing on some Stetson that I'd bought at the local Cunningham Drugs. Scott was attractive, but I didn't lust after him. I wouldn't have complained if something had happened, but his friendship was enough for me. It was like having a brother I liked.

We met up after school one day, and he drove us to his place. Troy had two halves. The richer side featured the fancier mall, the world headquarters of both Volkswagen America and Kmart, and homes with in-ground swimming pools. The side Scott and I lived on had homes with aboveground pools and was more modest but still comfortable. His house resembled one of those clean suburban homes featured in the opening credits of a sitcom: middle class with a two-car garage, a covered porch, and aluminum siding.

I couldn't wait to see what life was like for my friend, but I started off on the wrong foot—or, rather, shoe. When I stopped in his foyer and slipped off my shoes, he gave me the oddest look, which made me check my socks for holes. Thank God I'd remembered to wear my good pair. "You can leave those on," he said.

I was confused. Like most people in Asian households, as a sign of respect and cleanliness, I had been raised to take off my footwear before I entered someone's home. "Isn't it dirty?"

Scott said, "It's fine," so I put my shoes back on, still worrying they might have doggy doo.

As we headed down the hall, I observed another difference: Scott's house was quiet. There were no squabbling siblings or multiple TVs clashing or grandparents scolding in Cantonese. I could hear myself think. As my friend shut the door to his own room, his *own* room, I wondered how awesome it would be to have so much privacy and a door that locked.

Scott and I finished studying in thirty minutes and moved on to a few games of Risk. After I decisively won another battle campaign, my stomach growled. Usually, my after-school routine included a smorgasbord of snacks at the restaurant: egg rolls, wonton soup, pork fried rice. By now, I was so hungry, I was dizzy, but I didn't want to come off as a demanding guest. Besides, this might have been part of Scott's strategy to win.

Thankfully, he was famished too. "Want something to eat?"

I played it cool. "If you want."

Scott's kitchen was super-clean. There were no bags of Chinese roots or animal parts left on the counter, no stacks of bills and invoices. Everything was tucked behind closed cupboards. His kitchen even smelled nice, a hint of potpourri.

As we snacked on a bag of chips, his parents walked in. I don't remember what they did for work, maybe something in the car industry like everyone else, but they were older and dressed for white-collar jobs. I tensed up, hoping to make a good impression. I wanted them to like me. Our exchange ended up being brief but pleasant. They asked if I enjoyed school; I complimented them on their home. Scott said he had other homework to do so we had to wrap up. He drove me back to the house with the crazy Chinese family.

The next day at school, Scott and I had lunch at our usual table—a long orange one to the right of the vending machines—and told our friends from the science club about our afternoon. Citing my back-to-back-to-back Risk victories, I engaged in a little smack talk: "Scott kept giving up Siam. I was getting two extra armies every turn."

A demoralized Scott tried to change the subject. "My parents said they liked meeting you. I don't know why."

I chuckled at his joke. "Yeah, especially after I beat their son at Risk."

"They said you were the first minority they'd ever had in their home."

I stopped chomping on my turkey sandwich. Scott's words, quoting his parents, made things feel awkward. Suddenly, I felt different, like an outsider. I looked around to see if anyone thought it was odd. None of our friends, all of whom were white, said anything. My mind began to churn. I got frustrated. If Scott's parents had said something clearly racist, I could have called them out on it. But it was these borderline comments that left me tongue-tied. I don't recall how I responded, but I'm sure it was along the lines of "Oh, well, tell them I said thanks."

This wasn't the first time I'd found myself confused about race, not knowing how to bring it up or discuss it. Was I overreacting? Was it really just harmless? I guess it was the fact that I heard these types of comments so often. Initially, I was able to ignore them or respond with a witty quip, but after all these years of living in Troy, as well as the death of Vincent, I found it hard to just let these things go. Every minor incident—which I would later learn were called "microaggressions"—felt like the ancient Chinese torture technique of death by a thousand cuts.

The rest of the afternoon sucked big-time. I felt unsettled. In calculus, I couldn't focus on the equations written on the board. In third-year French, I couldn't conjugate a single verb. I kept wondering if I should have let Scott know that his parents' comment irked me. But I didn't want him to think I was overreacting. In truth, I was more concerned with protecting his feelings than unpacking mine.

At the end of sixth period, the bell rang, and all the students got up and rushed to the exits. I couldn't wait to get back to the restaurant. I could really use the comfort of some familiar egg rolls. I could already smell the plum sauce drizzling over the piping-hot cabbage filling. As I approached the bank of lockers by the stairs where Scott's locker was located, I ducked my head. From the corner of my eye, I saw him waving me over. "Want a ride home?"

I lived two miles past Scott's house, so that meant he would have to go out of his way to drop me off. He'd never offered before. Maybe he'd picked up that I'd felt awkward at lunch. Maybe he just wanted a rematch at Risk. I don't know, but I was still processing my feelings.

In truth, I didn't want to rock the boat. Life was great for me at Troy High. I did well in my classes. I had lots of friends. I had added the title of class president to my résumé. I worried that if I started making accusations of discrimination, my friends might look at me differently. Would the cheerleaders still say hi to me in the halls? Would my other classmates start to think I had a chip on my shoulder? Resolving my feelings wasn't worth risking what I had achieved.

So I decided to ignore the situation. I pretended not to hear Scott's offer and tried my best to blend in with the strangers rushing past me. Unlike in a standardized test, there were no simple bubbles to fill in.

R-5.

Following the incident with Scott's parents, I decided that there were two types of racism. While all incidents were dumb, some were dumb *and* mean, things like someone saying, "Go back to where you came from," and any sentence that included "You people." I could never forget any of them, but the dumb-only ones I could at least forgive. In the end, I didn't think his parents were trying to be offensive—in fact, they might have thought they were paying me a compliment— so I chalked it up to a misunderstanding, a hurt I could live with.

As my friendship with Scott rolled on, it was obvious that he was trying to figure out his own identity too. He was always suggesting we try new things. In addition to his fascination with haunted houses and professional wrestling, both of which I would never understand, he had recently gotten into midnight movies. The shows were late enough that I could finish my homework, help out at Chung's, and still have time to rush back to the house and shower off any restaurant stink.

In order to go out, however, I needed to ask my mom. Any request led to questions and then, inevitably, a huge fight. Detroit was a pugilist paradise, and the people of the city liked a good bout. During my junior year, six-time world champion Tommy "the Hitman" Hearns fought Marvelous Marvin Hagler for the middleweight championship, what some say were the three greatest rounds in the history of boxing.

Most marquee matches took place at the aptly named Joe Louis Arena, but our house featured quite a few bouts too. Mostly, my parents fought over money. My dad was terrible at managing it, in particular at collecting debts from friends who'd borrowed money and from customers who hadn't paid their bills. That's why our cash register had a big stack of IOUs. My grandma berated my grandpa when he took us to Emily's for Häagen-Dazs. Cindy and Clifford tussled over Cindy's Robotech figures. We all fought over the best way to make fried rice.

While Craig also battled with my parents about going out, my fight with my mom was the main draw. In one corner was my mom. After marrying my dad at seventeen, she had been thrown into the ring with her adversarial in-laws. Following Ngin-Ngin's lead, my dad's younger siblings liked to tease my mom by telling her that only people with college degrees could be successful in life. Outnumbered, my mom had to learn how to stand her ground. According to her, one night she grew so sick of their snark that she snapped, "Thomas Edison didn't go to college and *he* gave us electricity!" I pictured her turning out the lights as she exited the room.

With five siblings at the dinner table and only two drumsticks, I had to learn how to use my elbows. Admittedly, being a middle child, I might have suffered from a sense of feeling ignored. It didn't help that my family followed Chinese American tradition—which simulated an older Chinese tradition—by starting all the kids' names with the same letter, in our case, a *C*. (It was to help identify our generation.)

My siblings put out regular rankings of our parents' favorites, their own sadistic form of Nielsen ratings. The consensus was that Chris topped my mom's list. In fairness, he had a good case. He did help the most around the house; he cleaned and took care of the younger siblings, changing their diapers and packing their school lunches. And my mom was over the moon when Chris announced, in second grade, that he intended to become a doctor.

Calvin held the top spot with my dad. This was my theory on that: My parents had three kids in rapid succession right after getting married. After realizing they'd have to pay for college, they decided to space any future kids four years apart. Calvin was the first in this second set. He came at a time when my parents were older and more stable financially. He also represented a new beginning for them. My dad even bought him a Sanders Bumpy Cake on my birthday, which proves my theory.

Cindy came next on the list. She was bright, with rosy cheeks like my mom, and the only girl. Clifford followed her, since he was the youngest, and then there was Craig. He was the oldest, which should have made him the preseason favorite, but because of his temper and his knock-down, drag-out fights with my dad, he'd slipped a few notches. That left me in last place, nothing notable to my name. Again, this wasn't just my imagination. This ranking was voted on.

I knew I couldn't compete with Chris or Calvin, or even Cindy or Clifford, but I didn't want to be last. To try and leapfrog over Craig, I loaded up my résumé with noteworthy accomplishments: I placed fourth in a national orienteering competition, got paid to do graphic design work for a local car dealer, and was nominated for class brain and most likely to succeed. I thought that these achievements would earn me some valuable chips with my parents, which I might need to cash in if I ever came out.

Sadly, my plan backfired. The better I did, the higher my mom's expectations were. Any good news produced a reply of "What else?" I don't know how my siblings dealt with the pressure—especially Chris and Calvin, both of whom earned straight As their entire lives—but for me, it was too much. I was tempted to fail at something—even a pop quiz now and then—just to get some breathing room. But I was too competitive and couldn't stand the thought of not giving my best.

My most recent bout with my mom happened to be a rematch. The week before, Scott had organized an outing with our friends to see *The Rocky Horror Picture Show*. Somehow I had managed to convince her to let me go. She might have been confused and thought the movie was about an aging boxer, not some sweet transvestite from Transylvania.

It felt uplifting to see characters like me, gay ones, running around on the screen. It showed that we had wants and desires too. In addition to realizing I had a type—nerdy-cute, like the lead character, Brad, with his glasses and pocket protector—I finally got to see some man-on-man action. It confirmed for me that I was definitely a homosexual. Transylvania never appeared on any maps I saw, but I was determined to find it.

After my friends and I raved about the movie, Scott suggested we return for an encore screening the next weekend. I was surprised. I knew why I wanted to go back—to rewatch the bedroom scene—but why did he? I mean, I had noticed in the dark that he jumped up as much as I did during the film. Was there something more to his response? That got me curious.

As my siblings argued in the video-rental room in the Detroit Public Library (a few blocks from Chung's), I snuck off to do some research. I scoured the card catalog and located three or four promising titles on the second floor. Fearing that the librarian or Craig or Chris might see me in "that" section, I grabbed the books and moved to a different aisle. I quickly flipped through the stash. To my dismay, all the descriptions of homosexuality came off as cold and clinical. Not a single sexy picture in sight. One book said gays were 10 percent of the population. That seemed high to me, but even if it was 5 percent, that meant that there were twenty gay and lesbian kids in my grade at school. I wondered who they could be. My guess was they were in theater and band, but what about science club?

All week long in school, I hinted to Scott that if there was something big that he wanted to tell me, I would be okay with that. Heck, maybe I might have something important to tell him. But these bread crumbs seemed to go over his head. Scott had yet to say a thing.

Before leaving for our next screening, I wanted to be prepared. The first time we went, the audience had really gotten into my favorite scene, the wild and raucous wedding. My plan was to bring some uncooked rice. Why not? Our restaurant had bags of it.

As I put the grains in a Ziploc bag, my mom became alarmed. "Don't waste rice."

My mom kept a tight inventory of things. She took the baggie out of my hands and began to pour its contents back into the giant sack. I tried to grab it. "Scott and I need it. We're going to see *Rocky Horror* again."

"But you went last week." My mom had this strange idea that movies were an annual event, or, in our case, once in a decade.

While not getting into the specifics of the plot, I tried to sell her on the film. "It's a musical, like *Flower Drum Song*—you know, the one with Benson Fong. You have to watch it several times to get all the lyrics."

"You want to practice something? Practice for your SATs." It was getting to that stage of our high-school careers. Craig and Chris had already taken the SATs. Soon it would be my turn.

"I studied already. I'm done."

"No such thing," she said.

My mom was being a hypocrite. She often complained about how little choice she'd had with her own life, and now she was denying me the chance to choose. How could I have sympathy for her when she had none for me? I kicked the bag of rice, hoping for a knockout blow. "If education is so important to you, why don't you go back and finish high school yourself?"

My mom's expression switched from sternness to sadness. My

words had cut too deep. I realized I had gone too far. "I'm sorry. I'm sorry. I don't know why I said that. I'm so sorry."

Too late. She'd run off to the kitchen. I knew there would be no confessions from a friend that night and definitely no singing transvestites.

For a week, I tried to make amends—saying sorry and doing extra homework—but my mom's shoulder remained cold. Hell hath no fury like a tiger mom scorned.

A few weeks later, the stage was set for our next battle. My dad needed help at the restaurant, since Craig and Chris, our part-time dishwashers, had recently been promoted to managers. On Saturdays and Sundays, I now washed dishes, emptied trash, filled the ice machine, and cleaned the toilets. My mom hated the idea of any of us being so involved with the restaurant, but at least the money could go toward our college funds, and in my case, the long hours kept me from going out with my friends.

My new job presaged our upcoming melee. I sometimes got random tips for bussing tables or doing other odd side work, like sweeping the gutters outside our restaurant or unloading the bags of bean sprouts, but this was my first job with real money, twenty dollars a shift. With a steady paycheck, I no longer felt like a kid at the mercy of my parents' whims. I started thinking about my independent future, about being my own boss.

The big choice in the 1980s wasn't Pepsi or Coke, it was a Walkman or a boom box. The white kids in Troy wanted the handheld device so they could cover their ears and shut out the world, but the Black kids walking by our restaurant preferred to blast their tunes so loud that our windows shook. For me, the choice was easy. I wanted to make some noise.

Whenever my family went clothes shopping—twice a year, at the start of the fall semester and again during Christmas—we went down to the posh J. L. Hudson Department Store, Detroit's retail anchor, at one time the tallest department store in the world. It was where I planned to finally buy my boom box. But declining sales and increasing five-finger discounts thwarted my efforts; the store shut its doors.

The day Hudson's closed was one of the saddest days of my life. I cried. I can't remember if I actually shed tears, but I know I felt this extreme pain, a deep loss, and not just because the Santa on the twelfth floor was now homeless. It was because, more than anything, the store represented Detroit's lifeblood, the reason to hop on a bus and head downtown. Its demise felt like the end of an era, the city's final knockout blow, a fatal hit from which it could never recover.

Close to winter break, I asked Scott to take me shopping for a boom box. Outside of school, we hadn't seen each other much— he had made other friends, I think from his church. He did share that he'd gone to see *Rocky Horror* a few more times. He must have really enjoyed the singing and acting because he never mentioned any personal reasons for being obsessed with the film. Maybe I had wanted a deeper meaning, one that didn't exist.

Scott and I swung by Oakland Mall, the mall on our side of town. The sprawling structure with its food court and movie complex was packed. It seemed like half my high school was there throwing money at the latest trends: jean jackets, leggings, anything neon. After we stopped by the usual teen music store, Harmony House, and got sticker shock from the boom boxes' prices, Scott suggested heading to Sears, sagely noting that the brighter the lighting, the cheaper the merchandise.

As this was my first big purchase, I took my time perusing

the merchandise, comparing all the features. Thankfully, Scott was patient. An hour later, I returned home with my new Sears 512 LXI with its four speakers, two tape decks, and AM/FM stereo. The best feature, though, was the price. Not including the eight D batteries I had to fork over money for, it was under budget: eighty-nine dollars.

From then on, I spent hours in my bedroom mixing tapes. By now, my musical tastes had expanded to include Bruce Springsteen, Hall & Oates, Elton John, and even some country artists, although, to be fair, it was mostly Dolly Parton. The catchy beats bursting from my boom box brought me to another world, one where I could just dance with somebody who loved me. If only finding love were as simple as the lyrics to a Whitney Houston song.

Hoping to avoid getting any grief from my mom, I hid my new toy under my bed. Unfortunately, she said locked doors were bad luck. I don't know if this was true or something she made up, but the best I could do was keep mine shut. The volume never went above level four, and the device came out only when my parents weren't home or when I knew they were occupied with laundry. To buy Craig's silence—he was now at Wayne State—I made him a tape of R.E.M. and Beatles songs.

For the first week or so, I wanted to record a clean cut of Prince's "When Doves Cry." When it finally came on one morning, I pressed my ear tight to the speaker, waiting for the exact second to hit stop. I didn't notice my mom had come in carrying a stack of clean T-shirts and underwear. I wrapped my arms around my boom box, but it was too late. She dropped the laundry on my bed. "What is that?"

Bribery was my only option. I held up the boom box. "I was going to make you a mixtape. Anita Mui!"

My mom loved the Hong Kong pop star. She would often sing

to us when we were kids before she put us to bed. But she was not having it. She went all MTV and unplugged my box. "That money is for college!"

Before I could explain myself, she reached under the bed and pulled out my piggy bank, a repurposed Royal Dansk cookie tin. I'd been working for several months, and it was full of twenties and fifties. I guess she must've snooped and found it. "This goes in the bank tomorrow!"

I reached for the container, but it was too late. She was gone and so was my money. I felt so disempowered. I no longer wanted to listen to music. She had reduced me to being a kid again.

Before we drove to work the next day, my mom swung the car by the closest branch of Michigan National Bank. Inside, she deposited my money into my college fund. When she was done, she handed me the checkbook. "You will thank me later."

I doubted that, but I was too exhausted to fight anymore.

When we got to the restaurant, my mom went straight to work. It was then that I realized one of my mom's greatest strengths as a fighter, a skill that I would need myself in the future: no matter how difficult the matchup, she always outlasted her opponent.

R-6.

"Gimme my egg rolls for free and I'll show you my titties," said the redheaded prostitute in purple Day-Glo spandex. I was surprised there was more to see, but after eyeing the empty dining room, she leaned forward and exposed cleavage deep enough to rival the Mariana Trench. I wasn't sexually attracted to girls, but my family loved bargains, so I had to consider the deal. The local sex workers were some of our best customers. They were also some of my first teachers, at least when it came to sex ed.

My mom had a thirst for science education, but her syllabus for us had never included the birds and the bees. I couldn't blame her or any of the other adults in my family. Except for my dad—who had spent his teens and early twenties on the streets of Detroit cruising up and down Woodward—dating was a foreign concept to them. My mom and dad had two meetings in Hong Kong before agreeing to marry. My grandparents had even less foreplay; they'd met on their wedding day.

My older brothers were useless too. From day one, my mom forbade us to go out with girls. According to her, there would be plenty of time for dating after college—or, possibly, after grad school. While Craig was upset, accusing my parents of stunting his social life, Chris accepted the ruling, preferring to focus on his future medical career. I thought it was fine too since it took the pressure off me. I sometimes mused whether this moratorium on dating girls might have accidentally turned me gay.

Fortunately, our dining room oozed with dating experts. Once Craig and Chris got bumped up to waitstaff, I was promoted to manager, a job that consisted mostly of answering the phones, seating customers, and packing the carryouts. I started working nights. After sundown, our white-collar customers were replaced by the more colorful residents of the Corridor. This included the working girls who came off the street. With the city's deepening economic woes, prostitution seemed to be one of the few boom industries. However, I only ever saw one East Asian girl. Because we knew all the Chinese residents in town, I figured she had to be Korean or Japanese.

One day, I saw my mom leaning on the display case taking an order from a pair of girls. The unlikely trio amused me. My mom's clothing and demeanor were very different from the two girls', but the three were laughing like sorority sisters. After my mom left for the kitchen, I continued to eavesdrop. The two friends stuck to one of the most popular topics among the girls: the Middle East oil crisis. Actually, they were complaining about the rising cost of smokes and beer, which was sort of connected. A few minutes later, the girls switched to discussing their future plans. The white brunette with the curls twirled her hair. "Someday I'm gonna get me a family."

The Black girl with hoop earrings nodded. "I want a mixed baby. Drop in some Oriental."

The white girl pulled back her epicanthal folds. "It's them eyes. Makes them exotic."

"Mm-hmm," her friend hummed. She pulled back her eyelids too.

I couldn't tell if the girls were being offensive because they'd caught me listening or if they really needed a sperm donor. Either way, my fourth-year French textbook—I'd chosen to study the language because of Detroit's French roots, not because it was so sexy—suddenly seemed *très intéressant*. A few minutes later, my mom brought out their order, and the girls waved goodbye to her. "See you next time, Mrs. Chin."

As a young Republican, I couldn't be seen as condoning this illegal behavior, but it was nice to see these girls had ambitions. I wondered what my mom thought. She was aware of their profession; she'd seen them standing on the corner, fixing their hair in our lobby, paying for their orders with crumpled bills that needed a good wash. Other than telling me to ignore them, she never expressed an opinion. I wanted to know if she aligned with the moral majority. "You know what they do, right?"

My mom looked at me, realizing that I was old enough to know some things. "So?"

"It's against the law."

"We all have to put food on the table."

Though it surprised me at the time, my mom's attitude made perfect sense. Her arranged marriage was her first and only relationship. To her, love was transactional, a calculation of cost and benefit. Her response brought me some relief. I wondered if my mom wasn't as traditional as I'd thought. If she was okay with having sex workers as customers, maybe she might accept having a gay son.

At school, the topic of sex had grown in popularity too. By senior year, most of my classmates' hormones had mounted a coup. Despite the risk of sexually transmitted diseases and a high-profile campaign to just say no, my peers sounded as if they were reading lines from a John Hughes script, *Sixteen Candles* or *The Breakfast Club*. They openly discussed their horniness, which made sex seem real and achievable.

Luckily, I was able to avoid most discussions about my sexuality. I was the only Asian male in my four-hundred-person class, the only minority guy at all, and I don't think anyone ever saw me as a sexual being. I doubt they even knew I had genitals. Normally, invisibility upset me, but in this case, it became my superpower; it made it easier to stay hidden in my closet.

On the rare occasions that my sexual status came up—whether I had met a girl, how far we had gotten—I had several canned answers. Sometimes I reminded my friends that I was a Republican and my abstinence was my commitment to the party's platform. Other times, I cited my religion. "Sorry, Buddhism says no desire, not even ginger or garlic." If neither of those excuses worked, I blamed my parents. "My mom and dad are such prudes."

My locker was on the second floor, three down from my friend

Doug's. A member of the track team, he had a thin runner's build. With silky brown hair that complemented his button-down cotton shirts and docksiders, the future Fox reporter reminded me of a younger, cuter William F. Buckley Jr.

Now, as a senior, I was the sole Chin representative at Troy High. Craig was in his second year at Wayne State, studying business, and Chris had gone off to the University of Michigan to begin to fulfill his dream of practicing medicine. I'd inherited Chris's orange Chevy Camaro, the one my grandpa had bestowed on him for his general excellence.

Doug and I cofounded our school's Young Republican Club. Despite announcing thought-provoking topics like Reagan's Strategic Defense Initiative and Russia's boondoggle in Afghanistan, we were always the only two attendees at our meetings. Still, we tried. Afterward, I would offer him a ride home. When we were in the car, our conversation flowed naturally, as we shared a lot of core beliefs about individual rights and small government. Doug would have been the perfect boyfriend if I were out and he were gay.

Doug lent me a copy of his new manifesto, *The Fountainhead* by Ayn Rand. While my other friends were fawning over J. D. Salinger's *The Catcher in the Rye*, I identified with this book's hero, an idealistic architect. I too felt conflicted about the strict rules in my life and the obligation to maintain harmony in my world. I wanted to rebel but didn't know how.

One night I was skimming the book again, hoping to gain some insight, as my dad sat in the front booth, chatting with some diners. After observing him for years, I'd realized a truth about relationships. While some patrons came in every week and ordered the same dishes, others disappeared for ages, only to pop up unexpectedly and order something new. My dad welcomed both types of customers with the same level of warmth. To him, friendship wasn't about the frequency of visits but the sincerity of those moments.

This night, my dad was reconnecting with an older Jewish couple who had moved south but were back for their grandson's bar mitzvah. When they first arrived, my dad welcomed them warmly, but I was annoyed. The pair kept pushing me about my grades and test scores, and even worse, they wanted to know if I had a girlfriend. The only girl in my life at that point was Margaret Thatcher, and she wasn't very pretty or popular, so I kept mum.

Business was slow that night, so my dad continued chatting with his friends. He could talk for ages with any customers, especially, it seemed to me, the Jewish ones. They shared the same core interests—their businesses and kids—discussing them in minute detail. I didn't mind having to manage the floor by myself. My parents had always instilled in me their philosophy of mo yow siew. Swinging your arms was bad. If I was going into the kitchen, I had to bring something with me. That encouraged me to be efficient and good at multitasking.

After the couple finished eating, my dad waved at me to join them. As a kid, I was happy when my dad called me over to welcome our customers. I liked meeting all the different people. I met doctors and engineers, nurses and lawyers, factory workers and barmen, postal carriers and politicians. It was like a nonstop career fair. I enjoyed hearing about their lives and engaging with them. But now I was older. No high-school kid wants to sit and answer questions from his parents' friends.

My body clenched, fearful of their next inquiries. I didn't want to have to make up any imaginary girlfriends, so I held up my book. "Sorry, I'm studying."

My dad's hands flapped faster. "Come on."

I held my book even higher. By the time I picked up a second and third book, he was bouncing like he was on a trampoline. I resisted. "I have to study. Big test on Monday!"

In retaliation, Big Al pointed to the stairs that led to our basement. As front-of-house staff, we had plenty of additional side work—peeling peapods, refilling the soy sauce containers, organizing the menus. Checking the toilets was the worst. Like the bathrooms in most Chinese restaurants, the decor left much to be desired, but given the choice of fishing used tampons out of the toilets or playing another round of the Dating Game, I think I came out on top.

With most of the legitimate businesses in the Corridor shuttered, public bathrooms had become extinct. The neighborhood sex workers treated our pretty-in-pink women's room as their boudoir. The girls could perform their five-minute favors in the alley, run in, clean up, and within seconds be back under the streetlights. The quick turn-around time was key. Prostitution in the Corridor relied on volume business.

The sky-blue men's room paled in comparison to the women's; it had a single urinal attached to the near wall and a stall in the corner. The cold and cramped space didn't stop the heroin users from coming in and leaving a trail of syringes and bloodstained napkins, though. On bad nights, they clogged the toilet and flooded the checkered floor. On really bad nights, we had to call an ambulance.

Etched on the men's stall were scratches and symbols that looked like hieroglyphics—if the pharaohs had enjoyed dick pics, that is. I took out my wet, soapy rag and scrubbed. Buried in a collage of scribbles were the words *want dick*. The phrase excited me, but since it lacked proper punctuation, I wasn't sure if that was a question or statement of fact. Fortunately, there was a phone number and I had a pen.

My fingers pressed hard against the surface, removing all the ink, but not before I'd jotted down the digits. Satisfied, I sprinted up the stairs. I tried to return to my book, but the evidence on my palm burned with desire. My emotions jumped between fear and curiosity. Serious questions filled my head. What kind of person leaves his number in a public bathroom? Even worse, what kind of person jots down that number? The most important query, though, was this: What would Ayn Rand do?

Curiosity ruled, and I tiptoed to the phone in our lobby. With my back turned to my dad and his friends—far enough away for my comfort—I nervously twisted the phone cord until it choked my fingers. Whoever was going to answer or whatever he was going to say, I wanted to get it over with as quickly as possible. By the fourth ring, panic ripped through my body. What the hell was I doing? This was a family restaurant, *my* family's restaurant.

I slammed down the phone and ran.

A wooden partition with a giant painting of a dragon and phoenix separated the dining room from the kitchen. Our water and tea station stood behind it. I turned on the mini-faucet. As the blue ink streamed down my fingers, guilt and disgust filled my core. I wanted to rewind to the moment I'd bitten into that forbidden fruit, but before my hands could dry, the phone rang. I froze, and my body and mind once again scrambled. *That's odd. It's been quiet all night. Why is the phone ringing now? Right after I hung up?*

My dad got up from the booth. I was not letting him answer before me. My hands flapped up and down like the wings of an overheated emu. "Don't worry. I got it." I sprinted to the lobby so fast, I banged my shoulder against the wall. "Hello, Chung's."

To my relief, the caller answered straightaway. I'm not sure what I expected the person to say, but the guy only inquired about our hours and last call. I felt relieved. My imagination had gotten the better of me. The timing must have been a coincidence. I exhaled and told him we were closing in twenty minutes, which, thankfully, we were. If he wanted to place an order, he had to be quick. He said something about next time.

As I hung up, my emotions shifted again—this time to regret. I had always been a good kid. It was important for me to set a good example. I knew whatever I said or did would reflect not just on me or my family or the other Asian kids at my school but on every Asian on the planet. Now I was like almost everyone else who came down to the Corridor: a pervert.

I looked to see if anyone noticed my sweaty face, my dripping palms. My dad waved again for me to join his party. The couple smiled. I looked at our lobby. Dead as the night. Feeling defeated, I dragged myself over, ready to once again nod my head and say "Yes, sir" and "Yes, ma'am."

The restaurant was split between our side of the family, the Chins, and my grandpa's sister's family, the Chungs. Because my uncle Phil wasn't too keen on working, every weekend, he hired me or one of my older brothers to cover his shift. Still leery of surprise visits from any bathroom van Goghs, I hesitated to accept, but I could never pass up the fifty bucks.

Unless there was a show going on at the nearby Masonic Temple or Orchestra Hall, Saturday nights were slow, so my dad often stayed in the kitchen trying new recipes. My parents didn't have the time or resources to travel, so cooking became their way to see the world. Thanks to our food distributors, an endless array of samples—new products ranging from Mexican salsa to Middle Eastern hummus—arrived in our kitchen. My parents got to taste a panoply of flavors and spices. None of the dishes ever ended up on our printed menu, but we temporarily escaped Detroit through a bowl or plate.

Cantonese food tended to be on the mild side, but my dad loved spicier fare. One night, he was squirreled away in the kitchen whipping up a hot Indian curry. That left me in control of the dining room. Despite his large size, Frank, our security guard, was a picky eater. He didn't care for the group meals—the traditional Chinese dishes with fish heads and chicken feet—so he'd wait until everyone was done eating, then ask the cooks to make him a special order, something recognizable, like egg foo yung. Ngin-Ngin decided Frank's daily requests cost us more money than his services were worth, so she fired him. Our last remaining line of defense to keep out the riffraff was the buzzer my dad had installed for use at night. We had been robbed at gunpoint several times, so it made perfect sense to have one.

One night around nine, several taps echoed off our front door. I raised my head to see a young white guy in jeans and a denim jacket standing in our glass vestibule. He looked like one of those wholesome students from the ubiquitous college brochures now flooding my mailbox.

Wayne State stood a few blocks north. In the late afternoons, our dining room made for a convenient study hall. Students would commandeer our comfy booths and take advantage of the bottomless pots of tea and free shrimp chips. While this was on the late side and the guy didn't have a backpack, he was nice to look at, so I buzzed him in.

"Welcome to Chung's. Is this for here or to go?"

He stopped in the lobby, signaling this was a takeaway. I handed him one of our paper menus, listing over a hundred mouthwatering items, but his eyes were checking out the room. He tipped his baseball cap. "Slow night?"

My parents had taught me that when discussing the restaurant with outsiders, I should be vague. No point in letting everyone know our business. My mom would even pretend not to be the owner, especially if it was an irate customer complaining about something inane like the size of the entrée, the number of shrimps in an order, or the amount of MSG. She'd say, "Talk to Mr. Chung. He'll be in next week."

I looked over at the empty back table. No bags were there to be picked up. I didn't want to give away how slow we were. I didn't want him to know that I was essentially alone. "It's okay. We have lots of orders inside. So many orders."

The guy continued peering around. I started to worry. Had I misjudged what a criminal looked like? If I screamed now, would my dad have time to rush in and save me? I scanned around for potential weapons. Forks and knives were the only ones in reach. If only I had taken those kung fu lessons like my dad suggested. "This is to go, right?"

The guy pulled his hands out of his pockets. "Yeah, to go."

Phew. He wasn't armed. He also wasn't much bigger than me. My nerves settled enough for me to regain my professionalism. Since most of the ingredients used in our dishes had been precut in the morning and the woks were pretty hot, orders were quick to make. In fact, customers got their meals so fast, some assumed the food must have been sitting under a heat lamp. This time, I was counting on our speed to end this awkward encounter.

He perused our menu as if he were reviewing for a big test. After a long pause, he cleared his throat. "I haven't seen *you* here before."

I was still a little nervous, but I didn't want to alarm him. Muscle memory kicked in and my mouth produced small talk. "I just started."

The guy nodded. "You like working nights?"

Pointing to my books, I said, "I can get more done."

"Nights are nice."

I smiled before noticing his eyes walking up and down my body. He was clearly taking my measurements. I tried to keep things together by arching my back like a defiant peacock. I hoped my firm posture might scare him off. It didn't. The guy continued, "They're more fun."

Suddenly it clicked that he wasn't eyeing the valuable artwork or our cash register. He was cruising me. The only thing he wanted to take to go was my virginity. Adrenaline pulsed through my body. It felt like the scene from *Alien* and my chest was about to burst, but instead of my guts, my heart would spill onto the floor. Part of me felt violated, but another part felt eager. This was dangerous, but in a good way. How was my hair?

Catching my breath, I realized I should've known better. Lots of suburban guys came down to the Corridor for some action. (Everything was cheaper in Chinatown.) The men would drive up and down our street and park in the back alley to do their business. Maybe this guy figured we were part of the sex trade. Guilt by association. My grandpa had been the landlord of a sketchy Asian massage parlor a few doors down. Maybe he thought we were connected.

I gripped my pen in case I needed to jab his eye with it. "Know what you want?"

He folded the menu. "Two egg rolls, please."

Good choice. The delicious appetizers were hearty enough to make a cheap meal. That's what made them so popular with college students and even with the kids from Burton. I scribbled down the order and ripped the sheet off the pad. "No problem. Have a seat."

He pointed to the end of the hall. "Bathroom?"

"Help yourself," I said.

I headed back to the kitchen but turned and caught him standing at the top of the stairs. Suddenly I wondered if he had anything to do with the graffiti. Was that a Magic Marker in his pocket?

The kitchen was quiet. No rattling dishwasher. No whirling fan. No clanging wok. For once, it felt cooler than our dining room. After a few moments, I could exhale. My mission was to get that guy to leave. Right? I mean, that's what my brain was telling me, but my eyes, mouth, and other body parts were telling me to let him stay.

My dad popped his head through the hutch. "Did someone come in?"

"No. I mean, yes, but it's just egg rolls."

I ran to the fryer and plopped in a pair, rattled the basket to get them to cook faster. It took forever for the color to darken from cream to corn yellow to gold. I tried to distract myself by humming, but I never got past a song's opening bars. When the timer dinged, I bagged up the egg rolls in a red-and-silver pouch and ran out.

To my relief, the dining room stood empty. I sat down and waited for the guy to emerge from downstairs. I had no idea what was going on. I pounded my head with my fists. I was so close to the finish line, just months away from graduating high school. I'd be free to do whatever I wanted. Why couldn't I suppress my urge to follow the guy? Why couldn't I just say no?

Once again, my impulsive nature put me in danger. I should've been more careful. There was too much at stake. Not only could it get me kicked out of my family, but it would also end my political ambitions. Republican politicians and public bathrooms were not a good mix.

My curiosity gnawed at me. My legs wouldn't stop shaking. My fingernails were chewed down to nubs. To release the excess energy, I paced about our lobby. I kept turning back to the bag on the table.

It didn't seem fair for the egg rolls to get cold, so I headed down the stairs. At least, that's the excuse I gave myself.

Standing at the door, I pressed my ear against the cold metal. My usual dread of finding a dead junkie was replaced with the fear of meeting a live homosexual. Still, something pushed me to go forward. Curiosity. Desire. A nice tip. I didn't know if or when I would get this chance again. I had to go for it. I took a deep breath and pushed in.

The bathroom's harsh fluorescent lighting forced me to adjust my eyes; my nostrils filled with the smell of Glade and piss. In the chipped mirror, my reflection looked back at me. I didn't look half bad. I would do me. I turned to my left to see the guy standing at the urinal taking what must have been the world's longest piss.

The eight-foot gap provided enough distance for me to take in the full view. He was so near, I could feel his energy. I imagined walking behind him and wrapping my thin arms around his waist and chest but I held back. I tugged the bottom of my shirt. "Your order is up."

The guy nodded but said nothing.

I should've run, but my feet stayed stuck to the floor. Usually that meant spilled sweet-and-sour sauce, but this time my legs were numb.

The guy must have interpreted my paralysis as a green light. He took a step back, exposing his semi-hard penis.

I blinked a few times, just to make sure it was real.

Yep, that was a penis, all right.

Thanks to gym class, I had seen my share of pink dicks. During the two minutes allotted for showers, my classmates' manhoods would appear wet, soft, and fleeting. This one was awake and beckoning: *Welcome to Chung's.*

As the guy leaned his torso back, my body froze. Seeing a single penis was scarier than a whole gaggle of them. (Is that the proper word?) I replayed every second since his first tap on our door, making sure I hadn't misread any signals. I didn't need to know the terms *gay-bashed* and *hate crime* to understand that bad things happened to little gay boys who allowed their dreams to lead them into ignoring any obvious stop signs.

The guy seemed to be shaking as he breached the short length between his hand and my wrist. He made contact. His skin was soft. I felt embarrassed that mine was so rough from all my manual labor. His smile said he didn't mind.

As he pulled me into his orbit, my feet stumbled the few steps until our knees clipped.

His faint breath felt warm on my skin.

Fear of the unknown had long dissipated.

The bulge inside my jeans pressed against the denim.

Just then, footsteps thundered down the stairs—large, clomping steps, like an elephant pounding my eardrums. My head spun around so fast, it was like a scene from *The Exorcist*. Shit. I yanked back my hand and ran out. "I'll go get your order." The bathroom door slammed shut. I looked around, but the space was empty. Had I really heard footsteps or was that Nancy Reagan in my head, saying, *Naughty boy?* I could barely orient myself. My mind bounced between the two men—the stranger in the bathroom and my dad upstairs. I wanted to apologize to each of them for not being the kind of man either hoped I'd be.

I wanted to open the bathroom door again, see what would happen next, but I was already out, and there was no way I was going back in.

I ran upstairs. My dad was sitting at the back table, chowing down on the evening's experiment, a tray of golden curry. He lifted his spoon. "Bombay flavor. Wanna try?"

My eyes fixed on my dad, making sure he hadn't figured anything out. I could see he was focused on the hot food steaming in front of him. "That's okay. I'm not hungry."

"You sure? It's super-spicy."

Spicy was the last thing on my mind. "I said I'm not hungry!"

My dad pointed to the red-and-silver bag on the table. "Whose is that?"

I turned back to the stairs. Still nothing. "I don't know. But make sure he pays."

The kitchen was even more dead. I paced about, trying to find busywork to occupy my hands, but my feet kept sliding back and forth. I wished I hadn't gone down in the first place, but I was also upset that things hadn't gone just a little further. Maybe even a touch. I opened one of the refrigerators and stuck my head in. The smell of red meat permeated the air. I switched to the next one, which was full of bok choy, carrots, and broccoli. Much better. The idea of being a vegetarian monk suddenly felt appealing.

A crashing plate in the corral brought me back to reality. My dad was standing at the dishwasher. "I saved you some curry in case you want to try it."

This time, I snapped, "I'm not the one who likes spicy. That's Craig. I don't want it." I took a breath and let my shoulders drop. "Is he gone?"

"Who? The egg rolls?"

"Yeah—did he pick them up?" My dad called all our regulars by their first or last names. It sounded as if he didn't know him, which was good.

"He's gone." Still unsure who I could trust, I couldn't breathe. I peeked through the portal to confirm his departure. "He left you a tip," my dad added, holding up a couple of dollars.

I looked at the singles in his hand. Disgusted, I wanted to erase all evidence of my subterranean encounter. I wanted the guy wiped from my memory too. "It's okay. You keep it."

I crept into the dining room to avoid any more questions. The room was quiet except for the ramblings of some long-forgotten Motown song. My eyes drifted to the vestibule. That was empty too. I slid into my chair. My butt felt at ease.

As the minutes ticked down to closing, my normal breathing resumed, but my mind could not relax. Instead of feeling guilty, I started to ask the questions that really mattered to me: Why did this have to be our meet-cute? Couldn't he have asked me for my number? Or come by again so we could become friends first? Was this the only option for us? How would I meet my Mr. Right?

R-7.

My first boyfriend was the scion of a wealthy oil family in Denver. Though Steven Carrington and I lived in different states, and he was a fictional TV character, the two of us had a standing date every Wednesday at ten p.m. While I sat at the back of our restaurant chomping on egg rolls and fried rice, my dream catch frolicked in his palatial mansion, feasting on steak and caviar. Our worlds might have been different, but it felt reassuring to know someone else struggled like me to accept his homosexuality.

When the producers of *Dynasty* announced the addition of another stud to their stable, I went berserk. Hollywood heart-throb Rock Hudson, with his chiseled good looks, epitomized the all-American sex god. Unfortunately, when his character finally appeared on-screen, his face looked gaunt and pale. Gone were the dazzling dimples and hunky body that had made the country swoon. It reminded me that youth and physical beauty were short-term visitors.

Rumors swirled about Rock being sick with AIDS. In the heartland of the country in the mid-1980s, not much was known about the disease that was ravaging gay communities on both coasts. Any infected person seemed to be dead within days or weeks. My fears of coming out no longer centered on being disowned. They were about dying. It didn't matter that I was still a virgin and had said no to drugs. The Corridor was filled with high-risk individuals: gays, druggies, prostitutes.

As a science-geek wannabe, I needed to find the cause and cure. The textbooks in school were outdated, and the humongous card catalog at the Detroit Public Library had no new entries. The newspapers in our dining room became my primary source. It was rarely treated as front-page news, so I had to scour every section to find any info. Whenever a headline appeared, my initial excitement would wither with the details. Not even the early reports that Asians and Italians were immune to the disease made me feel better. The fake news only increased my fears about coming out.

One night at the restaurant, my mom and I were on duty. It was my senior year in high school. She again pestered me for an update on my college plans.

"I'm still thinking," I said. That was true. With applications costing as much as a hundred bucks each, I had to be strategic. Two Kroger's shopping bags full of brochures sitting in the corner of my bedroom made the choice difficult. The images seemed nice enough, but I couldn't picture myself on any of those green and ivied campuses. I figured it was like love—I would know the right suitor when he came along.

As I flipped through the latest batch of competitors, the TV teased an upcoming report on funding for AIDS. My ears perked up. It had been a while since I'd heard any news about research or stats. The lack of information only made me think the worst. I looked forward to the update, but I couldn't show too much interest. My mom was sitting right next to me, and I was so deep in the closet that I didn't even want to hear the word *rainbow*.

In those days, gays and lesbians received little support as a protected class, especially among members of my political party. The GOP didn't understand why the government should be doing anything to help these sinners. Some politicians felt that the gays were getting what they deserved. I wanted to bury my head in the sand too, but I was not budging from the chair. An abrupt exit would draw too much attention.

As usual, the report began with a photo of some random white guy wasting away in the hospital. The more handsome he was, the sadder the image. It was strange. I was in high school and constantly thinking about death. Why? It was scary to see so many young men dying, but to me, it was even scarier to see them dying by themselves, no loved ones surrounding them with love and support. That was my biggest fear. I didn't care how I went. AIDS. Gunshot. Overdose. I just didn't want to die alone.

The story switched to the meat of the piece. While the bipartisan Congress had allocated $190 million for research—much more than his administration's request—President Reagan was missing in action. The world was four years into the epidemic with thousands dead, and he was still having trouble even mentioning the word.

Maybe the Great Communicator needed to be pulled aside and given speech lessons.

When the segment ended, I searched my mom's face for her reaction. I wanted any clues to her views on AIDS and, by extension, homosexuality. The fact that she didn't flinch or throw up was a good sign. Maybe there was hope. Once again, my party politics forced me to proceed with caution, but I was too curious—and optimistic—not to ask, "So, what do you think?"

My mom paused, then offered a frown. "He's your president."

"He's everyone's president," I said.

"Then he should act like it."

I couldn't agree more, but I was handcuffed. The closet made me say things I didn't truly believe. I responded, "He's busy fighting the Russians. What do you want him to do?"

My mom shook her head. "Help." It was a simple word. *Help*.

My mom's answer surprised me. Personal responsibility had been her mantra. She'd always taught us to depend on ourselves. No hand-outs. But here she seemed to be saying it was okay to seek help from the government. In some cases, maybe even necessary. Was she re-evaluating the idea of welfare lines too? Was my independent mom becoming a bleeding-heart liberal?

Of all the junkies in the neighborhood, I was in the most trouble. My addiction was the news. I read several papers every day. Seeing the importance of information and how the same stats could be manipulated so differently, I developed a more critical eye toward the media. To avoid getting a biased opinion, I made sure to read both the liberal *Free Press* and the conservative *News*. That was the only way to be fair and balanced.

Our dining room resembled a newsroom thanks to a popular

$4.99 daily special for the almond boneless chicken with egg roll and vegetable soup. My dad loved to introduce us to every reporter. Bob Vito—famous for being the last man to interview Teamster president Jimmy Hoffa before his mysterious disappearance—was the nicest. Vito had started a new job as bureau chief for a start-up cable channel called CNN. He encouraged me to look into the Fourth Estate, adding there would be plenty of job opportunities now that the news cycle had gone 24/7.

It had never occurred to me to pursue journalism, or any type of writing, as a career. I didn't even know where to start. But the more I thought about it, the more it made sense. I liked following the news, and, from talking to the reporters, I thought the job might include travel, something I'd always wanted to do. Newswriting had one additional plus: in that field, if I came out, my sexuality wouldn't be an issue, not like it was for teaching, the military, or the priesthood. I had never heard of a reporter fired for being gay.

So I enrolled in my high school's one journalism class, led by the free-spirited Mrs. Shapiro. Class assignments included composing copy for breaking news, interviews, and profiles. It felt stimulating to stretch my literary muscles, to play around with words and sounds. Thanks to my acing all my homework, my teacher offered me a coveted spot on the school paper. After two years and countless rejections of my op-eds, finally, someone noticed my writing. My perseverance was about to pay off. I was finally going to see my name in print.

At the same time, I got a big promotion at Chung's. With Craig and Chris both in college, my parents bumped me up to the most lucrative position on staff: waiter. It was an easy transition. No additional training was necessary. I had grown up watching my dad and brothers wait tables; I could step right in. Best of all, on a good night, if there was a show nearby, I could pull in as much as 150 dollars in tips.

My ego received a boost: a lot of customers praised me for my fast service and friendly demeanor. I remembered little details about all of them, and they liked it when I asked about their jobs or kids or favorite teams. Some of them started requesting my section. I became their regular. I finally found my seat. I realized that a successful restaurant required more than just good food—it had to have great service too. That was me.

A few months into my new role, my dad and I were on the night shift. In the past, we hired two waiters to work the dining room after the dinner rush on weekdays. Now, we just needed one, plus the manager. With slower business, my dad needed to make some adjustments.

Looking over our menu at all the low figures, I suggested my dad raise the prices, but he refused, arguing that customers would pay only so much for Chinese food. Instead, Chung's had to cut costs. He switched from fresh lobsters to frozen and limited the number of free soy sauce packets. They were tightening their belts so much, I wondered if they had room to breathe.

To help out, I waived my wages and worked solely for tips. I also limited the number of dishes I ordered, especially anything with lobster, crab, or steak. I ate whatever everyone else ate for the group meals. I even stopped drinking pop and switched to tea and water.

Winter months were often brutal in Detroit. Snow and sleet blanketed the ground. Driving on the roads at night could be dangerous. Around nine one evening, a middle-aged couple tapped on our front door. The two of them, both white, were bundled in thick layers, and their hands rubbed each other's arms and shoulders. I was tempted to tell them that the no-tell motel was down the block, but we had only three or four other tables, so I buzzed them in.

Before I could offer our usual greeting, the woman pushed her way across the room. "Tea. I want tea. You got hot tea?"

The man laughed as he trailed her to the front booth. "The place is Chinese. Of course they've got tea."

It was important to stay on guard. I followed, waiting for any warning signs—alcohol, drugs—that I might need backup. Nothing. I was relieved. These two were just in a good mood.

The couple slipped out of their heavy coats. He sported a white button-down shirt and jeans, but she wore a sleek turquoise dress and had stylish hair and makeup. It was clearly a date night. She planted her hands firmly on the Formica tabletop to steady her weight. "Scoot in, hon." She tapped her menu on the table. "Fried shrimp. You got fried shrimp?"

Breaded fried shrimp was one of our bestselling items. The dish featured eight large shrimp shaped like bloated onion rings, then battered and fried and served with a side of Ngin-Ngin's homemade plum sauce and Colman's mustard. The woman prattled on, and her voice sounded husky and strained. Did she have a bad cold? Understandable, given the winter weather. Then it hit me. She was a man— a drag queen.

This wasn't too shocking. Of the dozen bars within walking distance, the Gold Dollar was the closest, and it had a permanent sign reading FEMALE IMPERSONATOR in the front. It was three doors down, but I never got to see what went on inside. Whenever our family walked past it, my mom told my siblings and me to look away. It wasn't so much the sign outside but the long-ago murder of a customer inside.

The pair's frisk-and-search operations continued. I was intrigued.

The few images I'd seen of gay people were associated with police reports, hospital beds, and funerals. Even if you survived, life seemed to be worse. Being in the closet might have been stifling, but at least it was safe. Coming out exposed you to a life of loneliness and sadness. Contrary to any definition on the SATs, nothing about being gay was "happy."

Seeing the couple snuggle in the booth filled me with a sense of warmth and safety, an image to hold on to. After a beat, I caught myself staring, so I did the only reasonable thing I could. I ran. "Hot tea coming right up!" I slipped behind the partition. As steaming liquid filled the pot, my mind brimmed with new possibilities. Maybe being gay wasn't a death sentence. Maybe there was life and even joy. What that might look like for me, I had no idea, but at least there was hope, and as a young gay teen trying to figure out whether or not it was worth coming out, that's all I wanted in the middle of a plague.

Heading back to the table, I skipped across our red-and-black carpet as if it were the Yellow Brick Road. I couldn't wait to reach my destination. They were the pot of gold at the end of the rainbow. To cement our bond, I brought gifts for the table, a side of lemon slices for their tea. Ngin-Ngin insisted we charge for the extras, but I didn't care. These were on the house!

The two were so engrossed in each other, they barely noticed me standing there and pouring them their cups of tea. But I took mental notes on everything about them—the way her arm slung over his shoulder, how they laughed at each other's jokes, the way their bodies connected. I couldn't get over how happy they made me.

The guy winked. "Can we get some menus?"

I pointed at the two on the table. "They're right there."

The lady laughed as she grabbed the one on top. "Where did these come from?"

I smiled. "Take your time."

Our menu had over a hundred selections divided into appetizers and soups, rice and noodles, entrées, and desserts. The dishes were mainly Cantonese with a smattering of Sichuan, Hunan, and Singaporean. A few of the fancier and more expensive items, like our worr dipp harr and lychee gai kow, had brief descriptions, but everything else was simply listed by name. New customers liked help translating unfamiliar dishes, so I stuck around.

Standing there, I thought of my dad and how good he was at making friends. He often just pulled up a chair and sat down with customers. I thought that was a bit forward, but for once, I wouldn't have minded being asked to stay. The couple were lost in their own world. Eager to be helpful, I pointed to the last page. "The specials are in back."

The woman snapped, "Hold on. We're looking."

I scanned the room, nervous that her raised voice might draw the attention of the other diners. Phew. Nothing. This was the Corridor. People knew to mind their own business. The woman ran her finger up and down the pages. I must have been staring again because she fanned the menu in my face. "You taking our order or what?"

"I'm sorry. What would you like?"

Her voice became shrill: "I'd like you to pay attention."

I looked at her, confused. I wasn't the one taking so long to figure out what I wanted—at least, not to eat. The man leaned forward. "We'll have the Dinner for Two."

Good choice. The prix fixe option came with a bit of everything— soup, egg rolls, pepper steak, almond boneless chicken, hot tea, and fortune cookies—so it required little thinking. I directed my attention to the man. "Anything else?"

He handed back both menus. "That's it."

EVERYTHING I LEARNED

I smiled, hoping our friendship was back on track. "Egg drop soup, coming right up."

As I headed to the kitchen, I tried to save time by filling out my pad. I had all the prices memorized as well as the Michigan sales taxes. As I reached the black door, a booming voice shouted across the dining room: "You better not be serving us dog meat!"

Dog meat—what?

I turned around in disbelief.

Did she really just…

I looked back at the couple. The woman was leaning over the booth with the smuggest look on her face. Yep, I had heard right. The perfect example of the mean kind of racism. To make matters worse, everyone else in the room, including my dad, was focused on me. I felt pressure to respond, but all I could do was run. Again.

In the hot, sweaty kitchen, I paced about, trying to mount my comeback. In French class, our teacher, Mr. Cornelius, had described a concept that seemed to afflict me from a young age: *l'esprit de l'escalier,* the clever saying that pops into your head only after you've left the party. This time, the only phrase that came to mind was *Bitch, I gave you lemon slices.*

Minutes earlier, my world had opened up; there was sunshine and air, and the three of us were best buds, members of the same alphabet-soup tribe. Now it had closed again. Shut down. I may have been staring, but so what? Why didn't she read my interest as admiration? Just because the Village People didn't include a Chinese waiter didn't mean I couldn't be gay too.

Kin Sook leaned against the stainless-steel hutch, twirling his toothpick.

I held up two fingers. "Lang ga nin tahn."

He knew exactly what to do. As he went about collecting the

164

vegetables to start the dish, my dad burst through the door. "What was that about?"

I dipped a ladle into the yellow and white swirly broth. "Nothing. Why?"

"You sure?"

My dad knew I was lying, but I had no choice. I felt trapped. The couple had shown themselves to be petty and vindictive. If they figured out my secret, they might out me to the rest of the room. That was not happening. I wasn't ready to come out yet and I wasn't going to let some strangers dictate how that would happen. If and when I chose to come out, it would be on my terms, not hers. "I'm just gonna get them out," I said.

My dad sighed.

I continued with my plan for damage control. Within minutes, I had converted our fine-dining establishment into a fast-food joint. Their dinner, bill, and to-go containers were all on their table. For good measure, I turned the lanterns over the booths up to their maximum wattage and raised the volume on the radio. I was sending a clear signal.

Unfortunately, the couple had planted themselves in the booth as if they owned the space. I was left to sit at the back table, stewing. It's not as if we hadn't encountered the mean kind of racism at the restaurant before. We often got phone calls with people making funny sounds; some kids from the neighborhood even opened our front door and did it live. But this was different. Despite all my efforts to kick these people out, they wouldn't leave.

For two hours, I kept giving them dirty looks, even an evil curse or two, but they kept laughing and joking as if everything were hunky-dory. Worse than her racism was her indifference. They both carried on as if nothing had happened, as if everything were normal. Maybe in their world it was.

Every now and then, my dad would look over at me. I'm sure he wanted me to speak up, but I was afraid of drawing any more attention to the situation. I was angry, but I didn't know what to do with that anger. My closet had left me helpless in the face of the racist attack.

When the couple got up to leave, I exhaled enough air to fill the *Hindenburg*. I couldn't wait to have our beautiful, safe dining room back.

The man headed out first. The woman followed a few steps behind, adjusting her coat. As I went to clear their mess, I spotted their bagged-up leftovers on the table. The woman was still in the lobby, peering out the window. Per my professional code of ethics, I grabbed the bag and ran over to her. When I got close, the woman swiped the bag from my hands.

I'd had enough. We were both different, but that didn't mean we were the same. I spoke slowly, as if I were in a first-grade speech class, and enunciated every word clearly and loudly enough for everyone to hear: "Thank you. Come again, *sir*."

Everyone else was flabbergasted, including my dad. Her, or rather his, eyes widened and his jaw twitched. I waited for his snappy comeback, but it never came. He stormed out speechless into the cold Michigan air. Three cheers! Long live *l'esprit de l'escalier*!

Though my response felt satisfying in the moment, I soon realized it was a mistake. My only motive was to hurt her the way she'd hurt me, but the whole incident was a sad reminder of how isolated I felt. Despite my best efforts to find connections around me, as a gay Asian kid trying to juggle multiple identities, I increasingly felt like the furry creature in a game of Whac-A-Mole. Safe ground for me to hide in was becoming harder to come by.

R-8.

One of our most loyal customers, Dr. Alan Canty, told us he was an ER doc. That's why he worked such odd hours and always ate alone. When the headlines revealed that he was a well-to-do psychiatrist who had been coming to our street to hire prostitutes, I was shocked. After spending over $100,000 on one girl, he tried to break off their relationship. Her pimp got so mad, he took a baseball bat, bashed in Canty's head, sliced and diced his body with a Ginsu knife, and scattered the parts all over I-75.

As Buddhists, my parents had taught me that life included suffering, but the amount we experienced in Detroit was ridiculous. Every few years, someone I knew was killed—a competing restaurant owner, a member of the family association, our neighbor's son from across the street in Troy, the sister of our hot dishwasher, a loyal customer. With the growing body count from AIDS and the haunting suspicion that one of the boys from the Birdtown pet shop was losing weight much too fast, I figured my life would be over by the time I hit thirty. Spending more time in the classroom made no sense to me. I was still eager to learn, but I just wasn't sure I had to do it through an institution.

Every January, when the snow and cold were most miserable and many Detroiters dreamed of moving to sunnier weather, Detroit hosted its annual auto show, where people could check out potential getaway cars. Held at Cobo Hall, the glitzy winter event, with its flashing lights and red carpet, tried its best to be our city's version of the Met Gala. It had lights and cameras and action. The only thing missing was Anna Wintour.

During the weeklong festivities, the entire city appeared to come alive. Even our dining room saw an uptick in business. Customers came in with their bags of swag, flashing the four-color brochures, the same ones my classmates in elementary school would bring in during show-and-tell to show off their parents' contributions. (I would bring in Chinese menus.)

During my senior year, Cobo Hall had once again been transformed into a giant showroom full of the latest models, the coolest concept cars, and the cheesiest Motown cover bands. Like most Detroiters, we considered only the American cars and trucks. For us, it was all about the Fords, GMs, and Chryslers. As I pictured the sleek new vehicles on the open road, my future after high-school graduation became clear. As a kid, I'd loved reading about different places in the *World Book*. Though my parents had managed to eke out a few family trips—a road trip to DC for the bicentennial, drives down to Dayton to visit my uncle stationed at Wright-Patterson Air Force Base, a couple of weddings in California—I wanted to see more. This would be my chance. Forget college. I was going to use my limited time on earth to see America.

Any road trip wouldn't be cheap. Thank God, I already had a head start on the finances. Apart from buying my boom box and going on the occasional Slurpee run, I had been saving most of my money for college. This included all the cash I earned tutoring French and doing graphic design, as well as money I was given for my report cards, birthdays, and New Year's. Since we celebrated both the lunar and Gregorian festivities, I got red envelopes twice a year. I had several thousand dollars at my disposal.

Early on, my plans hit a roadblock. I was waiting on some new customers who needed help with our menu. They were confused why our restaurant had kreplach but no dumplings. I explained that my parents used the Yiddish term to make some customers feel more at home. They still didn't get it. By the time I returned to my seat, my mom was holding one of the free travel guides from the Automobile Club I had left open on the table. "What's this?"

It was freakin' Texas. I panicked and tried to grab the guide. I'd been planning to tell my parents just as soon as I mapped out my itinerary. Now that I had a clearer picture and my mom had the evidence, I figured it was time to come clean. "I'm taking a road trip."

My mom tossed the guide on the table. "Why?"

"Because I want to. I'm going to do it this summer," I said.

"What about school? Don't you have to get ready?"

For months, I had been coy about the subject, giving vague answers about my plans. But now that some ahoos were dropping by and bragging about their grandkids—the ones who had applied early decision—my mom wanted specifics. I couldn't duck and cover anymore. I took a deep breath and steeled my balls. "I'm not going to college. I'm thinking of taking a gap year!"

Despite my gung ho delivery, my mom's face turned stone cold. The visible devastation was worse than the time I'd told her I was a Republican. "What is a gap year?"

"It's when you take a year off before going to college."

My mom narrowed her eyes. "Who came up with this 'gap year' shit?" Okay, she didn't actually say "shit," as I never once heard my mom swear, but I could feel the venom in her pronunciation. It was shit.

"My guidance counselor. She said some people like to take a year off before starting college." I didn't know if college was ever going to be in my future, but I figured throwing her this bone might buy me some time. It didn't.

"So finish college first."

I couldn't tell my mom my real reasons for not wanting to go—the anxieties I had about wasting my precious years and dying young. She never liked talking about death. She said discussing it made it happen, as if it were avoidable. I had to appeal to her compassion. "Please, I really wanna do this. I want to take a break. Can't I have a gap year?"

My mom folded her arms. "Gap is no good. Gap is bad. That's why we mind it!"

Okay, my mom, who came from British Hong Kong, didn't say that last part either, but I wish she had. It would've broken the tension. Instead, she kept rubbing her neck and shoulders, a not-so-subtle reminder of all the backbreaking, painstaking, feet-aching sacrifices she had made for us. Without saying a single word, she had still managed to crush me. Damn, she was good.

I felt guilty for being so selfish. How could I talk about taking time off to someone who had had very few breaks since coming to America over two decades ago? I knew she'd given up a lot of things for us—new clothes, dining out, big vacations. She had no problem reminding us. But wasn't that why she'd sacrificed so much? So her children wouldn't have to work as hard? Couldn't I start enjoying some of the fruits of her labor?

I had to stay strong. This was my future and I needed to take charge. Going to college had been her dream. Sure, I went along with it when I didn't have any ideas of my own. But now that I was figuring things out for myself, I had to take a stand. I had different priorities, like making out with a cute cowboy in Texas and humping some surfer dude in Hawaii. Yes, my plan to see America also included seeing naked men.

At that point, my dad came bouncing in with a big plate of almond pressed duck, a dish like our almond boneless chicken, but a different fowl. His smile collided with the ongoing tension. He looked at his wife and third child. Throughout high school, my mom and I fought, but he had managed to avoid being drawn in. "What?"

We retired to our corners and my mom gave my dad a quick recap before turning back to me for another round. "It's your friends, isn't it? I knew those other kids were no good."

My mom didn't have the greatest confidence in other people's kids. She worried that they would lead me to drugs and temptation. I sighed in exasperation. "They don't even know about this. This was my idea. I want to see the country."

My mom rolled up her sleeves, marched over to the front of the dining room, and pulled back the curtain. The big windows provided a full view of Cass Avenue with its urban landscape of graffiti, busted lights, and abandoned buildings. "That's America. What is there to see?"

I turned to my dad. "I don't know why this is such a big deal. It's just for a year."

Big Al had taken only a few classes at a community college before dropping out to do what made him happy, working in the family business. He never pushed us in school. I thought he would be a natural ally, but I was wrong. He shoveled in a few bites of the duck and put down his chopsticks. "Your mom's right."

"You're serious?"

"You should go to college." The only time my dad ever mentioned college before was in reference to a football or basketball game. Where was this coming from?

"Why? You guys didn't go."

"Well, now you have the chance."

Damn. I don't know if my dad said that to make my mom happy or if he no longer saw Chung's as an economically viable option and needed me to have a backup, but I could feel my plans slipping away. I had never felt so abandoned.

* * *

Over the next few days, my parents continued their full-court press. My mom tried to guilt me by weaponizing food and making my favorite American dishes: lasagna, meat loaf, creamed chicken. As my younger siblings and I devoured her offerings, she'd once again bring up our friends and say how lucky we were to have a mom who liked to cook and who made us what we liked to eat. Of course I swallowed every bite on my plate, but I did not make eye contact.

Meanwhile, my dad turned our dining room into a college recruitment office. The customers he introduced me to—all college graduates—urged me not to "throw away" my future. They raved about their own experiences living on campus, attending football games, joining clubs and activities. They made it sound like so much fun, I think my dad was regretting his own decision to drop out.

The pressure continued in school, where my friends were so excited. They loved sporting sweatshirts and hats from their future institutions—University of Michigan, Michigan State, Wayne State, Oakland University. Though I had had my doubts for a while, I had played along, going through the motions. I listened as they prattled on about their housing plans and future courses. It was as if my mom had called them and fed them their lines.

Feeling cornered, I came home from school one day and headed straight to my room to stuff my face with jelly beans. At the top of the stairs, there were two large pictures hanging in the hall. I normally passed them by without a thought, but this time, I stopped to look. The first featured my mom in her wedding dress. It was the traditional Western white, not the Chinese red. She was the same age then as I was now, seventeen, but she looked so much more mature.

The second came from the same photo shoot. The backdrop was pure white. My mom was seated, holding her bouquet, with my dad standing behind her in his dark-colored suit, hands by his sides. Growing up, I'd always thought how beautiful they were together: The flowing dress and sharp tie. The makeup on both their faces. But today, I took a closer look. They were so serious. I wondered what each of them was thinking. Were their hopes aligned?

The one thing my parents had most in common was their adherence to filial piety. It was due to the love of their parents that they'd both found themselves in that pair of pictures. Neither of them had been thinking of marriage. My mom was in high school, and my dad was having fun driving fast cars. But they both did what their parents asked of them. Without that sacrifice, I wouldn't have been born. None of my siblings would be around either. I wondered if this idea of choosing your own life was an American thing—more specifically, a white American thing. Where else in the world did young people get to do whatever they wanted without thinking of the impact on their families?

The image jarred an old memory, one I had long buried. When I was twelve, I went into the main kitchen to make myself a bowl of wonton and chicken noodle soup. It was my latest mix. I noticed my mom clutching the phone, her knuckles white. She was crying. After hanging up, she slow-walked into our dining room. I didn't know who or what could have made her so upset, so I followed her in. She was seated at the back table when I sidled up to her. "Is everything okay?"

My mom shook her head. "That was your dad's girlfriend."

That phrase might sound like it was out of the blue, but, surprisingly, it wasn't. Maybe it's because I knew how my mom and dad were pressured into marriage or because they rarely showed any physical affection. Or maybe it's because I grew up in the Corridor, where every car parked in the alley included some wayward husband. Or, more likely, because of the earring Chris found in the back seat of our Buick when I was five or six.

My mom mumbled, "She says he's planning to leave us."

Now I was lost. Sure, there were times when my dad would raise his voice or even blow his top, but everyone had their moments. Being together at the restaurant so much wasn't easy for any of us. It was loud and noisy and hot. We were all on top of one another all the time, with no space or privacy. I got it. But I thought he liked being part of our family. Didn't he love us? At least Calvin and Chris?

Suddenly, my mind shifted. I pictured this other woman. Who was she? Was she Black or white? Did he have other kids? I had to stop. I needed to pull it together. No matter what my dad's excuse was, I had to push those thoughts aside. My mom was crying and I had to focus on her. I laid my hand on top of hers. It felt cold. "Dad shouldn't do this. It's not right."

A long pause ensued. Too long. My mom's face looked like it belonged to a ghost, as if her life had already left her body. "So what do you want me to do? Leave him?"

Despite my reputation for talking too much, I had always been a good listener. I heard what she said. I was astute enough to pick up that my mom had said "me," not "us." She was going to leave my siblings and me.

Where would she go? California? Hong Kong? China? In the end, did it really matter? Yes, I would've missed my mom, but I had been raised with enough independence to know that I could survive. I could take care of myself. All that mattered was my mom's needs and safety.

"Yes," I said. "If he's not treating you right, you should go."

She wiped her tears. "But who would take care of you?"

The grotesque thought of Ngin-Ngin raising us flashed through my head, but not even that scared me enough to ask her to stay. I wanted to see my mom smile as if she'd won the biggest hand ever in mahjong. "If you need to go, you should go. We will be fine. Chris will be here. We can look after each other."

For years, my other siblings and I had been obscured by our family's brightest sun, Chris. In that moment, I appreciated having a perfect older brother more than ever before. I realized he wasn't casting a long shadow; he was protecting us with shade.

More yelling and crying ensued that night, accusations and denials, slamming doors and frantic calls to California, but in the end, my mom decided to stay. She did, however, get as far as my sister's room. My siblings and I joined her. We slept by the window, at the foot of her new bed, that first night and for many moons after.

For days and weeks beyond, my mom avoided any interactions with my dad. Except for Craig, who would lob nasty gripes at my dad, my other siblings and I tried to follow her lead and keep our distance. Our trips to Chung's were reduced to a minimum, and we went only when Yeh-Yeh called asking for help. We stayed at home, where my mom focused on us and our studies. Her lessons written on the page matched the ones on her face.

We all tried our best to make life better for Mom. Chris took charge of domestic duties around the house, helping to cook and clean. Craig and I tried to keep the volume down when we watched TV. Calvin and Cindy ate their vegetables. To my surprise, even Ngin-Ngin said supportive things to my mom, telling her to fight back and stand up for herself. Of course, it might also have been a chance for her to put down my dad, but no kindness was refused.

I'm not sure how or why it happened, but over time, the rift began to heal. My mom started accepting the little gifts that my dad left on the old dresser in my sister's room—a red silk scarf, some craft supplies for macramé, a bottle from Clinique. The two of them could stand to be in the same room together and even nodded good morning.

Then one night—I don't recall how long it took—my mom rejoined my dad in the master bedroom. By then, we had already returned to ours. With my parents back in the same bed, my siblings and I knew she had forgiven him. It was her permission for us to forgive my dad too. Some of us took longer than others, but we all eventually got there.

Back then, my mom stayed with the family because of her children. It was another check in a lifetime of sacrifices. Now it was my turn to return the favor. Her parents had disappointed her. Her husband had let her down too. I didn't want one of her children to add to the hurt.

My reasons for not wanting to go to college now seemed silly and spoiled. Yes, I had my own dreams of getting out of Michigan and coming out of the closet, but seeing and hearing everything my parents, both my parents, had given up for us, I had to take into account their happiness too. They'd devoted their whole lives to me and my siblings. Was four years asking so much?

By late afternoon, I had sorted through all the applications and placed them into piles of yeses, noes, and maybes, the latter two being larger. There were no surprises. All the schools wanted the same information. While I wrote my essay, I played one of my mixtapes. When Cyndi Lauper came on, I turned wistful. Even she and her girlfriends were allowed to have fun. When would it be time for me?

At first, I'd considered writing on some unifying event for my generation, like seeing the *Challenger* space shuttle explode on national TV or working on the upcoming Hands Across America, which Chris was helping to organize locally, but I thought it was better to go personal. I expanded on an essay I had written for the school paper. During my senior year, the producers of the hit game show *Wheel of Fortune* came to town to cast local contestants. I'll save the gory details for another day, but let's just say I nailed the sample test and won all three rounds in Los Angeles. I figured that name-dropping a few celebrities would help get me into a good school. After all, who doesn't love a happy Hollywood ending?

That evening, as the oldest kid left in the house, I drove my younger siblings down to Chung's to help with the dinner rush. It was midweek and the place was slow. Calvin, Cindy, and Clifford, who were more latchkey than restaurant kids, ran off to get a snack and then settled in to do their homework.

At the back table, my mom was folding paper napkins. Having exhausted most of her American recipes, she barely acknowledged my arrival. My dad was seated in the lobby. Thanks to the increasing number of dine-and-dash customers, he'd added a stool behind the display case. He pointed at the tray in front of him. "Beef fried rice?"

I wanted to take a bite, but my visit had a purpose. I slapped my dot-matrix printout of my essay on the table. "This is what you wanted, isn't it?"

My mom perked up. She picked up the paper. As her eyes scanned the information, she lifted her shoulders. "So, this means you're going to college?"

"It means I'll apply," I said, "but only to one school."

I was thinking Northern Michigan in the Upper Peninsula, the farthest I could go and still qualify for in-state tuition, but my mom had her mind made up. "Michigan! You apply to Michigan!"

For months, if not years, Ann Arbor had been her top choice. Not only was Chris there studying premed, but it had the highest academic ranking in the state and was not too far from home. Plus, she was a big fan of Bo Schembechler, the football team's legendary head coach.

I sighed. "Okay, but if I don't get in, I'm taking that gap year. Is that a deal?"

My dad crossed over. "Don't worry. You'll get in."

"I don't know. They don't take just anyone," I said.

My mom waved her hand, shooing away any negative thoughts. "They will take you."

"How do you know?"

"Because you're our son."

My mom headed into the kitchen, probably to go brag to whichever ahoo was hanging out in back with Ngin-Ngin. My grandma wouldn't care, but the ahoo might. My dad got up to follow, turned back, and raised his fist. "Go Blue!"

I raised mine too. "Go Blue." Blue indeed.

My dad might or might not have noticed the hesitation in my voice. I don't know. But he kept his fist raised. "Let's celebrate. I'll make you something to eat, anything you want."

I thought for a second. "Anything is fine with me. You guys decide."

Both my parents exited the dining room. The joy and relief I'd seen on their faces—a double happiness—made me feel like I had done something good. So even though going to college was not my first choice, I knew it was the right decision for all of us, including me. I still worried that life was short, but I knew it was never too short to make my parents happy.

MAIN ENTRÉES

M-1.

The crisp air punctuated the fall morning. My parents were making another huge delivery. They were dropping me off at college. As we unloaded the van, my dad kept an eye on his watch. A little after ten a.m., my parents would need to go back to the restaurant to open up, but my mom insisted that we celebrate as a family. Good yang chow fried rice or chicken chow mein was hard to find in Ann Arbor, so we settled for pizza.

Hordes of students and families crammed into the faux-rustic Cottage Inn. Eventually we were seated, but my parents barely had time to take two bites. My dad, the leftovers king, packed us the rest to go. The dorms had yet to install our minifridges, but he insisted we take it anyway. Some families had a five-second rule; my parents had a five-cent one: If it cost more than a nickel, we couldn't throw it away. "Go on. You might get hungry later."

Chris took the pepperoni. I grabbed the beef and mushroom. As my parents waved goodbye, they seemed relieved. Half of their kids were now in college. Maybe they knew what they were doing after all. Meanwhile, I was happy too. Though Ann Arbor was in the same area code as Detroit, the calls were long-distance, which made it seem much farther away.

Couzens Hall was one of the older dorms on the hill, overlooking a track and an open field. To save money, I'd signed up for a triple room with two friends from high school. Located in the basement next to the boiler and bomb shelter, the room was a tight fit but doable. Michigan must have thought it would be a good idea (or a cruel joke) to keep families together, so I was assigned to the same building as my brother and three of my cousins. Instead of creating distance from my family, I ended up living under them.

My two roommates, Tim and Steve, had similar profiles: blond, German, and premed. Their schedules were similar so they could share notes. As a third wheel, I decided to venture out and make friends with some of my other hallmates. There were about fifty guys down our all-male floor's corridor, and I wanted to meet all of them. During our first hall meeting, I noticed a couple of cute ones—a Black boy from the middle of the state and a white boy from the Detroit suburbs. I made sure to stand next to each of them and smile.

Unfortunately, that's as far as things went. On the first full weekend, some of the guys wanted to hit a kegger and the bars on South University. I decided to pass. I was never a big drinker in high school—I needed to stay in control, for fear of slipping up and prematurely coming out—so I wasn't too keen on getting wasted with a bunch of straight guys.

It turns out they didn't need alcohol to be assholes. My room was at the far end of the long hall, so I had to pass every other room on my way in or out. One day, I noticed an open door, so I popped my head in. Posters of NASCAR and Paris adorned the walls. The three guys and I shared a nice exchange until the one with the Jersey accent complained about the communal bathrooms. "Those curtains are so flimsy. Hope there are no gay boys down here."

Everyone laughed, including me. I felt guilty, but looking around the room at the glee on my new neighbors' faces, I didn't want to kill the party or be the outsider. I resented even being in this position. I had assumed these childish jokes would end after high school. I was wrong.

This further dampened my excitement about coming out. I was already being cautious, not just because I had so many relatives floating around campus but also because of a major Supreme Court decision over the summer. In *Bowers v. Hardwick*, the conservative majority upheld the constitutionality of a Georgia sodomy law, ruling that the Constitution did not confer a fundamental right for individuals to engage in "homosexual sodomy." In effect, depending on which state you lived in, it was still illegal to be gay. Michigan was a swing state, which left me blowing in the wind.

After Mr. Jersey's comment, I further retreated into my shell. I limited my interactions to my roommate Tim and a friend from Boys State who also lived in the dungeon. Otherwise, I kept to myself and a few other friends from high school who were living in other dorms.

I thought avoiding most contact would protect me from harm, but it didn't. On the whiteboard taped to our door—the one meant for pithy greetings and smiley faces—anti-gay words (I don't recall exactly what they were) appeared over the next few weeks. It happened only two or three times, but as I'd done with the graffiti at our home in Troy, I quickly scrubbed it off. The memories and fear dashed any hopes I'd had of coming out.

* * *

While I was dealing with homophobia, racism wasn't too far behind. Michigan was a *predominantly white institution*, a term introduced to me when I visited the campus at the end of the summer. As I was a *first-generation college student*, another new term, the school wanted to ensure my successful transition. The Office of Minority Affairs invited me to attend a two-day orientation for free. *Free?* That was a term I knew and liked.

Two hundred students, including me and my friend Angi, a spunky Indian American, gathered in a giant rec room in one of the dorms. The organizers began by advising us on how to sign up for classes, manage our meal plans, and dress for games at the Big House. School sounded fun. But then the topic turned serious. The staff kept referring to the Black, Latino, and Asian Americans in the room as "people of color." That sounded cool. The old term—*minorities*—had never made sense to me. There were more Black people in Detroit than people of any other race. How were they a minority? Did someone forget how to count?

After a quick pizza lunch, we broke up into small groups of twenty. Our leader, Roger, a sporty Black guy in a blue polo shirt with the school's signature *M*, spoke in a deep, calm voice. He discussed the challenges of living away from home and needing to create a new support system before warning us that the previous year, an anonymous flyer that read GET OFF CAMPUS and used the N-word had been tucked under a dorm-room door. The other members of our circle, who were mostly Black, stiffened their backs while mumbling obscenities. I felt bad for them. That flyer was terrible. I was mad too, but I wasn't sure how mad I should be. I glanced at Angi, who was seated across the room. She looked just as unsure.

My first encounter with the hateful word had come as a kid when our delivery guy Bernard, who was Black, called me and my siblings that whenever we hid his cancer sticks. For the longest time, I thought it meant "little rascals." I realized it stood for something worse after I called Craig the word in front of some customers, who proceeded to drop their chopsticks. My dad temporarily banned me from the dining room, so I knew it was something that should never be said, at least not by me.

Our circle pulled in tight as Roger continued his talk. He told us that we should expect to experience some racism, maybe from our hallmates, our professors, or even random people on the street. "I'm not trying to scare you. Just keeping it real." His warning reminded me of the talk my parents had had with me in ninth grade, after the Vincent Chin murder. I wondered if this lesson—on how to behave—would need to be repeated every time I entered a new situation.

I'd signed up for intro courses in economics and political science. I figured they were general enough that I'd need them no matter what major I ended up choosing. When classes began, I hoped for a little more diversity, like Chinatown, but I was one of the few Asian faces in all of my large auditoriums. College was starting to feel like an extension of high school, except instead of being locked in the same building for seven hours, now it was all day.

Outside of seeing family and eating, studying was the quickest and most effective way for me to feel grounded. Acquiring knowledge—even silly fun facts for *Jeopardy!* or Trivial Pursuit—always made me feel like my troubles were temporary and surmountable. I spent the rest of my freshman year in three locales. Most often, I'd be at the undergraduate library, which was appropriately called "the UGLI." When I wasn't there, I could often be found in the small computer lab in Couzens. Since most of the other students owned their own computers, there wasn't much of a wait, except to use the fancy new laser printer.

Finally, I hid in my room. Aside from my boom box, my few luxuries, including my microwave oven and portable TV, had been won as prizes on *Wheel of Fortune.* By eliminating any social life and focusing on my studies—although I did indulge in some Love in the Afternoon (*All My Children, One Life to Live,* and *General Hospital*) and the new shoulder-pad-infused talk show that followed them, *The Oprah Winfrey Show*—I excelled in school. I rocked all my quizzes and tests. My grades ended up being even higher than they were in high school. After that, I knew I'd be able to handle college, at least academically.

As part of my deal to attend Michigan, my parents granted me "gap summers." For June, July, and August, I could do whatever I wanted. For my first break, my mom booked a short visit out west to see her side of the family. My maternal grandparents had originally planned to join my mom in Detroit, but after experiencing the cold freeze—not the weather, but my grandma—they'd changed their minds and settled in the Bay Area. Best decision ever.

A family trip sounded great. I wanted to check out San Francisco. I had been there once or twice as a kid, but only to Chinatown. One of my hallmates had mentioned that the city had a large gay community. I had only completed my first year, but I was already planning my postgraduation life. The city moved to the top of the pile, since it had both my people.

When my mom booked our plane tickets on Northwest, I asked if I could stay on by myself for a couple of days. As usual, she had a barrage of questions: With who? For what? Why now? But since my grades were in good shape and I'd already committed to another year, she agreed to support my research trip. However, I had to cover my own costs.

Over several days, my mom's extended family crowded into the three-bedroom home in Menlo Park. The adults compared their children's academic achievements and played mahjong; my siblings, cousins, and I played spoons. We all chowed down on my aunt Rebecca's scrumptious Hong Kong dishes, including her red bean soup with condensed milk. I was stuffed. When my parents and siblings left for the airport, I took the ninety-minute bus ride into the city.

San Francisco was full of graffiti, trash, and druggies—in other words, it felt like home. I liked the urban jungle more than suburbia. Armed with my blue JanSport backpack, the same one I carried to classes, I checked out the city, picturing my future home. I avoided the tourist areas and went straight for the more downtrodden neighborhoods, the places I could afford to live if I chose to come out this way.

Except for all the damn hills, the streets didn't look or feel too different than Detroit's. It had the same inner-city issues as us, but the national press made it seem like Detroit was the only city in America with any problems. I wondered why we got such a bad rap. Did we need to come up with another catchy slogan?

Before my family left, my mom suggested I look up Mr. Mah. She'd always liked playing mahjong with the guy. I had happy memories of him too. It had been years since I'd thought about our former cook, but when his name came up, his hotness flashed in my head. His smile. His chest. His forearms. (The guy had the nicest forearms!) My mom said he had opened his own restaurant somewhere in Chinatown, but she couldn't remember the name. In Detroit, that would not have been a problem. In San Francisco, it was mission impossible.

Embracing the bustle of Grant Avenue and Bush Street, I wondered if this was what Detroit's version of Chinatown had looked like in its heyday, the 1940s and 1950s, before its inhabitants scattered and reconvened in the suburbs. After I'd trudged up and down even more hills over the next hour, my feet ached. I wasn't a big sweater usually, but now it was dripping down my back. San Francisco had its first strike against it. If I did move here, I would need to budget for better shoes and a hiking stick.

Chinatown was known for its scrumptious food. Each time I passed a roast duck or barbecue pork hanging in a shop window, my stomach grumbled. I needed a break. But which place to go? There were so many to choose from and they all looked good. Then I saw it, a place that looked busy but not too busy. It was a greasy spoon with fluorescent lighting and yellow-stained walls. It was just the kind of restaurant my parents would frequent, clean and cheap, so I headed down the few steps.

Inside, the place reminded me of Chung's. The waiters even wore red jackets accented with plum-sauce stains. There was one big differ-ence, though: the menu had both English and Chinese lettering. It reminded me how little of my ancestors' language I knew. Using my limited Cantonese, I tried to order a sam bo fan—a combo plate of soy sauce chicken, lap cheung, and fried egg. I thought my pronunciation was fine, but the surly waiter kept giving me the stink eye. Normally, I would ask a family member to step in and interpret, but my closest relative was at least an hour away. For the first time in my life, I felt on my own. And although I suspected the waiter was doing this to punish me, I sucked it up and pointed to the picture on the wall.

Abandoning any hope of finding Mr. Mah, I moved on to other potential eye candy. After years of passing by the adult bookstores back in Detroit, I'd finally gained the courage to pop into one now. Truthfully, I hadn't missed much. Most of the porn was straight; there were only a few gay titles. I perused them all: *Honcho, Blue Boy,*

Mandate. All the guys, who were, again, all white, were attractive but a bit too beefy for my taste. I didn't need a Big Mac. A cheeseburger would be fine for me.

I did pick up a copy of a gay travel guide called *Spartacus.* (The cover featured a hot, young pre-*Friends* Matt LeBlanc.) I was amazed that a book like this even existed. The guide had listings for gay bars, gay hotels, gay beaches. There were even gay hairdressers. The book also included a section of sexually oriented services: leather stores, massage parlors, bathhouses. The idea of paying for sex wasn't new to me, but the book was advertising guys, not girls. I approved of the equal opportunity.

I tried to figure out a game plan. I had no connections to get a fake ID for the bars, so that left the gay strip clubs. There were three or four listed. I can't remember the one I chose—or I've since blocked out its name—but I'm pretty sure it was in the Tenderloin, this city's version of the Corridor. When I arrived, the blinking lights on the marquee served as a beacon in the night. The men who slipped in reminded me of the ones who entered the Gold Dollar bar through the back door. I wished I'd brought a trench coat.

AIDS remained a concern, but thanks to another iconic Diana (Spencer, not Ross), there seemed to be more compassion and understanding. The People's Princess, whose wedding, when I was in middle school, had been watched by an estimated 750 million people worldwide, had recently visited an HIV/AIDS unit in a London hospital. Once she showed that it was okay to shake hands or even hug someone with HIV, the whole world, including me, breathed a sigh of relief. I realized that I didn't need to be scared. I just needed to be smart.

After pacing on the corner for at least thirty minutes, I decided to just go for it. I quickly walked over, paid my fee, and ducked in.

The dingy lobby reeked of smoke, mildew, and what I assumed to be semen. It was weird how I felt so out of place yet so comfortable at the same time. I continued into the theater space, where half a dozen silhouettes each had the luxury of an otherwise empty row. I slipped into a seat by the exit, using my backpack as a buffer between my body and the stained fabric.

On the stage, a series of male dancers took turns parading in the flashing lights. They'd start off in some sexy attire, stripping off piece by piece with every thump of music. At some point, they'd be completely naked. I tried hard to avoid staring at their groins. For some reason, I thought that'd be rude. Instead, my mouth salivated over their faces, chests, and arms. I found the whole experience thrilling, but by the fourth or fifth guy, some of that initial excitement began to wear off. The theater turned out to be another predominantly white institution. The chosen guys were attractive, but this was San Francisco. Where were all the Asians or other men of color? Didn't the club's bookers know anyone in Chinatown?

As I composed the words to my refund request, the night suddenly picked up again. The next dancer, who, no surprise, was also white, somehow managed to regain my attention. Attraction was strange like that. Does anybody know why some people just turn us on? This guy did it for me. His whole package just seemed to work: his sandy-brown hair, his lean body, the way he thrust his way onto the stage.

The emcee shared that the performer hailed "all the way from Montreal." Canada. That must've been it. I thought back to my family's dim sum trips across the border. No offense, but the guys in Windsor never looked this hot.

He was dressed in a black leather jacket and tight blue jeans— at least when he started—and I soon realized that the guy's appeal to me came from his attitude. He probably wasn't that much more attractive than the other dancers—it's not like he was Brad Pitt—but there was something in the way he paraded from one end of the stage to the other with all this chutzpah that drew me in. From the way he thrust his hips and the big smirk on his face, I could tell he knew he was a better cut of beef than the chuck meat at his feet. That was sexy to me.

During his set, he came off the stage and weaved his way through the seats of fans, pausing occasionally to collect his tips. I skimmed through my wallet, wondering if I could compete for his affection. I gripped a few dollars and slid my butt to the edge of my seat. I imagined myself fingering the fuzz on his chest. But I never got the chance. Some old dude in front turned the performance into a private show, stuffing in enough singles to make a small mortgage payment. At the end of his set, the sexy Canuck retreated into the wings.

As the next dancer gyrated onstage, I grew mad at myself. I had missed this great chance by sitting so patiently in the back row. Why was I always waiting? I realized that if anything was going to happen, I would need to learn to take charge. I was an adult now, and I could make the rules. I slipped out of the theater to see if I could find him in the lobby. Lucky for me, my dancer had stopped outside to chat with the burly bouncer. My eyes stared at the guy's ass; my tongue got stuck in my throat. He noticed me staring and strutted my way. Aiya!

"You like the show?" he inquired with an accent.

I pretended not to be scared. I thought back to my high-school French but wasn't sure I could say more than *Voulez-vous coucher avec moi ce soir?* I spoke the only language I knew he would understand: I pulled out a five.

The guy assessed the bill. He seemed amused, yet satisfied, as he slipped it into his back pocket. How was I supposed to know what the going rate was? That's what I'd heard they paid in Detroit. Maybe the cost of living was higher out here. I feared his next move would be an escape, so I stayed with my native English. "Can I kiss you?"

I don't recall if he answered yes or how I knew it was okay, but I lunged forward. Our lips locked. Time stopped. The energy from my body turned me into a human space heater. I'm sure I must've been glowing. I felt different. I felt like a grown man. I couldn't believe this was happening. I opened my eyes to see if he sensed our connection too.

No. The man's arrogance had turned into indifference. He had probably been through this scenario a hundred times before. So what if some nerdy fresh-faced kid from the Midwest just got off the bus and took one of the biggest steps of his life? What did it matter to him?

I was out of fives and didn't have the cash or balls to go any further. After our peck, the night shut down, at least in the romance department. There was nothing left to do. The guy walked past me and got on his motorcycle, and when he kick-started his hog, the ground trembled like a small earthquake. I wanted to chase after his bike, to tell him not to go or to take me with him, but he was gone.

Even then, I knew I would remember this guy long after he had forgotten me.

A hunger grew inside my body—this time in my stomach—but the kiss was my trip's one big splurge. It was too late to head to my grandparents' place, and even the cruddiest hotel room would've set me back thirty bucks, the equivalent of a few textbooks for school. So I decided to sleep out on the streets. Morning was just a few ticks away. I could handle this. Detroit's Corridor had an ever-growing number of homeless people. If those drunks and addicts could survive the cold Michigan winter, a summer night or two in California should be a snap.

I trudged up the hills in search of temporary housing, a hidden corner or private alley. After being chased out of several doorways by the other orphan occupants, I spotted a tall parking structure that looked dead enough. I slipped past the guard nodding off in the booth and snuck up to the top floor, where the smell of gas and urine was less prevalent. A few parked cars dotted the landscape. I crawled behind a big silver Cadillac, hoping that the fancy wheels would soften the rough night.

I swept the ground with my feet, kicking away any dirt, before I lay down. I converted my backpack into my pillow and felt a lump digging into the back of my head. I unzipped my bag, revealing a takeout container of leftover rice with soy sauce. The meat and vegetables that had come with it were long gone, but my dad had taught me never to throw away good food. I finished the last bites, then set it aside, hoping the smell wouldn't attract bugs or rats.

As I tried to catch a few winks, memories of the dancer played on a loop in my head. The hair. That jacket. Those lips. I might have been homeless and hungry, but I was happy.

Soon, my attention drifted up to the cold night sky. Too much light pollution was generated by the city for me to see any celestial bodies, but I knew the stars were out there somewhere, just waiting to be found, admired, and even kissed.

M-2.

I stood on the corner of Cass and Peterboro with my mom, who peppered me with a new set of questions: "Are you sure it's safe to drive at night?" "What's the speed limit on the highways to Massachusetts?" "Do you want an egg roll for the road?"

I said yes to the last query, but all the others led me to check my Swatch watch and wonder where the hell my ride was. It was getting late and we had a nine-hour drive ahead of us. I wanted to get on the road. When the red sports car finally pulled up in front of our restaurant, twenty minutes late, I jumped in and headed off with my new friend.

I had landed a summer job working out east—or, rather, my dad had helped me land it. (I had tried looking myself, but I didn't have any contacts, and the ones the university offered led nowhere.) My dad had been talking to our kitchen-equipment supplier, who'd told him that his nephew had landed a gig at a summer camp in western Massachusetts. My dad mentioned it to me, and after I'd applied there and gotten hired, I arranged to go with the guy's nephew, Steven.

Splitting the gas and taking turns behind the wheel, Steven and I sped through a trio of states, chatting about our different colleges and families. I don't remember much of what he said, but like my dad, I was always happy to listen, and Steven was happy to talk. I was too excited to sleep. After my kiss in San Francisco, I wondered if the East Coast boys were just as loose.

Our destination was down the road from Tanglewood, the summer home of John Williams and the Boston Pops. As Steven's car pulled past the thick wooden gates, my pits began to sweat. My only prior experience with the outdoors was the time my parents had signed up Craig, Chris, and me for one of those do-gooder programs that shipped inner-city kids into the wild. When one of the other campers had pulled out a knife he'd taken from the mess hall and threatened to kill himself, my parents had reasoned that we'd be safer in the city.

Built on a pristine lake, Camp Mah-Kee-Nac turned out to be a sports camp for highly educated Jewish boys from good families. Given the clientele of our restaurant, I expected to feel right at home.

As the camp's staff—a hundred men and two women—gathered around the flagpole for orientation, I was excited to see so many potential new friends. The other counselors were mostly white jocks from the Midwest and a handful of Brits imported to teach their version of football.

Steven and I were both wearing jeans, but most of the other guys, who'd probably arrived a day earlier, were dressed in shorts. Spotting all the muscular thighs, I prayed for a hot summer so my coworkers would have to take off their shirts too. But to my chagrin, the guys spent the icebreaker discussing subjects that were foreign to me: girls, cars, and beer. It felt like the basement of Couzens Hall, the same rampant machismo. Once again, my hopes of coming out were dashed.

I was thankful that I was at least out of Michigan and getting paid a nice sum, but I was out of my comfort zone, and the summer soon felt like it was dragging. I tried to make the best of my situation, but it wasn't easy. My only release was jerking off, but even there, my options were limited. I could duck behind the giant kiln in the art room or wake up before everyone else and hit the showers, but the risk of being caught was too great, and I liked sleeping in.

On alternating weekends, I caught a ride into town with whoever had room in his truck. At the local dive bar, my fellow counselors pounced on the girls from our sister camp as I looked for ways to kill time. After exhausting the two good songs in the jukebox—"Sweet Caroline" and "Dancing in the Dark"—I resorted to drinking. The taste of beer still grossed me out, but it was better than hearing the drunk guys spew their horniness and misogyny. I slowly nursed my mug, but lacking the proper enzymes to metabolize alcohol, I didn't need much to get wasted. At the end of the night, I would stumble back to my cabin alone, tripping and falling, hoping not to step on my own vomit.

The diversity at camp was limited: two Black counselors, an Irishman, and one other East Asian, James, a twenty-something English bloke who'd recently quit his job at the BBC to sightsee across America. When the fit Brit introduced himself on day one, I was excited. He was attractive with a sexy accent, and I thought, *Cool, another Asian who wants to travel.*

But James and I had little in common. We came from different worlds. While I was trapped in the dingy art cabin with the nerds and misfits, the hunky midfielder frolicked outside with his fellow jocks. The white guys from Texas and Kansas were amused by the fact that an Asian guy knew how to kick a ball. They liked him so much, they nicknamed him "Charlie."

Every time the guys used that slur, it triggered my PTSD from elementary school. Those stereotypes were already fifty or sixty years old when they'd been used on me. If they were going to be racist, they should at least try to stay in this decade.

While I felt like a hypocrite since I never spoke up to defend myself, I wanted the slightly older James to be braver than me. I wanted him to stand up and fight for all the smaller kids who had ever been bullied on the playground. Instead, he laughed along, the same way I'd laughed at fag jokes in the dorm. After another catcall during lunch, I had had enough. I cornered James at the drinks station. "You know that's racist, right?"

He stopped pouring the cherry bug juice. "Excuse me?"

"They're making fun of you," I said. "It's from those Charlie Chan movies from the twenties and thirties, the one where the fat white dude puts on offensive makeup and plays the wise Asian detective. It's like calling you Bruce Lee or Long Duk Dong."

James surveyed the packed room of boys and men, all jamming their mouths with hot dogs and chips, before nodding to me with an ever so proper "Thank you." As he walked over to his junior campers, he looked back and shook his head at me. "Why is everything about race with you Americans?"

My shoulders jerked back. What was his problem? I was trying to help a brother out. Did they not have racism in England? Or was he afraid of being relegated to the kids' table, like me? Either way, I guess the guy didn't want a little thing like racism to ruin his American summer.

Over the next few weeks, James and I rarely spoke. I stayed in the art cabin messing with the pile of clay while he played the beautiful game with his friends. We had each made a bargain with ourselves and learned to live with the consequences. If I'm being honest, maybe a small part of me was jealous that James had been given this opportunity at friendship. Would I have taken the same deal if it had been offered to me? Could I have been happy playing Charlie?

As the summer wound down, I figured it would still be nice to stay in touch with James. When I saw him outside his cabin cleaning his cleats, I asked him for his address in London. It wasn't a sexual thing. It was just to be friends. He hesitated before telling me that it wasn't necessary, that the camp would be sending out a directory of all the staff. I was surprised but excited. The camp hadn't said anything about those plans. At least, I hadn't heard about them.

A week or two later, I returned home. I looked forward to receiving his information so we could become pen pals, but no packet ever arrived in the mail. It turns out that James should've been called Dick.

Fortunately, in the fall, my social life at Michigan improved. Tired of trying to hitch free rides home, I stayed in Ann Arbor and got a part-time job in the dorm. I moved up to a double on a co-ed floor with one of my freshman roommates, Tim. Though the engineering major and Depeche Mode aficionado sometimes resembled an even more anal-retentive version of Mr. Spock, we got along well.

Our new neighbors were nicer too. Alicia, a Black premed major who wanted to increase the number of Black students on campus, and Janet, a Palestinian American architecture student who advocated for a Palestinian state, lived next door. We often shared meals. Of course, after years of being a Republican, I liked riling up liberals, which wasn't hard to do. I sometimes took extreme political positions, the opposite of theirs, just to watch them choke on their spinach salads.

Though my major, like my sexuality, remained undeclared, my classes leaned toward prelaw—economics, English, and political science courses. My GPA was a 3.8, so it felt like I had room to breathe. I missed being socially active like I'd been in high school. I decided to join a club or two, but I wasn't quite sure where to start in this liberal bastion.

During my first year, I had sought out the College Republicans, but they were MIA. Either Michigan didn't have a chapter or the members were in hiding. I sent in sample articles to the college paper, the left-leaning *Michigan Daily*, but never heard back.

In truth, I wasn't too upset. Despite the way I teased Alicia and Janet, my allegiance to the Reagan Revolution had softened during my senior year in high school. It started after I attended Boys State, a select summer program for aspiring politicos. The attendees came from every corner of the state, including the rural counties, home to the Michigan Militia and Dutch Reformed Church. As we debated current events, I realized I might have considered myself a "conservative" in the Detroit suburbs, but to the rest of the state, I was practically Phil Donahue.

South Africa and its segregated system of apartheid presented the first sign of a schism. A huge international push existed to get the United States to divest itself of its holdings in the pariah nation, yet Reagan defended the white supremacist government. I couldn't believe anyone, let alone the leader of the free world, could support colonial-era policies, but I was wrong. The guys at Boys State pointed out that South Africa was the most economically successful country on the "dark continent." Our debate then shifted to Detroit and how it was a "giant shithole" as corrupt as a "Third World nation." To my surprise, I found myself getting angry and defending Mayor Young.

AIDS further expanded the rift. Reagan's silence equaled death, but the words coming from some of the students at Boys State made me wish they would just shut up. They said Rock Hudson was at fault for "choosing" that lifestyle. Given my own struggles, I knew it was not a choice. My sexuality had been hardwired since I was born. Now that I was in college, the Ryan White case—where an Indiana teen with AIDS was denied the right to attend seventh grade— proved the party to be plain cruel. "Compassionate conservative" was just clever branding.

Now that I was in college, apartheid and AIDS were joined by a third *A*—abortion. The only visible conservatives on campus were the ones protesting the landmark Supreme Court decision *Roe v. Wade*. At first, I followed the party line. I was adamantly pro-life. I could afford to be. The contentious issue meant nothing to me, since the chances of me getting a girl pregnant were nil. Besides, why couldn't these young people practice abstinence? I certainly was.

But after being tag-teamed by Alicia and Janet for weeks, I conceded the issue had bigger implications. It had to do with the freedom of choice, allowing women to do what they wanted with their own bodies. I'd like to think that it was compassion that got me to switch my position, but the truth is that I didn't want to feel like a hypocrite. As a closeted gay man, I was striving to do the same thing: control my own body. The only consistent position was to evolve and be pro-choice. Of course, I waited weeks before telling Alicia and Janet that they had opened my eyes, just to prolong their ire.

I can see, in retrospect, that the signs that I was at the wrong party were always there. It's like that famous quote a pastor wrote about the Nazis: "First they came for the socialists," then the trade unionists, then the Jews, and each time, he said nothing, so when they came for him, there was no one left to defend him. I still believed in working hard and in individual agency, but I couldn't leave out having compassion for others. I had heard the liberal media and activists calling out the Republicans for their austere policies, but I wasn't ready to hear their criticism.

The thing is, I was a gay person of color from a religious minority and a working-class background; I was an outsider trying my best to fit in with the cool kids. And though members of my own party had clearly been coming after me, or people like me, for a while, I had refused to acknowledge what was going on. I wanted to believe they weren't talking about me, that I was one of the "good" ones.

Looking back, I regretted that I had given so much time and energy to my first political home, but it was better that I figured out these things now. As a newly independent voter, not tied to any party, I had a newfound freedom. For the first time in my life, I could figure out where I fit in, at least politically. I wanted to challenge the many assumptions I had and explore some new ideas.

Angi, my friend from high school and the minority orientation who happened to be Hindu, was interested in joining Talk to Us, a comedy-improv group sponsored by the Jewish organization Hillel. I had never auditioned for anything before, so I was surprised that

I got in. We both did. The troupe—which traveled to the dorms, performing skits on racism, homophobia, and antisemitism—was a new experience for me. It forced me to get out of my head and think on my feet. There was an electric energy being onstage.

The next summer, Camp Mah-Kee-Nac invited me back for another season, but my plans changed when Keith, a friend from the improv troupe, asked me to come out with him to San Francisco. Of course, he didn't mean *come out*, come out, since I still hadn't told him—or anyone else, for that matter—I was gay, but if things went well, that might be a good summer goal.

Michigan's summer break began in late April, so until I headed west in June, I planned to stockpile some big cash by waiting tables at Chung's. For the next few weeks, I took every open shift in the dining room. I even washed dishes and made delivery runs. While most of the money was earmarked for tuition and room and board for the fall semester, I figured some of it could be used as play money. If I was lucky, I might even be able to afford something more than a kiss.

As my exit date loomed, I often stayed up late to research my trip. Despite its hills and dirty, overpriced parking garages, San Francisco grew more appealing as a postcollege destination. One travel guide mentioned Harvey Milk, the first openly gay person to be elected to public office. It was a nice surprise. I had never heard of a gay civil rights leader before. It had never occurred to me that gay people might deserve protection and equality. It made me happy. Maybe I could be gay and still be involved in politics.

One night a week or so before my departure, I heard a noise coming from the kitchen at home. Usually that was my grandpa brewing up a late-night cup of Ovaltine or Craig yelling about some bad play on a West Coast game on TV. Annoyed by the racket, I stumbled to the archway. My mouth was ready to cuss someone out when I saw my dad helping Ngin-Ngin put on her black slippers. I rubbed my eyes. "What's going on?"

Yeh-Yeh was standing by, looking lost, as my dad lifted Ngin-Ngin to her feet. "Nothing. We're just taking Grandma to the hospital."

The hospital? That was odd. My family might not have officially homeschooled us, but we were definitely home-hospitaled. In our restaurant's back kitchen, my grandma had a giant metal cabinet stocked with preserved roots, rare herbs, and dried animal parts. Any health issue with anyone in our house, or even in Chinatown, was treated with one of her soups or stews. If that didn't work, we had jars of Tiger Balm and bak fah yeow. My grandma's problem must have been serious.

My dad led Ngin-Ngin to the door. "Don't worry. Go back to bed."

"Are you sure?"

"Yeah. Yeah." The stutter in his voice unnerved me. My dad was not the biggest talker, but when he did speak, he was straightforward. "We're fine," he said. I didn't quite buy it, but I was tired, so I let it go.

The next morning, we learned that Ngin-Ngin had suffered a major stroke. True to form, she'd put in a full day's work, then stayed late to play a few rounds of mahjong. She never mentioned the tingling in her arm or dizzy spells she'd experienced throughout the day. It was only that night when Grandpa heard crying from the single bed next to his that anyone suspected any trouble. Now she was in the hospital, and my dad was stuffing her nightgown and kung fu slippers into an overnight bag.

As word of Ngin-Ngin's condition spread through Chinatown, friends and family filled our back kitchen, dropping off trays of sesame balls (lucky desserts made with dough and red bean paste) and boxes of dan tat (fresh Chinese egg tarts originally from Portugal). The ahoos shared funny stories about Ngin-Ngin, like how she used to skip her English classes at Burton to run across the street and play mahjong; they wondered when she would be able to play again. Despite my impressions of my grandma, it was nice to know that others had a different point of view. Everybody should be liked by somebody.

Two days later, my dad brought Ngin-Ngin home in a wheelchair. I hardly recognized our family matriarch. She seemed mentally out of it. She had lost the use of her right arm and leg. Her booming voice, which once rattled the bottles and shook the fan, was gone. I had no idea who this person was.

The rest of the family stepped up to provide home health care. My dad played chauffeur, driving her to physical therapy and picking up all her medicines. Chris did research, trying to find information on the best care. Calvin served her hot tea. Cindy took her to the bathroom. Clifford lifted her in and out of the car each night. Even my mom pitched in, making the egg rolls, almond cookies, and white rice so my grandma could remain on the payroll.

Me? I still wasn't ready to show her any compassion. I knew she had had a hard childhood—she'd grown up fatherless after her dad's head had been chopped off by deadbeat debtors whom he was trying to collect money from as part of his job; that's why she always threatened us to jom ne ga how—but I still couldn't muster any sympathy for her. In retrospect, this may come off as harsh, but it was how I felt. She'd never shown me any signs of affection. Why should I give her any? Just sharing the same last name and blood didn't mean we were truly family. Your family, I thought, were the people who loved and nurtured you. That didn't describe her.

During my breaks waiting tables, I'd stand in the narrow hall between the main and back kitchens and watch my grandma sitting and staring at the grease-stained walls. I wasn't gloating, but I was paying attention. It was ironic that after all these years of her calling me and my siblings useless, it was my grandma who had become mo-yung.

With all the drama, everyone seemed to have forgotten that I was leaving in a few days. When I asked my dad to help me get traveler's checks from the Automobile Club, he surprised me by insisting that I cancel my plans and stay home. That made no sense to me. There were already so many people hovering. I would just be in the way.

But my dad, who shared the same birthday as Ngin-Ngin, wouldn't abandon his zodiac twin. I shouldn't have been surprised. He had always prioritized his mom over us. At dinnertime, he scooped her a plate first. When the weekly lobster delivery came in, when we still ordered them live, he saved the largest for her. Of course he was going to make me abandon my plans.

But I wasn't ready to give up. I figured my mom might be a useful ally, since she and Grandma had never embraced each other. Lately, my relationship with my mom had vastly improved. Our fighting had ended, and since I'd started at Ann Arbor, she hadn't once tried to pressure me into pursuing one of the big three Asian American professions: doctor, lawyer, engineer. I think she was just happy that I was in college.

One afternoon, after my younger siblings had settled into the back office to do their homework and my dad had taken Ngin-Ngin to physical therapy, I approached my mom in the back kitchen. She was taking out another tray of cookies. Even after all these years, I still couldn't get enough of them. I picked up one of the bigger samples. It was hot to the touch. "Man, I am going to miss these when I'm in San Francisco." My mom didn't reply as she put in the next tray. I tried again, in case she hadn't heard me over the slamming oven door: "I'm leaving next week. Maybe I can take some with me."

She walked over to the refrigerator. "Did you talk to your dad?"

"About what?"

"You know, San Francisco."

I took a giant chomp of cookie. "He thinks I should stay, but I don't see the point. There's already so many people here." I waited for an answer but got only silence. I wasn't sure what was going on. I expected her to be asking me a million questions like she usually did. Instead, she seemed to be ignoring me. "Is everything okay?" I asked.

"Your grandma's not doing well."

"I know. But there's not much I can do."

She pulled out the milk and poured me a glass. "She is your grandma."

The few hairs on my skin bristled. "So? What's that got to do with anything?"

"Maybe you can go to San Francisco next summer."

The hot blood reached my head. Summers were mine. That was the deal. I raised my voice: "Why is everyone making such a big fuss about all of this? None of us even like her."

My mom slammed the refrigerator door. "That's not true!"

I could have gone into a litany of incidents, but I figured my mom had her own list of grievances. "What has she ever done for us? Do you even care about her?"

"Of course I do."

"Why?"

"She's the only mom I've ever known."

My mom's response devastated me. She would never come out and openly say it, but I knew she resented her own mom for abandoning her as a one-year-old in China and then—after the two reunited in Hong Kong for a few short years—sending her off to marry a stranger in Detroit. But it wasn't like Ngin-Ngin had ever been maternal to her. In fact, she gave Cinderella's evil stepmother a run for her money.

How badly had my mom craved a mother figure, someone to keep her safe? Maybe the reason my mom was so protective of her own children was that she'd never had anyone looking out for her, telling her she was loved, that her presence was needed. Maybe in all these years, she was trying to be the mom she'd never had.

I retreated to the dining room to review my options. My parents believed that our bodies needed to be balanced, like yin and yang. Right now, I had too much yeet hay, or hot air. I needed something cool, so I ordered a plate of steamed bitter melon with black beans. Kin Sook looked surprised. This wasn't one of my usual dishes. He gladly made me my comfort food. As I slowly consumed the soft and soothing bites, I began to feel more centered. I wondered if I hadn't been too hard on my grandma. Maybe I needed to practice more compassion. If I wanted my family to understand and accept me for who I was, then I needed to do the same for them.

An hour later, my dad returned, wheeling Ngin-Ngin into the back kitchen. I followed with a pot of tea. "What did the therapist say?"

My dad looked happy. He had been so depressed since the stroke. It was nice to see the color return to his cheeks. "She's doing great. She can even move her arm a little."

I looked over at my grandma. I think she even gave a slight demonstration.

The family stood around as if we were waiting for a baby to take its first steps. Everyone wanted to believe we saw something. A few orders came in, so my dad had to rush back to the other side. My mom returned to work too, scooping more rice. Calvin, Cindy, and Clifford had gone back to their homework, so this left me to tend to Ngin-Ngin.

Seeing her there, so many past memories came forward—the yelling, the screaming, the whippings from her feather duster. When I was growing up, my dad would never let us say anything negative about my grandma. According to my mom, it was best to ngin hey, or hold our breath. (So many of her lessons were about breathing.) I could've said something to her then. But I didn't. I held my tongue, not because my dad ordered me not to say anything, but because it felt right. Despite everything I had been through with my grandma, I decided to be the bigger person.

On the table, I noticed the bowl of jook—rice porridge with stewed pork, sliced ginger, and thousand-year-old preserved eggs, which I once thought contained baby pterodactyls. I assumed my mom must've left it there for Ngin-Ngin. I picked up the spoon and lifted it to her mouth. As my grandma slowly lowered her bottom jaw to eat, I pressed the curved utensil against her lips. For once, I believed in karma, both the good and bad.

M-3.

When one of the ahoos suggested that shark fin soup could speed Ngin-Ngin's recovery, my grandpa resolved to feed his wife back to health. The rare ingredient cost too much to stock at the last Asian grocery store in Detroit, so my dad offered to drive Yeh-Yeh to Toronto. I still yearned to see America—even if this was Canada—but decided to pass. Being stuck in a car for eight hours with my grandpa, who loved eating stewed cabbage with soy sauce, would've given us the wrong kind of gas.

The two snuck back across the border with fifteen hundred dollars' worth of the now-banned animal part, and my grandpa went into the kitchen and strapped on his white apron. He scrubbed the hard, scratchy fins for hours, soaked the ground shrimp and dried mushrooms, strained the chicken broth and ginger. I jotted down the recipe for future use.

Despite some early success in physical therapy, Ngin-Ngin's arm remained flaccid, matching the side of her face. Previously, my grandma had carried a little extra weight, thanks to all the snacking she did as she made her own treats, but now she had lost thirty or forty pounds. Embarrassed by her appearance, she'd banned any visitors. She relented only after another ahoo suggested mahjong might help. With only one good limb, she took forever to play a tile, but her friends held their tongues. After watching my grandma play in slo-mo, I figured out her strategy was never about winning but about stopping other people's success.

Even worse, during my cruel, cruel summer, Detroit was suffering through a historic drought. In the hundred-degree weather local deejays thought blasting the Martha Reeves and the Vandellas classic "Heat Wave" would be funny. It wasn't. Ignoring my mom's mantra to work hard, our air conditioner went kaput all the time. My dad had to bring in table fans for our guests. Those became our most popular seats.

Mimi, my fellow Wolverine and longtime friend, came to my rescue. As the only two Chinese kids in our high-school class, the sporty girl with short hair and I ran in the same science-club pack. Her family, who spoke Mandarin, resided on the more affluent side of town. She liked to make fun of our Cantonese, which sounded more guttural, pretending to hack and spit. She even claimed that the southern Chinese had less class than the people from the north. Other than that, she was great.

Mimi was driving up to Ann Arbor for the annual art fair and invited me to tag along. I was searching for an excuse to get out, so I said yes. We arrived on campus after lunch. Like me, she hated paying for parking, so we circled the same set of blocks half a dozen times before finding a spot near the Hill Auditorium. As we headed on foot toward the crowds on State Street, she surprised me by asking when and where we were meeting up later. The cheapskate wasn't planning to hang out with me. She'd just wanted someone to split the gas money with!

Abandoned and alone, I was still glad to be out of the restaurant. While my parents had convinced me to cancel my plans to go to San Francisco by stressing the importance of family, I realized they weren't being fair, since Chris had been allowed to go on with his own arrangements. Thanks to my mom's younger brother Tony, my brother had an internship in Los Angeles with TRW, a big defense contractor. The double standard made my skin crawl. Sure, defending the country was important, but so was eating Ghirardelli chocolate.

The art fair turned out to be fun. The atmosphere reminded me of the old Autumn Moon Festivals we used to have in Chinatown when Peterboro was filled with locals and visitors. They'd line up at our restaurant's food stall and at the game booths and performance stages. We'd stuff our faces with delicious moon cakes. It had been years since our community had had the numbers or energy to pull off such a large affair. I missed those big gatherings. I perused the stalls of macramé and tie-dyes, searching for something to send my parents a message that I mattered like Chris. The rows of street vendors presented me with several options: A tattoo. A mohawk. A complete glam makeover. But all these changes seemed too over-the-top. I wanted to get my parents to notice me, not give them an ulcer.

Then the perfect stall appeared on the corner. Among a wide selection of trinkets and baubles, I noticed a small gold stud earring. This was it! For my parents, especially my mom, the precious metal symbolized success and prosperity, as well as good luck, something I sorely needed. I would get my ear pierced. I made my purchase with glee.

Soon it was time for me to head to our rendezvous spot, Drake's Sandwich Shop. I had never been to the place before. The 1950s throwback featured a milkshake machine, a soda fountain, and jars of hard candy. A quartet of girls dressed in sky-blue smocks tended to the packed room of customers. Their style, split between goth and bohemian, was too cool for me. I retreated to the stool at the end of the long counter.

I fidgeted for five minutes trying to get a waitress's attention, so it was no surprise that a HELP WANTED sign sat in the window. After a few more waves of my hand, a light-skinned Black girl, her hair stuffed under a polka-dot scarf, approached with her pad and pen. "Yeah?"

Concerned about breaking any health codes, I pointed at the trash in front of me. "Could you clean this up, please?"

The girl harrumphed, pushing aside the crumpled napkins. "Happy?"

Her nasty attitude startled me. At Chung's, most of our business came from repeat customers. To convert new diners into regulars, you had to make a good first impression. If my dad had ever heard me speak to any of our guests like that, he probably would've made me apologize and refuse to accept any tip. My body shriveled. "I'm waiting for a friend."

"You still gotta buy something."

I looked around to see if anyone else was witnessing this dreadful customer service. After another clerk barked at a little boy for being too slow to pick out his gummy worm, I realized the rude attitude was meant to be part of the store's charm. Judging from the number of customers, it must have worked for them. "Fine. What have you got?"

She pointed to the back wall above the sink. On circular blackboards, written in white chalk, were drink lists. In addition to typical soda-jerk selections, there were over a hundred varieties of teas. I was amazed. They had English breakfast, Irish breakfast, Russian breakfast, even Kroger's breakfast. (At Chung's, we had two options: oolong and green.) The price, fifty cents, appealed to me too. "I'll try the samovar. Are refills free?"

The girl rounded the worn wood counter, mumbling death under her breath. I pegged the odds at fifty-fifty she would spit in my drink. As I searched for a pen and paper and a suggestion box, Mimi popped up from the crowd. "Ready? Let's go."

I perked up. "We're not staying?"

Mimi rolled her eyes at the rowdy kids. "It's too crazy here."

I peered over the counter. "Cancel my order."

The girl, still searching the shelf, snarled, "What?"

As we exited, Mimi pointed to the bag in my hand. "What did you get?"

From the cheer in her voice, I could tell she was hoping it was something sweet from the store. She pulled out the box, revealing the earring. "Who's this for?"

"Me," I said.

Mimi handed back my purchase. "So why didn't you get your ear pierced?"

"The lady was charging five bucks. I'll do it later."

"Don't be so Cantonese," Mimi sniped. That could've meant a million things, but I assumed it meant "cheap," which was strange coming from the girl who'd spent half an hour trying to find free parking. Anyway, I hated how some of my friends assumed that five dollars was no big deal. I worked hard for every cent. That was at least two tables' worth of tips.

I turned to the clock on the Burton Memorial Tower, the art deco building designed by famed architect Albert Kahn. It was approaching five. "We should get going. I told my parents I'd help with dinner."

"Don't worry. We'll be quick."

"Quick doing what?" I asked.

The two of us headed up State Street toward Huron Avenue and the medical school's campus. Mimi was enrolled in the university's prestigious combined premed/med-school program, which gave her access to the labs. Visitors weren't allowed on weekends, so we snuck through a side door.

On the second or third floor, we found an open room. She pointed at an exam table. "Sit here."

My heart pounded like a dribbling basketball. My experience with doctors was limited to the creepy pediatrician in the Corridor who always fondled my balls. I was not falling for that trick again. "What are we doing here?"

Mimi grabbed a pair of gloves from the drawer. Whatever she was doing, at least she practiced good hygiene. "We're piercing your ear."

My body stiffened. "That's okay. We don't have to."

"You said you wanted it done."

I looked into Mimi's eyes, wondering why she was pushing so hard. She probably thought that if it were left up to me, the earring would stay in the box forever. She was giving me the extra shove I needed. Maybe that's why we were friends. I hopped on the table. "Fine."

"So, which ear? Right or left?"

I froze again. I had no idea. From watching TV, I knew the

gays had secret handshakes, secret handkerchief codes, even a secret language called Polari, but I couldn't remember which ear signified "big fat homo." I felt like I was in the hot seat with no lifelines left. I went with door number two. "The right one."

"You sure?"

I wasn't, but I figured this was my one shot to get it done. I closed my eyes. "Just do it."

I sweated, hoping I was doing the right thing. This rebel stuff was new to me. I was afraid of going too fast, too hard. There were no brakes. A second later, I opened one eye to see Mimi grinning. She tugged my earlobe, evaluating my face. "My first surgery. Not a bad job."

And just like that, I was a metrosexual.

By the time we left Ann Arbor, the day's heat had given way to a dusky balminess, and the sky had changed to a royal orange-purple. Chung's was forty minutes away, so we had to jet. Luckily, Mimi was an aggressive driver, and she kept her foot pressed to the pedal. As we cruised down the empty highway, I kept checking the stud in the car's vanity mirror. The earring was the perfect size and fit. I just hoped it was the gay side.

Mimi flipped up my visor. "Stop. You'll get it infected."

I leaned back in my seat, satisfied. "I can't wait for them to see this."

"What's the big deal?"

Mimi wasn't stupid. In fact, she was one of the most astute people I knew. She was also one of the most liberal. In high school, she often interrupted my Reagan quotes with threats to form her own Young Democrats club (which she never did). Her words now seemed to be a clear sign to me. She was telling me it was okay to open up. I hadn't planned on coming out to her, at least not there and then, but the vibe, the two of us alone in her warm and heated car, told me it was time.

"You know I'm gay, right?"

As the words slipped from my mouth, my chest caved into my spine. *Shit.* I'd done it. I'd come out. I'd shared my big secret with someone else, and it felt great. And powerful. And exhilarating. And just plain awesome! For the first time since I was nine and my cousin confronted me about my attraction to Rudy, my lungs could fully exhale. The fear that had gripped my body for over half my young life was suddenly gone.

But then I noticed Mimi's silence, which seemed to last forever. She wasn't saying a thing. As my emotions boomeranged, I was suddenly scared again. *Shit.* What the hell had I just done? Why had I risked our friendship? Why did coming out feel like a kamikaze mission?

Those next few seconds were the longest of my life. My eyes stayed fixed on the open road as light beams from the oncoming cars flickered across the dashboard. I couldn't stand to look her in the face. As my teeth began to chatter, a soft, calm voice emerged from the stillness.

"I am too."

Phew! Words! Sounds! I could breathe again. My path to freedom had taken a giant step and I was...wait a minute. Did Mimi just say she was gay too?

I turned to my friend. I couldn't believe my luck. Sure, she lived in the artsy East Quad, had short hair, and played rugby, but it had never occurred to me that she wasn't straight. I was so concerned with hiding my own sexuality that I had forgotten that other people were on their own journeys.

I searched Mimi's face. Now she was the one avoiding eye contact with me. She continued, "Those friends I was meeting, they're gay too."

By now, my heart was doing cartwheels. This was my dream scenario. The love. The acceptance. The generosity. Why hadn't I come out sooner? What had I been waiting for? What hip parties had I missed? I adjusted my seat. "So why didn't you introduce us?"

"They hate Republicans."

I flinched, caught under my seat belt. "Well, I'm not one anymore."

"I mean, they *really* hate Republicans. Like, they want to kill them."

"Okay, I get it. No more elephants ever again. Promise!"

My friend nodded. "Right."

She sounded a bit doubtful, but this was no time to fight. I had crossed a big bridge the size of the Mackinac and I wanted to savor the view. Like the Model T, the old Curtis had been retired. Long live the new version. The window was rolled down. The whooshing air whipped against my face, and the wind whisked away my barbaric yawp: "Ahhhhh!"

For the next few miles, as we sped toward downtown, Mimi and I played twenty questions. To our surprise, we shared even more similarities. When did we first know? Elementary school. Did we suspect the other was gay? No. Had we told our families? Not yet. Did we like George Michael? Definitely, post-Wham!

Mimi gripped the steering wheel. "Are you going to tell your parents now?"

My butt shifted. "We'll see."

Coming out in the 1980s was a much bigger deal than it is now. It involved more caution and calculation. There was no network of support groups, no guarantees that "it gets better." It wasn't out of the question to be disowned or even killed by your family.

As Mimi talked obsessively about the blond left-winger on her team, my mind drifted to all the men I'd loved before. The what-ifs that might have happened if only I had been braver, more confident.

Rudy, my first crush; Gary from the pet shop; Greg, our African American dishwasher; Mr. Mah, my favorite cook. My thoughts then turned to the men I had yet to meet. I wondered what they might look like. My tastes had been all over the place. Who would be my first?

Rows of abandoned buildings outlined Chinatown. Half the streetlights were busted. The number of cars parked in front of Chung's gave me a good indication of the number of diners inside. It looked like a slow night. Still, I was happy I'd offered to help.

Mimi's car pulled into the open spot in front. She left the engine running. As I got out, my nerves returned. I poked my head through the passenger-side window. My parents had taken a liking to Mimi. During my high-school years, they didn't allow my brothers and me to date, but if they had, my sense is that they would've preferred our partners to be Chinese, or at least Asian. That's why they were so happy when Mimi went to prom with Chris. If I brought her in with me now, it might put them in a good mood. "Are you sure you don't want to come in and say hi?"

Mimi turned up the radio. "It's okay. Call if they kick you out."

Her flippant response threw me. Maybe I had let the success of my first coming-out cloud my sense of reality. I had no idea what would happen. My hand stayed glued to the car door. It wasn't too late to get back in and take off. "You think they'll do that?"

"You never know," she said.

I bit my lip. Why was my friend torturing me? Before I could respond, she rolled up her window. "I'm sure it'll be fine. But call if you need me."

With that, my one gay friend pulled off.

I breathed in the muggy air while surveying the street. Across from Burton sat the gutted carcass of the James Scott Mansion. The Victorian castle with its white stone turrets had always been my fantasy home. I used to wonder who was lucky enough to live in a place so big that everybody got their own room. After a fire consumed half the structure, I discovered it was occupied by a band of squatters. If my parents kicked me out, would the homeless make room for me?

Red is a lucky color to the Chinese. That's why Chung's had a red awning and why our waiters wore red jackets. We were even in the red-light district. I pulled open our red door and tapped on the glass in the vestibule. My dad buzzed me in. I surveyed the dining room. Only a handful of diners sat in a few of the booths. I nodded to no one in particular. My mom was at the back table reconciling the day's credit card receipts. Due to recent changes in banking regulations, more customers were charging their meals. My mom hated the extra paperwork as well as the idea of living on credit. To her, life was a cash business.

My dad, who was restocking the display case with dinner mints, looked over my shoulder toward the door. "Where's Mimi?"

I wasn't in the mood for small talk. It was better to cut to the chase. I held my head up, hoping my dad would notice my new addition. "She had to get home."

He bent over to throw away the cellophane wrapper. "Oh."

My mom looked at my empty hands. "Did you get your books?"

"My books?" I had forgotten the original excuse I'd given them for needing to go up to Ann Arbor. I had to cover the lie with another lie. "They didn't have what I wanted."

My dad pointed to the dining area. "You can set the tables."

My mom was the more observant of the pair, so I turned to her, but her eyes remained glued to the sliding beads on her old wooden abacus. As I walked toward the tray of silverware, regretting that I hadn't bought the bigger, flashier hoop earring, I thrust the right side of my face in their direction. "Anything new going on?"

They both continued doing their own thing. "No. Why?"

I tilted my head even more. "Just asking." I was about to tip over.

My dad closed the sliding door to the display case. "I'm gonna go check on Grandma. She wasn't eating her jook before."

He walked past me. My mom packed up her folder and followed him out. I stood alone on the dining-room floor, wondering what it would take for my parents to see me for who I was.

Or maybe they had, and that's why they ran.

M-4.

The following fall, Mimi and I, along with six friends, moved out of our dorms and into a big red house on Ann Street that we dubbed "the barn." To reduce costs, I shared one of the five bedrooms with Dale, another member of the Scandinavian American clique from high school. Calling it a "room" was generous, as it was an illegal attic space with exposed fiberglass.

The money from my two scholarships—both for writing political essays—had run out. My attention turned to the income side of the equation. My parents didn't believe in loans, so that meant my getting another job. The previous year, I'd worked on the residential staff at Couzens. Twelve hours a week, I'd sat at the front desk selling meal passes, checking out the gym key, and flirting with the security guard with one glass eye. The job was easy but too white-collar for my taste. The way I was raised, I wasn't working unless there were blisters on my fingers and my back was sore.

I'd grown up as a restaurant kid, so a job in food service seemed to be a natural choice. But working at China Gate or Empire Szechuan, the two Chinese restaurants on campus, would have made me feel like a traitor. There was a huge difference between eating at another establishment and serving their food. Besides, it wouldn't have been fair to the customers at these other restaurants. How could I recommend any of their dishes when I knew my family's egg rolls and soups were so much tastier?

In addition to working at Chung's, my dad sold restaurant supplies—paper products, fortune cookies, bags of rice—to the area's Asian businesses, including Donburi, a small Japanese place on State Street. Most of my dad's efforts to open doors for his kids fell flat, so it was fulfilling whenever one succeeded. I went to the interview he'd arranged, hoping to score him a victory. But when I arrived, the owner—a sweet Japanese woman—informed me she was fully staffed. She had only agreed to the meeting because my dad had said such nice things about me. As consolation, she comped me my chicken teriyaki.

With my rent coming due, I remembered the HELP WANTED sign at the sandwich shop. My first visit to Drake's had been frosty, but the place was close to my classes, and the selection of teas impressed me. After acing my interview with the buxom goth manager, Connie, who appeared to be white underneath all that makeup, I was hired to bus tables, stock shelves, and refill the ice machine. Back to square one.

With over a decade of experience at Chung's, I picked up the job in a snap. By week two, Connie, who always wore dark baggy tops, had put me behind the shop's grill. I hesitated at first. Given my past kitchen nightmares, I expected to get canned. But much to my surprise, I managed to make everything on the menu. Granted, working a single plug-in stove top was easier than cooking with a wok, but it still required skill. I synthesized my parents' contrasting styles of cooking—combining recipe-following and improvisation—and it turned out I made a mean tuna melt.

I had a full-time job and an eighteen-credit course load, so heading home on the weekends was no longer feasible. My mom and dad left choppy messages on my answering machine, checking in about my classes and laundry. I was still upset at them for nixing my summer plans and not acknowledging my earring, so I almost never returned their calls. When I did, it was during the lunch or dinner rush, when I knew they would be too busy to talk.

As time went on and I got to know the staff at Drake's better, they became my new chosen family. Connie, who was only a few years older than me, played mother hen, making sure the students on staff finished their homework and got to class on time. A few older diners acted like aunties and uncles, expecting us to remember their orders and serve them first. Like siblings, the coworkers had rivalries for the best shifts, the longest breaks, and the lion's share of the tips.

The lone holdout was the clerk from the art fair, Marsha. Since we were the only two minorities—I mean, people of color—on staff, I'd assumed we would click, but she had no interest in forming a rainbow coalition. She barely acknowledged my existence. Her rejection only pushed me to try harder. To paraphrase Miss Diana Ross, I was going to make her love me.

As my dad showed me at Chung's, a connection could always be made. I just had to find it. Every time we shared a shift, I complimented Marsha on her skirts, her tennis shoes, the consistent angle of her sneer. I jumped up to help any customer so she could stay on her cigarette break. Nada. I wondered if she would ever warm up to me. Just like my dad's efforts to woo my grandma, nothing I did worked. Maybe some people just aren't meant to be friends.

One day, sensing my growing frustration, Connie pulled me aside and explained that ever since Marsha had dropped out of school due to finances, she had been extra-grumpy. I wasn't sure that was the only reason she acted the way she did, but I was happy for the additional context. Money issues challenged me too. I didn't feel comfortable bringing up my tight finances with my old friends from high school or my new friends at Michigan, but with Marsha, I figured we could at least joke about thrift shops and instant ramen recipes. And when Connie provided me with more intel on Marsha, including the fact that she and her family hailed from Detroit, I got even more excited. This was my opening to make our connection. On our next shared shift, I raised my hand. "Fellow Detroiter in the house!"

Marsha lifted her eyes from her doodling. "You from Detroit?"

"I grew up in the Corridor. My family owns Chung's."

According to Connie, Marsha had gone to Cass Tech, the elite public school five blocks from the restaurant that accepted only the brightest kids from across the city. The school's alumni included such luminaries as Lily Tomlin, Della Reese, Ellen Burstyn, John DeLorean, and one Diana Ernestine Earle Ross. Marsha lifted her chin. "So which high school you go to?"

"I didn't go to high school in the city."

"Why not? Where'd you live?"

"In Troy. But we were downtown all the time. It's where my siblings and I grew up."

Marsha flicked the toothpick in her mouth. "Freakin' Troy."

I sensed a little resistance. I brought up my stint at Burton—complete with complaints about the soggy mac and cheese and unsafe water fountains—but she wasn't sold. Thanks to the rise of hip-hop artists like Public Enemy and Run-DMC and basketball stars like Michael Jordan, a growing number of middle-class kids from the suburbs, mostly white, were adopting "urban" (that is, Black) culture. To her, I was just another poseur trying to gain some street cred from an association with the inner city. She sneered while walking off. "You ain't from Detroit."

Marsha's smackdown reminded me of the old question I grew up being asked by customers, friends, and even teachers: "No, where are you *really* from?"

Once again, questions about my homeland arose. I'd been born and raised in Detroit, same as my dad. My family worked at the restaurant all the time. I played on the streets of Chinatown more than the ones in the suburbs. I knew the shops that were safe and the ones to avoid. The city might not have been where I slept, but it was where I lived. Who was she to define my place of origin?

Fortunately, my other coworkers were more accepting. Our politics were different—at least when we first met—but they never judged me. We could have heated discussions about hot-button issues and still share a fresh limeade. That made me want to open up more and hear their perspectives. Our differences didn't define us. We found a way to accept one another.

After the success of coming out to Mimi, I wanted to expand my circle of gay friends. If a journey of a thousand miles began with one step, I had taken that first one and was eager not to just walk, but to run. I figured that if I doubled the number of confidants every month, I would be done telling everyone by the end of the school year. I'd never have to come out again. That was how it worked, right?

Matt, the only other guy working behind the counter, was the low-hanging fruit. The tall blond with floppy hair tinted with lavender-lilac streaks appeared to be one of those flamboyant gays who had probably been out since the obstetrician slapped his butt. Every shift, he sat at the counter waxing on about his big old gay life: whom he found hot, whom he didn't; when he had sex, when he didn't; when he was the pitcher and when he caught. He made baseball sound interesting.

Matt shared the most intimate details of his sex life, the kind that made the girls on staff wince but that secretly thrilled me. To me, too much information was impossible. Hearing someone be so sex-positive about being gay excited me. I envied him. I hoped to be like him when I grew up. Maybe not when it came to the explicit sex acts, but the attitude of being proud and unafraid. I wanted to live in a world where I didn't have to hide or lie anymore. No more pining after unavailable straight guys. I would be free to be me.

One day, Matt was standing in the stairwell checking out the schedule. He was twirling a blue pen in his mouth as if he were making love to a tall Smurf. This was my chance. I took a deep breath and slid in. Like a birthday balloon popping, I blurted out: "I'm gay too."

Matt turned his head and landed his soft blue eyes on me. "Good for you."

I waited for him to say more, but he turned his attention back to jotting down dates. Perhaps nothing more needed to be said. As with Mimi, the world didn't end. In fact, it got bigger. My overhead bin space had increased. It felt like first class. Once again, I wondered why I was making such a big fuss about all of this. What was I afraid of? I threw a quick wave. "Okay, then. Have a nice day."

As I turned, Matt tapped the pen on his lip. "I thought so."

My feet stopped, as did my heart. "Thought what?"

"Oh, honey. I'm blond, not blind."

Matt's answer made me a little nervous at first, but then I chuckled. Was it my earring? Or my trimmed haircut? But who cared, really? His suspicions offered me some relief. It saved me the stress of having to worry about his reaction; it was a sign that my interior and exterior meshed. They were now part of the same whole person. Maybe I was closer to coming out than I'd thought.

Thanks to Matt, the entire staff knew by the next break. I'm not sure what I expected, but again, no one cared, at least not negatively. In fact, it was the opposite. My coworkers seemed to like me even more. Connie hugged me and said she had a gay younger brother. Two other girls boasted that they were bisexual and thinking of dating. Everyone said they loved belting out "I Will Survive."

I couldn't believe my luck. I'd come in looking for work, but Drake's had turned out to be so much more. Back then, other than the bars and students' clubs that specifically catered to the gay community, I didn't know of a place that openly welcomed gays and lesbians. Everywhere else, I had to be guarded. Before I could relax, I had to send out a trial balloon to see if it was safe. At Drake's, it was okay to be myself. Being different made me normal.

As we were the only two guys on staff, Matt loved pairing us together as BFQs, or "big fucking queens." While the camaraderie warmed my heart, the wording made me cringe. No one had ever called me a queen before. It felt wrong, as if that put a target on my back. I was okay being called gay—that word was safe and pleasant.

Matt also liked to tease me and call me straight-acting, but I wasn't faking anything. I was from the Midwest. How I acted was how I acted. After he used the term *butt pirate*, I'd had enough of his teasing. "Enough with the names, Matt. They're not cool with me."

"Oh, the baby fag is mad."

My eyes nearly popped out of my head. I had spent a lifetime dodging these words, living in constant fear of being labeled. And now he was throwing them around as if they were confetti at a gay-pride parade, which I had never even been to. "These words—they're so offensive."

Matt got up from his seat. "Only if you let them be. Don't give them that power. Take it back. *Queen. Queer. Friend of Dorothy.*"

Matt's words made me recall my mom's old phrase about being hurt by sticks and stones. Maybe I had a choice. Maybe they didn't have to hurt me. His point started to make sense. I had no idea who the hell Dorothy was, but it was clear I still had a lot to learn about being gay.

One night at closing time, I was running around, setting up my small cooking area for the next morning. Having grown up watching the cooks at Chung's, I knew the importance of mise en place, prepping the kitchen the night before, making sure that the refrigerator was well stocked and all the cooking utensils were cleaned and within reach. This way when the first customers arrived, we could hit the ground running.

Matt, the other clerk on duty, was prepping for another hot date. I'm not sure where he found most of his suitors—the bars, the bathrooms, the frozen section at Kroger's—but I loved perusing the personals in the paper. I never replied to any of them. My mom had always told us to live our lives before settling down. I extended *settling down* to include having sex. Abstinence-only was the one policy I retained from my Republican past. I didn't mind saving myself for the right guy. Reading the silly requirements in the personal ads only confirmed to me that this was the right decision.

Matt was putting polish on his nails. I had already wiped down the counter, so I tossed him a towel. "Watch it. You're gonna get that crap all over the place."

"It's not *crap*. It's Maybelline."

"Whatever. Keep it off the counter."

Matt picked up his mess. "You know, it wouldn't kill you to put in a little effort."

Not this again. Matt often teased me about my look, or lack thereof. I wasn't one of those gay guys who were into reading fashion magazines and knew the name of every designer. The simpler and cheaper, the better. That's why I was excited to discover there was a popular style known as the gay clone that consisted of a simple white T-shirt, Levi's blue jeans, and a pair of Doc Martens. That I could afford, so that's what I wore every day.

Matt thought the look was boring. He squinted his eyes and tilted his head. "I bet you would look good in drag."

I unplugged the hot pots for the night. "No, thanks." My only experience wearing a dress had come when I was six or seven. Craig, Chris, and I were in my grandpa's office. The space contained an old desk, an even older couch, and dozens of bottles of cognac of indeterminate age. As we searched the mahogany wardrobe for the extra set of mahjong, we stumbled upon some silk cheongsams. We decided to try them on, along with one of my grandma's black wigs and some of her baby powder. While we looked fabulous, the barrage of whips from my grandma's feather duster discouraged any repeat performances.

As usual, Matt loved his own idea. He got up from his seat and skipped behind me. "Your skin is so pale and smooth. Have you ever tried using makeup?"

I rolled my eyes and lied. "No."

He grabbed the hand I was using to set up. "Oh my God. Let me do your nails."

"No way," I said. Matt leaned over to look at my ass. "What are you doing?" I asked.

"Checking for that stick up your butt."

"Shut up," I said.

"If you're gonna call yourself gay, you might as well have some fun."

I looked at the cooking station. The place looked immaculate. Maybe Matt was right. Maybe I could afford to loosen up a little bit. "Okay, fine. Just one hand. That's it."

Matt bobbed in delight. "You won't regret this." He pulled a few options from his bag and placed them on the counter. "Welcome to Chez Matt. Your selection, please."

The three or four bottles all looked scary to me. "I don't care. You pick."

Matt didn't hesitate. "Vicious Red it is." He twisted off a top and grabbed my hand. I tried to pull away, but he tightened his grip. I had never been touched this way by another guy. His skin felt warm. "Just relax," he said.

As I shut my eyes, Matt's brush glided over my index finger. The touch felt really intimate. I imagined this was what it felt like to have a boyfriend. It was too bad I didn't see my friend that way. Yes, Matt was the boy-next-door type, but only if you lived next to a cabaret. Still, it made me reconsider. Maybe it was time to loosen my chastity belt too.

With my eyes still closed, I heard the bell on the door ring, followed by a male voice. "Hey."

"In a sec," Matt hollered. He was the worst employee, always prioritizing his own needs over any customer's. "The menu's up there. But hurry, we're closing soon."

The other voice said, "I'm here to see my brother."

"Your brother?"

Shit. I knew the voice had sounded familiar. It was Chris. I totally freaked out. It had been ages since we'd seen each other on campus. Our family's golden child had enrolled in Michigan to pursue medicine, but after screwing up organic chemistry and a few other courses during his first year, he switched to business, a decision that shattered my mom's dream of one of her sons becoming a doctor. I never asked him how he felt about that, but I assumed it must've been hard for him. I had never seen him fail at anything except in fourth grade, when he'd screwed up the big spelling bee by misspelling *restaurant*.

What the hell was he doing here?

I opened my eyes and yanked my hand back from Matt's, hoping my brother hadn't noticed. I forced a smile. "What's up? How are your classes?"

"Good," he said. "I'm taking business administration courses. I like them."

"That's nice," I said. Chris sounded happy. After returning from his internship at TRW, he'd mentioned that our uncle Tony was so impressed with him, he'd offered to get him a permanent job. I was sure my brother had other offers too, all of which would pay him beaucoup bucks. I didn't begrudge him his success. At least he'd be in a position to take care of Mom and Dad if things got really bad with the restaurant.

His eyes shifted to the truffles. "Mom said you had a new job."

I knew it. My parents had sent the snitch to spy on me. Whatever. "Tell them I'm fine. If they're worrying, they can stop."

Matt turned to touching up his own nails. "Curtis is doing fine. He spends all of his breaks reading and studying. He's kind of a *drag* like that."

The dick. Matt knew I wasn't out to my family, and he didn't approve. His theory was that if every gay person came out, there would be zero homophobia. I didn't agree with his math, nor was I ready to test his hypothesis. Thank God his pun went over my brother's head. Chris shifted his attention to the display of hard candy. "Good."

I peeked down at my fingers. Matt had barely begun, but the nail polish had still smudged everywhere. It looked like I had stabbed a small bunny. I hid my hands behind my back. "Well, thanks for coming. Good luck with the rest of the semester. Glad you're happy."

Chris picked up a jar of giant gumballs. "So, what's good here?"

"Nothing. It's all bad for you."

"I could use something sweet."

Of all the six kids, Chris had the biggest sweet tooth. On weekend trips to Eastern Market with my grandpa, he'd stock up on gummy bears and Twizzlers. I bagged up some of his favorite goodies as fast as possible, careful to keep the towel over my hand. To avoid having to give him change, I nodded at him and said, "It's my treat."

"Thanks," he said.

"Okay, see you."

As Chris pulled a few gummy bears from his bag, he looked at me. "Don't forget to call Mom and Dad. They want to hear from you." Chris exited. I flipped over the CLOSED sign.

By now, it was really time to close. Matt wrapped up his beauty salon. Our little makeover was done. He handed me an extra towel. "I can't believe that was your brother."

"Really?" I asked.

"Yeah, you two are nothing alike."

But Matt was wrong. My brother and I were very much the same. We were both going through our own metamorphoses, becoming the creatures we were always meant to be. Emerging from our cocoons, reincarnated, we were both embracing our new identities while also hoping that the relics of our former selves would still be recognizable the next time our growing wings flew us home.

M-5.

Days after I got my ear pierced at the art fair, my parents still hadn't said a thing. Calvin, Cindy, and Clifford, who were bonding as a trio just as we three oldest kids had, at least offered a cursory "Cool" before returning to their respective summer reading. Craig, after years of fighting for his own independence from my parents, had transferred to a school out west, so he was still unaware, and Chris had responded with "Did you tell Mom and Dad? What did they say?"

But that was the point. They hadn't said a freakin' thing. The tension was awkward. I finally had to confront them in the main kitchen at work. Their response was "Oh."

It was a total case of "Don't ask, don't tell, don't even look."

Out of hurt and frustration, I retreated to Ann Arbor. There, my closet door had busted open, and the flood of light invigorated me. The warm embrace of my sexuality by my friends felt like a sharp contrast to the shadows at home.

Still, I knew at some point I would have to explicitly come out to my family. Whenever I pictured my life as an out gay man, there was a boyfriend or a partner. (This was long before the country even discussed marriage equality. The idea of a man having a husband was unheard-of.) Whoever this person was, I wanted to be able to bring him home. I wanted him to be part of my family, to have a seat at our table, to eat our great food, and to join in the fight as to which franchise was better, Star Wars or Star Trek.

In figure-skating terms, coming out to friends had been a simple jump; having the same conversation with my family would be more like a quadruple axel. The stakes were too high. Failure was not an option. To prepare for the talk, which had to be done face-to-face, I wanted to get some expert advice. I had seen flyers for the school's gay and lesbian center. I decided to go to a meeting. I figured I'd meet an expert gay there, maybe even a future boyfriend.

After work, I showed up at a small office on campus to find a dozen students, evenly split between men and women. The moderator, a short, butch lesbian, asked us all to introduce ourselves and say why we were there. I'm not sure what I expected, but the meeting was surprisingly boring, nothing like the images of gay gatherings on TV or even what Matt described. Of course, he could have been joking about the dungeon, whips, and chains.

Almost everyone came from Michigan, though different parts. They talked about their own coming-out processes. While they all seemed nice, I felt self-conscious. I had never been surrounded by so many gay people before. Maybe it was because I was the only person of color, or perhaps it was the fact that they all seemed to know one another, but I felt like a surprise last-minute arrival at a party to which I hadn't been invited. In retrospect, I probably should have given the group a second chance, but I decided that I would try to figure out how to come out to my family on my own.

The following weekend, my coworkers Carla and Sarah had tickets to see a band at St. Andrew's. The hip concert hall in Detroit was not too far from Chung's, so they offered to drop me off. This seemed like a good chance to come out to my parents. I had briefly considered doing a trial run and telling my younger siblings first. After all, they'd seemed to handle the earring best. But out of respect for my parents, I figured I should start at the top.

Hailing from the East Coast, Carla and Sarah, who were both white, had never been to the city before. The whole ride down, they kept droning on about the musical act. Meanwhile, I was lost in my own world, too busy thinking about my own upcoming performance to even remember the band's name. My biggest priority was not to worry my family. They were already going through enough troubles with the business and my grandma, as well as my grandpa, who seemed a bit lost and depressed about Ngin-Ngin. I didn't want to add to their burdens.

We pulled off the freeway and passed the usual carcasses of buildings. Reagan's War on Drugs, which began when I was in high school, had yet to yield positive results, at least in the inner city. In fact, with policies like expanded penalties for possession of marijuana, mandatory minimum sentencing, and civil-asset forfeiture, life in the Corridor seemed to have gotten worse. Now even the teens and preteens were trouble, running around with their beepers and coming into our restaurant, flashing their cash, and ordering extra shrimp with every dish.

Carla interrupted my mental monologue with a screech: "Eww, it's just like *RoboCop*." She was referring to the recent hit movie that depicted Detroit as a crime-infested cesspool. "Better lock the doors."

"Don't worry. Everything's fine," I said. Frankly, I was tired of hearing all the bad jokes about my hometown. Most of the people I'd grown up with in the suburbs avoided it, made fun of it, or just rolled their eyes. The latest headlines heralded the firebombing of crack houses as vigilante justice. I gave it one more college try. "Everything looks worse in the dark."

"I'm pretty sure this looks just as bad in the daytime," Sarah said.

We turned onto Cass, and I almost screeched myself as we approached the Birdtown pet shop, or at least the site where it once stood.

Arsonists had recently firebombed the store. (No one knew why, but it did cross my mind that it might have been gay-related.) In addition to the hundreds of exotic birds and tropical fish that had perished, a charred human corpse had been found in the ashes. I feared that it might be Gary or one of the other familiar faces, but it turned out to be an elderly lady who'd lived above the store. I'd breathed a sigh of relief. Not that I didn't feel bad for the woman, but I had seen enough death in the city to know that my grief would be saved for the people I knew.

As we approached Chung's, I could already taste my first home-cooked meal in months. It had to be shrimp with lobster sauce. The stir-fried crustacean was served in a white sauce made with chicken broth, garlic, green onions, minced pork, and scrambled eggs. The dish had a smooth texture and savory taste that melted in my mouth, but I was confused as to why there wasn't any actual lobster in the sauce.

My special guests could be a good excuse to order something nice, something I hadn't done in a while. Before I could invite them in, Chung's new facade came into view. Gone were our beautiful glass windows; they'd been replaced with ugly gray cinder blocks. There was even some illegible graffiti tagged on the side. I guess we were lucky the building hadn't been burned to the ground, but it still looked awful. What the hell had happened?

Shocked but also embarrassed, I got out of the car and waved off the girls without an explanation.

As they sped off to their show, I stood outside, surveying the last standing structures in the area. Being away for weeks had provided me with a new perspective. My happy childhood memories of play-ing with friends and cousins on the street might have clouded my impression of Detroit. The suburbanites might be right: anything good about the city had gone *poof*.

I banged hard and fast against the vestibule glass, which rattled. I whipped open the door and made a beeline for my parents. They were sitting in their usual spots, acting as if nothing had changed. "What happened to our windows? Who did that?"

My dad, who sat closest to the door so he could be the first to greet the customers, was taking the last bites of his late-night snack. "You hungry?"

Of course I was, but that was irrelevant. I had to pretend I wasn't, just like they had to say they were doing fine.

When my siblings and I were growing up, my parents faced a lot of hardships that they tried to keep from us—mostly unpaid bills, but also some minor health issues. I was hoping that now that we were all older, we could be more honest with one another, that they could tell me what was really going on. "When did this happen? Why didn't you say anything?"

"Don't worry. We're fine," my mom said. I guess my hopes were useless. No matter how old I was or how independent I had become, my parents' instincts were still to protect me.

My dad took another bite of his chow mein. "Guess who came in last week—Mayor Young. He's running for reelection. He said to send in your résumé."

Once again, my mom and dad were avoiding a difficult subject. Just as they'd turned a blind eye to the gold ball lodged in my ear-lobe, they were refusing to talk about the cinder-block wall. But they weren't getting off so easily.

I stormed back to the lobby and grabbed the phone. "Did you guys call the police? Don't you know some people at the station?" My dad often comped the cops their meals to curry favor with them. I guess that hadn't helped.

Big Al looked up at the few diners. They were too busy eating and chatting to notice us. He motioned with his hand. "Stop. Worry doesn't help."

My mom looked at my dad, then at me. "It's okay. Your dad called both times."

I came back. "Both times? What do you mean, both times?"

This was scarier than I'd thought. In fact, it was too much. I hadn't even had a chance to ask my dad about his friends at the Birdtown.

Irony aside, I wondered what else my parents were hiding from me. Why couldn't we be straightforward with each other? My knees buckled, and my butt landed on a seat. I rubbed my throbbing head. "Can someone please tell me what's going on?"

My mom sighed and explained that the first incident had happened a few weeks earlier. They had come in one morning to find a giant rock in the middle of the dining room, surrounded by shards of broken glass. On Leong had agreed to fix the damage, but when an even bigger rock landed the next week, they'd chosen to cut their losses and install the cinder blocks.

My whole life, my mom and dad had stressed the importance of loyalty, of sticking by the people and things that mattered to me. They never gave up on anyone, not even the friends who owed them money or the ones who went to jail for selling drugs or killing their wives. That commitment was a belief they both shared. I tried to live by that adage too, but now I wondered if it was time to give up.

As much as I loved my hometown, I couldn't bear the thought of anything bad happening to either of my parents. I couldn't let pride get in the way. I slammed my hand on the table. "That's it. You guys can't stay here anymore. You have to call it quits."

Big Al got up and headed for the register. "C'mon. Don't," he said.

"Don't c'mon me. I'm serious." My eyes turned to my mom. She had never cared for the restaurant life. She married into it. If it had been up to her, she would have moved out to the Bay Area to be with her folks a long time ago. "What do you say, Mom? Don't you want to move?"

My mom shrugged. She'd never had the strength to follow her own ambitions. It probably had something to do with her abandonment issues. She always deferred to my dad. Asking her to change now might have been too much. I shifted my attention back to him. "Detroit is dead. You have to move on."

Even as I spoke, I thought, *Move on to what?* I wasn't sure, but not this.

I turned to the tray of filled water glasses, which was how we tallied the number of customers each day. The glasses were still on the tray, but the ice was melted. At this rate, I wasn't even sure if my family was making money. "Why are you being so stubborn? Why won't you listen?"

I waited for the light to click on in my dad's head. I knew this decision wouldn't be easy for him. He was a restaurant kid like me. He had grown up cooking and serving our customers too. But surely he would see my point, right? The damage and danger were everywhere. No one would blame him or criticize him if he chose to close down. Not even Ngin-Ngin. We'd had a good run. Decades. There was no shame. He had fought the good fight. Our whole family had.

But my dad wasn't done fighting yet. He clenched his teeth. "Quit it, will you?"

"No, you quit," I said. "You have to leave before someone gets hurt or killed." *Please, no more suffering,* I thought. *I'm tired.*

With a final wave of his hand, Big Al went to check on the remaining parties. The cheerful tone in his voice and skip to his step told me he had moved on. I turned to my mom, who shrugged. She'd probably known his answer even as she was on her knees cleaning up the broken glass both times. After twenty-three years of marriage, they understood each other fully. They would sink or swim together.

* * *

When I got back to Ann Arbor, my appetite withered, which had never happened. I had trouble focusing in class. My grades began to slip. Worst of all, I couldn't sleep. I started having this recurring nightmare. It was like the scene in *Batman* with Bruce Wayne's parents dying on the ground in some back alley, but it was me and I was away in Ann Arbor. A late-night phone call from the police told me that my parents had been shot, but I had no way of getting home.

I started calling my parents every night around closing to make sure they had an exit strategy for the day: who carried the money bag, who turned out the lights, who locked the door, whether one of the employees had family members who could watch them from their apartment window across the street. I realized that my relationship with my mom and dad had flipped; now I was the one playing their guardian.

Unlike Chris, I'd never developed a sweet tooth. The number of sugary goodies on Chung's menu was limited, just cookies and canned fruits, lychees and peaches. I once asked my dad why we didn't serve cakes or pies or even ice cream. He said it was because only restaurants with bad food needed good desserts. I could see his point. However, surrounded by all the chocolate and candy at Drake's, I turned into Willy Wonka to relieve my stress.

To further reduce my chances of getting an ulcer or having a heart attack, I had to lighten my course load. I kept the maximum number of credits—I was paying for them anyway—but I looked for classes that might be less stressful. Connie, an aspiring poet, suggested I try taking a writing workshop in that genre. She thought it might be a good chance for me to work out my feelings. "And poets are way more easygoing than your poli-sci classmates."

Connie's encouragement made me think. I had always liked

writing, albeit nonfiction pieces like articles and essays, but I did have some experience writing poetry. In high school, for my advanced English class, I had written some sonnets and gotten an A plus. I guess I never took it seriously because it seemed more like a hobby than a job. I didn't know many poets, especially not any who looked like me or wrote things relatable to my life. Still, I thought I'd give it a shot. I thought it would be an easy A.

The poetry class ended up being even more stressful than my political science courses. Instead of sitting in an auditorium with several hundred blank faces, I was now in a room with twenty people looking straight at me. They even knew my name. On top of that, the instructor, a twenty-something graduate student, expected us to critique one another's work. I had never been asked to judge my fellow students' writing before. Who was I to say what was good and what was not?

The class assignment was to turn in fifteen poems. I figured if I wrote haiku, I could whip them off on a single napkin. But the instructor expected a little more. She encouraged us to infuse our words with our feelings and emotions. This was new to me. In my family, we were taught to keep our lips shut tight and soldier on. *Be quiet.* Given my past writing experience, mostly with my high-school paper, I approached poetry like journalism. Big mistake. The poems were dry, full of facts and reason. I even considered adding footnotes.

Meanwhile, the other poets treated class like a confessional. One guy had defeated testicular cancer; another shared how her cousin had raped her in the back of her family's hardware store. And this was all in an intro class. I sat back and marveled at how my classmates could be so open and vulnerable with people they'd just met. They encouraged me to do the same, to let my guard down and allow people to see the "real me."

It wasn't comfortable, but I tried my best.

As it turns out, poetry saved me. It gave me back a sense of control, arming me with a new set of tools to express myself—metaphors, alliteration, enjambments. Through stanzas and couplets, I pushed myself to explore what it meant to grow up in my family's restaurant and on the streets of Detroit, to be a middle child in a crazy Chinese family who struggled to be heard, to understand what it was to be Asian American and working class. And though they remained nameless and gender-neutral, I wrote about my sexual desires. Every vision and revision took me one step closer to understanding my own narrative.

Toward the end of the semester, our instructor passed around a flyer. Michigan was launching a new creative-writing concentration for undergraduates majoring in English. I was prelaw, or at least that was still my claim, so without even looking, I handed the sheet to the next person. When one of my classmates pointed out that the program was accepting only twenty writers, my indifference felt justified. Considering the size of the university, the odds of me getting in would be slim. Why apply just to get rejected?

By then, I was working full-time at Drake's. The sandwich shop had become my *Cheers,* the place where everybody knew my name. But more accurately, it had also become my Chung's. Every time the bell rang, I looked forward to seeing who came through the front door. The delighted look on the customers' faces as they scanned the menu or the display of chocolates reminded me why I loved working in food service.

To my surprise, one afternoon as I was completing an order for a double grilled cheese sandwich and tomato soup, Connie grabbed the work schedule and crossed out my name.

"Um, I wanted those shifts."

She tossed her long black hair. "You're working too much."

"No, I'm not. It's forty hours." In my family, that was considered part-time, but it was enough for me. Michigan cost only fifteen hundred dollars a semester. My take-home pay could cover all my bills and even a weekly stop at Dave's Comics, my one form of paid entertainment.

Being financially independent wasn't just a pride thing for me. Yes, it felt good not to feel like a burden. My parents would have helped if I'd asked, but they had five other kids and I didn't want them working any harder than necessary, especially with the difficulties around Chung's. More important, I needed to know I could take care of myself in case my parents ever did disown me. Having a job would make it easier for me to come out. It was my insurance.

"You should apply for that new program," said Connie. One of the other writers on staff must have told her what I'd said. Connie looked me in the eye. "Don't use this job as an excuse to not write."

"I like my job," I said. "It makes me happy."

"But writing makes you happier. I see you after your class."

Connie was right. I loved reading, writing, and discovering new authors. And for the first time in my life, I could see there was potential. I had grown up surrounded by so much death—the floundering auto industry, crack, AIDS—that I didn't think I would get to live past decade number three. Now that I was in college and doing okay, I figured I might have a few more years than I thought. Maybe I could start planning for a future. Besides, it was only an application. Getting in was still a long shot.

Hunched over in one of the back booths, I sorted through my poems, trying to assemble a through line. Much of my writing was inspired by the artwork at Chung's. The most interesting piece there was a mahogany carving featuring the Eight Immortals, the gods of longevity and prosperity. Eight was a lucky number to the Chinese; a triple eight was even better.

The Eight Immortals featured a team of six men and two women—like my family—who'd sailed off on the Bohai Sea. Despite the dangers of Detroit, thanks to the protection of these powerful deities, our restaurant's dining room had always felt safe to me, a contrast to the world just beyond our red door. Once again, I turned to these gods to help me chart my next journey. They proved to be the inspiration for my collection of poems.

Several weeks later, a small crowd gathered outside the English Department's office in Angell Hall. Peeking over the heads of the other hopefuls, I scanned the board. The first names posted were, of course, the fiction writers. They always got top billing. At the bottom were the three poets, two of them writers from my class.

To my surprise, the third name was mine. Shocked, I had to read the list twice just to make sure. But there it was: *Curtis Wing Chin, creative talent of the country.*

Back at Drake's, everyone congratulated me. Connie said, "I told you so."

Even Marsha managed a quick "Good job."

The future had cracked right open. I had a little more direction. The only thing left to do was to let my family know that I was switching majors. My financial security had always been their primary goal. I didn't know which truth would be more difficult to reveal—that I was gay or that I was going to be a poet.

M-6.

With just twenty students admitted into its creative-writing program, Michigan hoped to create a tight-knit community of artists. Instead, the selection process caused ripples in Angell Hall. Through the grapevine, I heard that some unsuccessful white applicants had griped that my inclusion was only to help "bring some color" to the cohort. Never mind that all nineteen of the other writers in the program were white. Somehow, I was the one taking their seat.

The lack of respect fed my insecurities. Could I be an impostor? I had been writing poetry for only a short period. How good could my poems be? I'd applied to the school's prestigious Hopwood Awards but hadn't won, placed, or shown. Maybe I did suck. Maybe these whiners were right and I was taking the spot of a more deserving white writer.

The episode reminded me of an incident that had occurred in high school. After I had been selected as one of two representatives to attend Boys State, one of my friends and my future college room-mate, Steve, had seemed upset. He could barely look me in the eye to congratulate me. He was valedictorian and captain of the swim team, so he'd probably expected to list this on his application to West Point. Despite my own credentials—class president, president of the National Honor Society, member of the science club, staff writer on the school paper, all-around nice guy—I think he wondered how I was picked over him.

I had no idea what to say to my friend, but after attending the program and meeting the other selectees and people representing the sponsor—the conservative American Legion—I realized my selection probably had a lot to do with my involvement with the Republican Party. But never mind that. To him, it was due to the program's need to find someone who looked different.

Once again, Drake's became my happy place—only this time, it encouraged my artistic ambitions. A lot of writers, both staff and customers, found refuge here. Together, we shared our work and swapped ideas. Our little cabal, a community of creatives outside academia, made me realize that it wasn't necessary to be enrolled in school to be a better writer. It was just important to be surrounded by other writers who weren't afraid to show you their shitty first drafts.

One afternoon as Connie and I traded our latest poems, a short Asian American girl wearing a gray winter coat came in. It was my turn to help the next customer, so I put down my pen and got up. "Welcome to Drake's. What can I get you?"

She perused the display case. "You're here all the time. You in school or what?"

I took a second look. The girl had straight black hair that draped over half her face. She didn't look familiar. "I work and go to school."

She waved her hand, as if my answer bored her. "Okay, but what are you studying?"

"English," I said. "Why?"

She flicked her hand. "Right. Right." Peeking from behind a strand of hair, she pointed to the boxes of chocolate on the top row. "Samples are free, right?"

As much as I loved getting freebies myself, it was annoying when anyone else asked for them. I handed her a cherry cordial, one of our least popular items. "Anything else?"

"You're not at any of the Asian American club meetings. You a banana or what?"

The hairs on my neck stood up. "Banana?"

"Yellow on the outside, white on the inside."

She clearly had the wrong fruit.

I'd grown up in Detroit, so my political awareness had come early and often. The issue of race seeped into every discussion, not just because of the city's history, but also because of its current state as America's most racially segregated city. As an Asian American, I was constantly being asked to pick a side, Black or white, whether it was on the playground or even in our restaurant, where our cooks teased me for being too much on both sides.

I pegged this girl as one of those holier-than-thou liberals, the kind that gave the left a bad name and made me hesitant to join the school's active Young Democrats. Ann Arbor was full of these loons. Dressed in T-shirts with pithy sayings and a faint hint of weed, they camped out in Haven Hall preying on innocent first-years. I had no interest in supporting her agenda, so I snapped my fingers at the other customers. "Who's next?"

"Okay, I get it. You're busy, dude." She handed me a flyer. "You should join our club. Not the Asian American Students Association. They do fashion shows and shit like that. Come to UMAASC. The Asian American Student Coalition. We're just better." As she headed to the door, she flicked her hand once more. "By the way, I'm Vicky."

Her last-minute introduction caught me off guard. "I'm Curtis."

"Yeah, Curtis Chin. I know."

Before I could ask how she knew my name, she slipped out into the cold.

Since arriving on campus two and a half years earlier, I hadn't made any special effort to seek out Asian American friends. For starters, there weren't many of us, less than 5 percent, with a big chunk in engineering on the north campus. Also, if I had to be honest, I wasn't sure if I'd like any of them. Mimi and Angi had no problem with me being gay, but the other Asian Americans I knew at Michigan, including my brother and cousins, were pretty traditional. Would they or people who looked like them be okay with my open queerness?

I did have room in my schedule. I had dropped out of the improv troupe after the organizers refused to let me skip a rehearsal to go home for Lunar New Year. I pointed out that we had taken breaks for the major Christian and Jewish holidays, but they said my request wasn't religious. Sorry, but to me, anything involving my family and food was holy. If I couldn't go home to have one of our famous egg rolls, what was I fighting for?

Still looking to keep busy and hoping to make more political friends, I decided to give UMAASC a shot. Meetings were held at the Michigan Union, the ivy-covered student activities building down the street from Drake's. Twenty people sat around a plain office with protest signs propped against the wall. I introduced myself to the attractive check-in girl. To my surprise, she had me on the list. "Vicky said you might show up."

I asked about our mutual friend. The girl explained that Vicky had too much homework to come that night. I couldn't believe it. I was being stood up by my stalker. I wondered if this had been her plan all along.

I was about to leave when I spotted Japanese candies being served. I took a seat.

For a little while, the group discussed a recent incident where some Asian American girls had been called racist slurs at a frat party, but they spent most of the meeting strategizing about how to establish an Asian American studies program on campus. I didn't know that could be a thing, but it sounded cool to me. Back in high school, I had wanted to learn more about our history but couldn't find anything, not even in the massive Detroit Public Library.

A guy in a denim jacket mentioned the Vincent Chin case as something we should be learning about in school. That also sounded good to me. Since college, I had paid less attention to the case. According to the elders in Chinatown, many of whom were immigrant and working class, they had been pushed aside and into the closet. The younger college-educated Asian Americans from the suburbs, and even from out of state, thought that On Leong's reputation as a tong might scare off outside support. These new activists wanted a squeaky-clean image, so our back kitchen ceased being the community's town hall. Despite the family losing all their appeals in court, the case had become a rallying cry for these students.

For some reason, I didn't mention my personal connection, our family association, or the fact that one of my uncles was his best man.

After the meeting, the business and engineering majors rushed back to the library and their cubicles. I would have gladly joined them, but my parents had taught me to stay and help clean up, so I collected the trash and reorganized the chairs with the remaining students. As I suspected, most of the attendees were premed, prelaw, or pre-something-six-figures. Once I heard that Vicky was in the same program as Mimi, I knew the source of her intel.

A chirpy girl rocking a New Order T-shirt mentioned the club had lesbian and bisexual members but no gay men. I could've been upset at Mimi for sharing my personal business, but it turned out she'd done me a favor. I had been worried that these other Asian Americans might harbor some unspoken homophobia, but they didn't. Like my friends at Drake's, they seemed totally cool. Maybe in my fear of being prejudged by the group, I had done the same to them.

I returned the following week, this time with a bag of chocolate hearts from work. Still no Vicky, but one of the bisexual guys did appear. He must have heard that at the last meeting there was a *gold-star gay*—a term I'd learned from Matt to describe a gay guy who had never had sex with a girl. He must've wanted to check me out.

Tim turned out to be a grad student from Queens. A short Jamaican Chinese with a man bun, he cornered me after the meeting, in which we'd further discussed the studies program. "So, you looking for an Asian boyfriend?"

Tim had a Vietnamese girlfriend, so I knew he wasn't proposition-ing me. Still, it caught me off guard. I had never considered race when thinking about a boyfriend or partner. Growing up at Chung's, I'd lusted after men of all races. Like our kitchen, I was open to serving anyone. "They just have to be normal."

Tim pouted. "You should date another Asian."

I looked around the room to see if this was the popular consensus. If it was, nobody flinched. "Really. I'm open to any race."

"Sticky rice is better."

"Yes, but what does that have to do with our conversation?"

Tim explained that in this case, *sticky rice* meant "Asians who date other Asians." *Wow,* I thought, *yet another term not on the SATs.* Also, why was everything about food with Asians?

Since any boyfriend or partner was still hypothetical, I didn't argue with the guy. If he was willing to help me jump-start my nonexistent love life, he could impose any rules he wanted. Heck, he could even be a Spartan. But I drew the line at a Buckeye. I did have some standards. "Fine. Find me a boyfriend. Make him sticky." (That came out wrong.)

It had been years since I had taken a math class, but the odds of matching me with another gay Asian guy seemed to be slim. Michigan was big, but not that big. As luck would have it, Tim had a candidate in the wings. "His name is Jeff. He's in the law school. He went to Yale. And he's Ko-re-an."

I didn't think it was possible to get hard from a résumé, but there it was. Ann Arbor had one of the top-ranked law schools in the country. Anyone who'd gotten in had to be smart and, as I said, smart guys turned me on. I knew my mom would approve. Perhaps this guy's Ivy League degree would soften the blow when I came out.

I had never met another gay or bisexual Asian guy before Tim. Prior to seeing the character Omar in *My Beautiful Laundrette,* I thought I might be the only one, a proverbial unicorn. I didn't think there was anyone who could relate to all my different issues. Now that I was about to meet someone from my own tribe, I was excited. Would he look and dress like me? Would we have the same taste in music?

Suddenly, UMAASC competed with Drake's as my regular hangout. I attended every general meeting and several subcommittees too. The work was challenging. Our club was only a small voice on campus, and the college deans seemed more interested in supporting Asian groups that organized socials and food festivals. And if the Black student groups, with their large-scale protests, weren't being heard, how could we, with our smaller numbers, have any success?

Still, I continued to attend the meetings. Dressed in a clean T-shirt and fresh jeans, I sat by the door at every meeting, hoping to be the first to greet the guy if and when he showed up. But as much as I chanted at home, he never appeared. The little slip of paper containing my phone number remained folded in my wallet.

One sunny afternoon, Tim and I headed across the campus to his apartment, where he stored his large collection of old typewriters. He said the traditional devices were better for writing than computer keyboards and wanted to lend me one. The physical act of seeing the ink hit the blank paper, he claimed, helped commit the words to memory. I thought back to all the failed op-eds I'd typed up in the restaurant. I was starting to send my poems to literary journals in hopes of getting published, and I wanted to ensure better luck.

As we passed the mammoth limestone Rackham Building, Tim's face lit up. He bolted toward an Asian guy who was just walking out the door. I was embarrassed. Was my love life so pathetic that my friend was now approaching any random Chinese or Korean guy on the street?

Tim gestured. "This is Jeff. He's family."

Family. Another new term, but much more appealing than *sticky rice.* Then it clicked. This was Mr. Yale Michigan Law, born in Cleveland but raised in Chicago. He was a little shorter than me, but he had a cute, clean-cut face. Most important, he was dressed like a Young Republican. Ding! Ding! Ding! (Okay, some habits die hard.)

Tim grabbed our arms and pulled us together. My palms were already wet. For some odd reason, my thoughts jumped to Hong Kong twenty-three years earlier, when my mom and dad first met. Was this how they'd felt on their setup? Awkward and shy? Did arranged marriages really work? Did ancient rituals really beat modern conventions?

Tim bounced on his heels. "I was beginning to think this day would never happen." I smiled at Jeff.

No response.

One thing Chung's taught me about was meeting strangers. I always tried my best to be friendly, but sometimes, no matter what I said or did, the new customer didn't respond. I realized that if someone wasn't open to my kindness, it might not have anything to do with me. It might be more about themselves, their personalities, or just the day they were having. I learned never to take rejection personally.

I reached out my hand. "Nice to meet you. How are things going?"

Jeff's initial response was a haze, as was Tim's, as both continued to rattle on. Nothing registered in my brain. I was too busy naming babies to hear another word.

Jeff pointed in some random direction. "Sorry, I've gotta go. Nice to meet you."

My heart sank. Was it something I'd said or done? Was I not his type? Was I not attractive enough? Or maybe this out-and-proud gay guy didn't want to deal with a closet case or a twenty-one-year-old virgin.

Too bad, I decided. I had waited this long and I wasn't letting this moment pass. "Maybe we're headed the same way. Where are you going?"

"Japan. I'm leaving next week."

Okay. That was a bit far.

Tim slapped Jeff on the chest. "What? Where are you going?"

Jeff explained that he was going on a one-year sabbatical to study in Japan. And that was it. He took off. Tim and I stood on the steps of the building.

Tim felt bad for me, but I was okay. In fact, I was feeling pretty good. Jeff's reaction wasn't personal; I could have been Chow Yun Fat, and he still would have left. The most important thing was that at least I'd tried. I'd put myself out there. And like my dad, whose first setup was also a failure, I just needed to find the next candidate.

UMAASC failed to boost my love life, but it did reignite my other passion: politics. Once again, it felt rewarding to be working with civic-minded people committed to making a difference at school and in the world. Although I was now doing it from a different side of the aisle, it was the same satisfaction I had felt being a Republican. Both entities claimed to love America. They just had different versions of its past and visions for its future.

The club managed a small library filled with the kinds of material I would have loved to have had growing up, books like *The Big Aiiieeeee!*, *The Woman Warrior*, and *America Is in the Heart*. I learned about Asian American history, including the origins of the model-minority myth and how it was first used by the *New York Times* in the '60s to pit Blacks and Latinos, who were still struggling economically, against Japanese Americans, who were seeing some success despite having just been released from internment.

The best part of the collection was the journals from the West Coast: *Amerasia*, out of UCLA, and *Tea Leaves*, from Berkeley. The young editors inspired me to launch my own journal in Ann Arbor, one geared toward our experiences in the Midwest. Recognizing the lack of diversity in my writing classes, I opened up submissions to all writers of color. I couldn't wait to hear the other voices. Thanks to the student activities committee, I had the funding to put out two issues. I was going to be a publisher.

Meanwhile, back in Detroit, my parents had reduced their hours even further after my dad got carjacked on a delivery run (another long story). Once open as late as four a.m. for the post-bowling crowd, Chung's now closed at nine p.m. While I was concerned about my mom and dad's safety, this meant my parents could alternate with Uncle Phil, sometimes leaving after the dinner rush at seven. This change reduced my anxiety tenfold.

With this new spare time, my parents might have tried in the past to pull together a mahjong table, but with fewer Chinese living in Chinatown and even fewer coming down on the weekends, it had been months since they had fielded a quartet. My mom and dad started socializing with some of their white and Black customers, going out to the movies or taking boat rides on the river. According to my siblings, my parents were even acting like teenagers, holding hands.

The reduced hours also meant they didn't need me to work as much over the summer. I was a little sad to miss our egg rolls, but it did open up my schedule. When the term ended that spring, I decided to stay in Ann Arbor. The men's basketball team had just won the Final Four, so the campus was in a damn good mood. I figured I could take a few extra courses and work on the journal. I wasn't sure how my parents would react to my plans, but they turned out to be happy. Their Wolverine pride was at an all-time high.

When I told my dad about the journal, he tried his best to help out. Detroit wasn't a major publishing hub, but he managed to introduce me to a few of the editors who came into Chung's. One of his contacts even came up to Ann Arbor and took me out to lunch—in retrospect, I think my dad might have inadvertently set me up on my first gay blind date (that's also another story).

Though I did miss being able to eat my favorite foods at the restaurant, my summer in Ann Arbor proved to be really fun. In addition to acing my classes and helping to train the new workers at Drake's, I dove right into putting together the journal. I was still new to the game, but using my mom's mantra of "working hard," I put in a 100 percent effort.

Publishing a journal turned out to be a team project. Luckily, I was able to find the perfect coeditor standing next to me at Drake's. A statuesque African American from Grand Rapids who had recently joined the staff, Darci was a no-nonsense journalism major who had been developing her own literary projects for Black high-school students. We both decried the lack of literary role models we'd had growing up and decided to join forces. Though she did challenge me on my own privileges of being male, Asian American, and able-bodied, we got along pretty well. She was the first writer I knew who thought about race as much as I did.

Ignoring Connie's pleas for us to stop debating the Western canon and get back to work, Darci and I executed our mission with precision. We split every duty, from finalizing the call for submissions to finding a designer to signing up sponsors, like Borders bookstore. By the start of the fall, we had sixty-four pages of poems and fiction from students, professors, and the local literati. And thanks to my dad, we'd secured an introduction to the journal from March Fong Eu, who was California's secretary of state, the country's highest-ranking Asian American government official at the time—and a new Chung's customer.

The first edition of *Backgrounds* was gorgeous—especially the table of contents. All the writers were Asian, Black, Latino, or Indigenous, and there were a good number of queer voices as well. After archiving a few copies, Darci and I sent the rest out to high schools around the state, hoping to inspire other young writers.

As I held my copy of the journal in my hand, I felt something I hadn't expected to find in college: a synthesis of all the different parts of myself. This journal, whose inception I could never have predicted, represented the part of me that appreciated the importance of education and academia, the part of me that was curious about people and their stories, and a space where I could be a more open book.

M-7.

Being a creative-writing major made me the literary expert at Chung's. That was inevitable, as my dad asked every customer, "Have you met our number three? He's the writer in the family." Every time he mentioned my program, the number of students accepted got smaller and smaller. At some point, I expected him to say I was the only one on campus allowed to own a pen.

One week, one of our waiters was out sick. My younger siblings were busy with their weekend activities, so I was the one called in to help. I jumped at the chance to have some home-cooked meals for a few days. I was running around the dining room, refreshing our customers' silver teapots, when a white middle-aged woman reached into her oversize bag and pulled out a colorful hardcover. "Have you read this book? It's so good."

The Joy Luck Club, the recently released novel that featured a bunch of old sassy Chinese ladies who liked to eat, gossip, and play mahjong, could have been set in our back kitchen. Every time I came in to help at the restaurant, another diner, usually older and female, cited the most memorable characters, lines, and scenes. They all wanted to know if I was working on something similar. I was writing poetry, but they didn't care. To them, all writers were the same. They would squeal, "You could be the next Amy Tan!"

My mom turned out to be the biggest pusher. She rarely had a book in her hand, but the success of *The Joy Luck Club* convinced her that her life was a bestseller too. She followed me around the dining room, dropping stories from her childhood—the same ones I'd heard growing up, but now she recounted them as if she was auditioning for her book on tape.

One night, after seeing how our waiters sometimes pooled tips together, my mom shared an oldie.

"When the Communists marched south, they targeted my family. My uncles and grandpa were rich in America, so the Red Guard called us traitors. My stubborn grandma didn't want to leave her big home, so when my parents escaped to Hong Kong, they left me behind to keep her company. The Communists hated me and my poh-poh. When I was four, they made me watch as they forced my grandma to climb the old banyan tree in our courtyard. Then they pushed her off into a pile of broken glass." For a visual, my mom rubbed her knees.

Another time, standing at the water station, she launched into her own nautical tale: "When I was five, my uncle in America paid twenty-five thousand dollars in renminbi—a king's ransom in people's money—to a local fisherman to ferry our remaining family out of China. After a long ride tucked under the planks of his fishy fishing boat, we came up for air. But we weren't in Hong Kong. The traitor had turned us in to the authorities. In jail, I had to sing Communist Party songs to earn extra rice for me and my grandma!"

Another chapter came as we stood beneath a painting of the Chinese countryside: "When my poh-poh and I were freed from jail, we found that the officials had given away our home to peasants. We were forced to live several villages away in a dirt hut with three other families. Whenever we went out for a pail of water, my grandma had to bend low, to keep her head below the soldiers'." Once again, she gave me a demonstration, this time bowing her head.

Granted, my mom's epic saga interested me. Who wouldn't be intrigued by tales of prison cells, guns, and stolen ransoms? Even the parts about her mundane life in Hong Kong after she was reunited with her parents and siblings were amusing. But these were her stories, not mine. She had to tell them. Not me. I was in school to find my own voice. I sat and listened, but that was as far as it would go.

Toward the end of the summer, as I was at the back table sipping my red pop, stockpiling poems for the upcoming semester, my mom sat down. Before I could say anything, she started talking. "I was a top student in Hong Kong. When Pepsi came to town, they held a big contest for students to draw a picture of their own school. Mine was the best at Sacred Heart. I won six cases. There were so many bottles, I had to give some to the nuns—"

I threw down my Parker pen, the one I'd treated myself to after getting into the program. "Yes, and they kept burping all day. It was so funny. You've told me that story over and over, and I don't even like Pepsi. I prefer Coke!"

My mom's shoulders shriveled; the shine faded from her rosy cheeks. "You don't want to hear my story?"

I tensed up. "I do, but I'm behind on my own stuff."

Between Drake's, the journal, and saving the world, my schedule was packed. On top of that, my workshops in the fall were advanced. Still insecure about my place in the program, I'd put pressure on myself to create more interesting writing by staying up late and scribbling in my notebook every detail of my life. But no matter how hard I tried, "working harder" could not produce a better poem.

My mom lifted herself off her seat. The glint in her eyes orphaned me. Her forty-two years of life flashed before my eyes. She'd gone from Guangzhou to Hong Kong to Detroit and spent the past two decades raising her six children in a hostile foreign land. She'd tried to prove her life had worth, that it hadn't gone unnoticed, and here I was, the ungrateful son, writing it off. Her lips quivered in a soft murmur.

I hastily picked up my pen, backtracking. "Go ahead. I'll write it down this time."

My mom bowed her head as if I were one of the soldiers holding a gun to her temple, ordering her to sing. "You go on. Do your own thing."

I reached out my hand, but by then she had disappeared through the black swinging door, leaving only the rattling from the kitchen— the clanging woks and rumbling dishwasher.

I sat there, upset at myself for being so inconsiderate. Everything I had done in the past three years had been for her, but it seemed as though I had failed the final test. My education wasn't just to help me get a better life; it was for my whole family. We were a team. We were the eight immortals. How could I let them down? I needed to make things right, but I knew that, like most disappointments in our house, apologies were never spoken. Only deeds would bring about reconciliation.

When I went back to school for my senior year, four housemates and I downsized to a smaller rental a few blocks farther from campus. The sky-blue home added ten minutes to my walk, but at least my room was guaranteed asbestos-free. The neighborhood also felt more creative—Arthur Miller, the playwright who'd penned *Death of a Salesman* and *All My Sons*, had lived in a house just around the corner. Hopefully, I thought, his working-class perspective could provide me with some much-needed inspiration. That's if he hadn't been a dick to his mom too.

The apartment suited me perfectly. I was growing tired of eating tuna fish sandwiches at Drake's, and I couldn't afford to eat any-where else, so I decided to use the small kitchen, stocking it with basic supplies from Chung's: frozen noodles, a bag of rice, a jar of MSG. Initially, it felt odd to be alone in the kitchen. At Chung's, cooking was loud and communal. Everyone pitched in. Now, alone in my kitchen, I realized that preparing a meal could be quiet too—a private conversation between the food and its maker. There was only one mouth to please, and that was mine. Suddenly the pressure to perform was gone and I could finally enjoy the art of supper.

The sole critic in our house was Dale, my former roommate now turned housemate. He had become a health nut in freshman year. He didn't approve of my Chinese food, calling it unhealthy and oily, but I didn't care. I loved my food and it felt good to no longer fear the wok.

For the first time in my life, I also had my own room. It wasn't huge—just big enough for a bed and desk—but it was mine. I also had a lock, one that I could use. I'd never realized how much I enjoyed being naked. I even nicknamed myself "the Nudist Buddhist."

On a small box in the room's corner, a picture of Guan Yin, the goddess of compassion, sat alongside a jade pendant. Before writing each day, I would burn a joss stick of sandalwood. The fragrance of our back kitchen and funerals conjured childhood memories, flooding me with warmth and peace. The self-imposed pressures of being a good writer, a good son, a good human floated away with the spiraling smoke.

I had a full work schedule, so my classes were limited to early mornings, late evenings, and independent studies. One of my coworkers, Linda, a sassy blond pothead from Romulus, over near the airport, mentioned she was taking a fiction-writing class on Tuesday and Thursday nights. The class was open to any writer, no experience necessary. That sounded great to me. Lately, I had been eschewing poetry and thinking in terms of short stories. After finally reading *The Joy Luck Club,* I recognized the beauty of the longer form and how it gave me even more space to explore personal themes. I thought this might be a good chance to get my feet wet. "So who's the instructor?"

"Some lady named Tish something-something."

"Is she any good?"

Linda rolled up her paisley scrunchie. "I don't know, but her husband is some big muckety-muck in history or something."

"Well, what has she written?"

"Her husband's famous. What else you gotta know?"

I guess that was it. It was only a low-level fiction class. What could go wrong?

On the first night of class, I came straight from work. The room was half full. Smelling like bacon, I took a seat on the side with fewer bodies. Some more students trickled in, including Linda, performing her usual Motown strut. To prepare for the new genre, I'd composed a list of anecdotes from Chung's that were too complicated to fit in a poem, memories like when my grandma had boiled our pet turtles and when my grandpa had been forced by the tong to carry a handgun.

The instructor walked in late. A husky woman with white hair, bland slacks, and folded arms, she dropped her leather bag on the chair before planting her butt on the edge of her desk. After introducing herself and talking about her newly released book, a collection of short stories about her Irish ancestors, she went on to explain the course requirements. Each student had to submit a hundred pages of new material. *A hundred pages?* I gulped. That was more than everything I had written in a year of poetry workshops.

The class had no formal assignments, but the instructor did suggest that, as young writers, we should challenge ourselves by adopting different voices. We would then read our pieces aloud for feedback. Some students followed the prompt by writing as characters from past centuries or as members of a four-legged species. As they shared their drafts, I tried to find something positive to say. I figured the good karma might come in handy when it came time for me to read my first attempt.

Except for me and a Japanese guy from the residential college who rarely spoke up, the class was entirely white. Three or four of the other students tried to write from the perspective of Black or Latino characters. I don't recall the specifics, but I do remember feeling uncomfortable. More experienced writers might have been able to pull that off, but the novices in our class relied on stereotypes. I waited for the instructor to say something about challenging assumptions or to push them to do more research, but she just nodded her approval.

I didn't want to be labeled as angry, but my inner voice urged me to speak up, especially after one ambitious white girl with neon-purple glasses wrote a story from the perspective of a lower-caste boy in colonial India. The young narrator was described as admiring his own brown skin and having almond-shaped eyes, with some unexplained reference to a lurking Bengal tiger. My fellow classmates praised the colorful descriptions and exotic location, but to me, it felt like she had just recolonized the country.

I turned to Linda, aghast. My friend gave me one of her *Don't do it* looks. I shouldn't have been surprised. Whenever I mentioned UMAASC at Drake's, she rolled her eyes and called me a lefty. I had never been so insulted in all my life. Just because I advocated for a program in Asian American studies so I could learn my own history didn't make me a leftist. The education would be open to everyone.

Linda kicked me in the shin.

I couldn't worry about my friend's discomfort. I already knew how I felt, and it wasn't good. Bottling up my feelings adversely affected my mental health. It made me second-guess myself, made me feel guilty for even having these questions, like I was the bad guy. I had to get it out. And so my hand went up. When the instructor finally called on me—only after she'd exhausted all her other options, I noted—I asked my fellow classmate, "So, what made you write that story? Have you been to India?"

"No, but the culture sounded so cool."

Again not wanting to come off as the aggressor, I took a deep breath and chose my words carefully. "Something about it seemed off to me. I know lots of Indians and Indian Americans. I don't know if any of them would—"

My instructor bolted to her feet. "Stop. She's using her imagination and being creative."

Fine, I thought. But who really got to do that? Wasn't it important to hear from writers who had a connection to that world? Wouldn't that provide an added layer of depth and understanding? I raised my hand again to add my further points, but the instructor's focus had shifted to the other side of the room, and she was not turning back to our side.

A few weeks later, my chance to read came up. I considered writing in a different voice, but I didn't know which one to choose. Instead, I followed the advice of another one of my writing professors, Charles Baxter. The kind and gentle soul had given me a waiver to take his graduate-level poetry-writing workshop. After inviting the class into his living room, he advised us to pay attention to the small details in our own lives—the people and places—and mine them for pieces. I figured I had a million stories on my grandma alone!

My fiction debut centered on a story from the fourth grade. My mom had sent me to the Chinese-language school at Burton to improve my Cantonese. All the other kids were native speakers, so my classmates were younger than me. The brats had laughed at me for my poor pronunciation, so I'd taught them a few choice words in English. The piece went on to explore the issues I was personally dealing with—most important, fitting in and speaking up.

I practiced and practiced before reading the story in class. Unlike poetry, where the other writers were pensive, the fiction writers were more emotive. They laughed and smiled, which caused my confidence to grow. With each paragraph, my voice built before reaching its spectacular conclusion, me standing all alone in the school gym, staring at the basketball net.

Scanning the happy faces around the workshop, I thought, *Hell, I could be the next Amy Tan. The boy version. With a better haircut.*

Throughout the critique, my instructor stayed mum. I figured she didn't want the praise going to my head. I was sure her appreciation would register in my final grade. Two more students needed to read, so we moved on. I was so happy with the response to my piece that I don't even recall what they wrote. When class ended, we all flooded out like a flock of starlings. My instructor stopped me at the door. "Mr. Chin, can you come by my office tomorrow?"

Oh, well. She was probably mad that I hadn't followed her writing suggestion, but I didn't care. After thinking about my goals as a writer, I realized that as a kid, I'd never gotten to read stories from people like myself, so I wanted to write about my own experience, not someone else's. The overall response from my classmates made me think I was on the right track. "Sure. Is there a reason why?"

"We'll talk tomorrow."

The next day, when I arrived at her office, the lights in the hallway were off. She opened the door to reveal a tiny space smaller than my grandpa's office. There was barely enough room for her desk, book-shelf, and two chairs. I took a seat and said hello, still upbeat from the comments from class. When she failed to offer any pleasant greeting, I knew this wouldn't be a social call.

"I need to talk to you about your participation in class." My butt shifted on the hard plastic. "You don't speak up, and when you do, you seem to be stuck on certain issues."

She was clearly referring to race as if it were a four-letter word, but she was wrong. As a young bard, I commented on other things too—usually the more poetic aspects of the work, like rhythm and language—but that must not have registered with her. To her, once I'd mentioned the topic of race, that's all she ever heard.

For the first time, my instructor's age became clear. Her white hair had made me think she was much older than me, more experienced. In reality, like my other lecturers, she was in her late twenties or early thirties. She was almost my peer. This wasn't a generational issue. It was cultural. I sat up in my seat. "I comment on all things, but these things matter to me too."

"Well, it stifles creativity. Writers should be able to write whatever they want. You need to focus on the more important things."

Her disregard for my concerns infuriated me, but arguing was pointless. She had already signaled what she thought of me. No matter what I said, she had put me into her box. I decided my time would be better spent working on my next submission.

Before I could get up, she continued. "I want to discuss the story you read."

The tension subsided, as I thought she was going to end the meeting with a little praise to balance things out. She leaned back in her chair. "This story is too good to be from an undergrad. I want to know where you stole it from."

I did a quick double take. *Did she really just say what I think she said?*

A typhoon of emotions ripped through my body. Shock and disbelief overtook me, as well as a bit of pride. *Damn, she thought my story was that good.* I composed myself enough to reply, "This is my story. I wrote it."

"I don't say this lightly. Tell me where this came from."

At that point, I became the angriest Buddhist ever. I wanted to leap across that desk and perform some tiger-crane batshit. If nothing else, I wanted to say something so biting she would find God, or at least another job, but any clever comeback died in my throat. *L'esprit de l'escalier.*

My temporary paralysis led me to repeat my defense. "This is my story. I wrote it."

We had reached a stalemate. From her rigid body, it was clear she wasn't going to be moved. She folded her arms. "Fine." Whatever came out of her mouth next, I didn't hear it. I'd blanked out. My body burned with so much disgust and hate. I didn't feel safe. I needed to get out. I stood up and left.

The hallway remained dark. I paced up and down, but I don't recall for how long. Five, ten minutes—who knows. Nothing made sense to me. I felt lost, unsure of what to say or whom to turn to. Why did she praise the other students for writing as other people but question the authenticity of my voice?

At some point, she popped out to check the drop box on her door. I know she saw me, but she didn't even acknowledge my existence. She just closed her door and went on her merry way.

As I crossed the university's central plaza, the Diag, my body remained tense. Sure, good people sometimes unintentionally say dumb and hurtful things—that's forgivable. But this woman thought this through. She had carefully composed that hateful thought in her head and said what she wanted to say. I considered lodging a complaint with the department—one of my many outraged letters— but given the power imbalance and lack of previous success with my op-eds, I wasn't confident anything would come of it. In fact, I assumed nothing would. When has an Asian person's words been more powerful than those of a white person?

I went to Drake's in search of support and advice. Connie was busy with a customer and Darci wasn't on duty. Neither was the first Matt or the second one who'd joined our staff. Linda, who was sitting in a back booth with some of her fellow potheads, would have to do.

After pulling her aside, I explained the situation. Linda's eyes glazed over. I wasn't sure if she was bored or she had smoked something bad. When I finished, she shook her head. "Yo! Why you gotta be so political all the time?"

I was stunned. "That woman just accused me of stealing my story."

"But you didn't, did you?"

"No, of course not."

"Then write another one. It's not a big deal."

Now I was more upset at Linda. Instead of trying to dismiss my reaction, she should have accepted what I was saying. Even if she didn't understand why the situation was so problematic because it had never happened to her, as a friend, she should have had my back and trusted me. But obviously, my word wasn't good enough for her.

Linda placed her hand on my shoulder. I think she was trying to steady herself. "Listen to me, mano a mano, writer to writer, what you need is some good pot."

"Is that all you have to say?"

"It's really good."

So much for allyship. Once again, my friend had let me down. I threw up my hands and walked out.

Over the next few days, my mind bounced between resignation and revolt. My parents probably would have supported me either way, but I decided to follow the advice of another great Chinese philosopher, Sun Tzu, who wrote *The Art of War*. The book viewed conflict through a cost-benefit analysis. It was my senior year. I had a few more poems to write for my graduating thesis as well as my overall grade point average to consider. This was just a side class, an experiment. The amount of energy necessary to defeat this monster was not worth the effort. I would stick to poetry.

To cement my decision, I left the house for some fresh air. I crisscrossed the campus, even going as far as the law school. Twenty minutes into my walk, my feet were standing under some Chinese lettering and a neon OPEN sign. China Gate, the only half-decent Chinese restaurant near campus, cast its shadow. I had never eaten there before, but in a pinch, it would have to do.

The space smelled of grease, warm and familiar. The owners had placed big mirrors next to traditional lanterns and paintings to form an optical illusion and enlarge the space. It didn't work. The place still felt small. On the back wall, a photo display of their selections lit up the room. An older Asian woman serving a table of other students nodded. I grabbed one of the booths. My eyes watched her every move. Perhaps she was like my family, low wah kiu, the old travelers who came to build the railroads and clean the laundry. I wondered what stories she might have to tell.

After finishing with the other table, she approached me with her pad in her hand. In her accented English, she asked, "You stay or take to go?"

It was a variation on my dad's old greeting but a question that was familiar. It was one I had grappled with for years, before I even had my driver's license or could name all the countries in the United Nations. As my eyes panned over the pictures on the wall—the moo goo gai pan, the almond boneless chicken, chicken with cashew nuts—the answer became clear.

It was time for me to go.

M-8.

After escaping the fiction-writing class with a B plus, the lowest grade I'd ever received for writing, I committed myself to finding a safe place to further my poetry writing. My poetic muse at the time was fellow Wolverine Frank O'Hara. His whimsical style taught me to lighten up, to have fun with my words, even to be flirtatious. Before he died in a freak car accident on Fire Island, he was an out gay man who worked at the Museum of Modern Art in New York.

Hoping to emulate his creativity, I applied to work at a few cultural institutions in Manhattan too.

Over spring break, Mimi and I took a quick road trip to the Big Apple for several interviews. I didn't land any full-time jobs, but I did get a summer internship with a museum in Chinatown. It had a small staff, only five or six employees. I would work to help them establish an Asian American bookstore and reading series. It seemed like a dream job. After that meeting, walking through Manhattan, I saw plenty of cafés and bookstores. I was ready to get out my pen and paper and French beret.

Before I broke the news to my parents that I would be moving to New York after graduation to try my hand at being a writer, I wanted to make sure they were in a good mood, so I asked them to meet me for dinner. I had to choose someplace nice. My family rarely ate out, but when we did, it was always Chinese. In addition to preferring the cuisine, my parents got to see their friends and check out the competition. At other restaurants, my dad would glance around the room and take mental notes of the dishes ordered by the other tables. If something seemed popular, he would add it to the next week's specials.

With support from Chris, Calvin, Cindy, and Clifford—whom I'd filled in on my postcollege plans a few days earlier—our family met at our regular karaoke place. (Bad news always went down better with a little Jacky Cheung.) Ping On, three times the size of Chung's, was located in the suburbs. A small cluster of Asian businesses had sprung up around Fifteen Mile Road. It was the city's new version of Chinatown. As usual, the place was packed. I couldn't identify the other patrons by name, but I could ID them by their businesses: "Those are the Dragon Inn folks." "They run Empress Gardens."

The playlist that night included all of our usual go-to numbers: a smattering of Motown, Canto pop, and songs from British invasions one and two. I waited until our stomachs were full and we'd all gotten in a few songs before breaking the news. We'd had plenty of family dinners, but there had been few family meetings when we discussed a serious matter, maybe around Vincent Chin or my dad's infidelity. I proceeded slowly.

Of course, my mom had a million questions—What exactly did a writer do? How much did poetry pay? Was I going to starve?—but in the end, she and my dad both supported my decision. They had six kids. I guess they figured they could afford to lose one. Besides, our family's education assembly line was proceeding nicely. Craig was getting ready to graduate from Loyola in Chicago; Chris had realized he still wanted to be a doctor and was considering taking classes at Oakland University in anticipation of applying to med school; Calvin had been the valedictorian of his class and was on his way to Yale; Cindy and Clifford were doing well in middle school and elementary school, respectively. That was a pretty good track record for my parents, two people without college degrees.

My internship began at the end of May. That gave me a few weeks to wind up the Ann Arbor chapter of my life. I divided my collection of poetry books, keeping my copies of *Leaves of Grass* and the *Chuang Tzu* and donating the rest to the UMAASC library. I stopped by all my usual writing spots—Café Royale, the law library, Zingerman's— wringing out any last drops of Michigan inspiration.

Walking through the Diag and the main campus, I had a chance to reflect on my college experience. I had arrived my freshman year with low expectations, but I'd grown to appreciate Ann Arbor. Over four years, I had changed as a person. Not only had my confidence grown, but I was more compassionate, especially to myself. In addition to accepting who I was, I now felt I had a road map for my life.

The world had changed too. Between the fight for democracy in

Tiananmen Square last spring, which my family and every Chinese person I knew had watched religiously, and the fall of the Berlin Wall a few months later, the march of progress was upon us. Denmark had become the first country to legally recognize gay relationships. Apartheid was coming to an end in South Africa. The future looked so bright, I had to wear shades.

The majority of my final day on campus was spent at Drake's. The friends I'd made there helped me come out to myself as both gay and a writer. I had to say my goodbyes. As usual, Connie was organizing the work schedule; Linda was being loud; Marsha was snapping at the customers; Matt number two was sketching in the back booth. Darci and I discussed our graduation and the future of our journal. She'd found our replacement, an editor who'd happened to be in my journalism class in high school.

Mimi stopped by, offering to give me a proper send-off. For the past four years, I had been too busy studying and working and then being a student activist to have much of a social life. No concerts. No first-run movies. No dates. That night, nothing could stop me from letting my hair down, not even the fact that I had short hair.

We decided to go to the hottest club on campus, the Nectarine Ballroom. As a member of UMAASC, I had boycotted the place for perpetuating stereotypes of Asian hordes with their "Asian Invasion" nights, but I figured I could set aside my politics for one night. See? Progress. That's how much I'd grown.

Mimi and I met up with Alicia, my old neighbor in the dorms. The three of us arrived a little after ten p.m. The place, which resembled a Studio 54 knockoff, with its disco balls, flashing lights, and fog machine, was packed. The clientele mirrored the university—half men and half women, mainly white. One or two Black patrons and a smattering of Asians, including me and my friends, provided some color.

I'd already packed up most of my clothes, so I'd put on what I had, a clean cotton button-down and jeans. I thought I looked pretty good standing off to the side. When "Bizarre Love Triangle"— the song we'd hoped they would play—came on, we all squealed. Due to a rugby injury, Mimi had to bob her head as she stood on the side, but Alicia and I managed to squat a sliver of real estate, packed between bodies, shoulder to shoulder.

A medley of crowd-pleasers bounced us through the night: Michael Jackson, Prince, the Cure. I had a move for every song, even Madonna's latest hit, "Vogue." Despite my aborted diatribe against her in high school, I had grown to appreciate the Material Girl's catalog. As I tried to strike a pose, Alicia tilted her permed head and short body to the right. I was concentrating on giving good face, so I didn't notice any talent scouts hoping to sign me. "What? I look cool."

Alicia jerked her neck. "That guy. Over there."

From a sea of white faces, a potential paramour emerged. Okay. Not bad. The guy's eyes were so focused on me, it felt like he was trying to have my baby. I didn't mind. Before we left, gay Matt had predicted I would be considered "fresh meat." He told me to enjoy it, and I did. It felt nice to be the center of someone's attention. This was my moment. I earned it.

After we'd bobbed our way through waves of songs, Alicia had had enough. Too many people stepping on her toes. I followed her off the floor, but the sound of a saxophone pulled me right back. David Bowie was on fire, and this young American was not going anywhere. As I danced and hummed along to the Black girls singing background on the track, my not-so-secret admirer slipped in front of me. I went on high alert. After scanning around for my friends and not spotting them, I checked to see if anyone was reacting to the sight of two guys dancing together. Then I remembered this was Ann Arbor. Who the hell cared?

The music continued pounding. The guy leaned in. I think he said, "I like your dancing."

I shouted back, "Thanks."

He boldly went where no man had gone before, placing his hands around my waist, then pulling me toward him. We were so close I could smell his sweat and cologne. "I'm Mark."

I looked closer at his face. He was definitely on the cute side, but truthfully, once again, it was his confidence that turned me on. Any guy could win me over if he was assertive enough. This was all so new to me. I think I just wanted to have a teacher, someone else taking the lead. "I'm Curtis."

We continued bouncing for the next several tunes; some Culture Club mixed with old-school ABBA. His sexy prance tempered by his sweet, Midwestern innocence chased away all my unease. Every now and then, he leaned into my ear. Each time his breath brushed my cheek, I lost my air. I either pointed near my lobe and shouted, "I can't hear you," or pretended that I'd heard and nodded.

When the deejay started hawking next week's specials, the regular lights came on. Mark grabbed my hand and led me to the side. We finally had a chance to formally meet. He was from out of town and lived twenty minutes away, in Jackson, the home of the state prison. I had one reference point. "That's where they took the kid who lived across—"

Before I could finish, Mark blurted out, "Wanna come back to my place?"

Oh my God. This time, I heard him loud and clear, and I was smart enough to know he wasn't inviting me over to play Risk. This was happening. No question about it. There wasn't a shred of hesitation in my body. I was already hard and we hadn't even left the club.

The midnight air was full of promise. Sweaty coeds crowded East Liberty Avenue as the night's revelers plotted their next moves amid the scant options. Alicia looked like she'd been ready to leave an hour ago, as Mimi dangled her keys in my face. "McDonald's?"

Earlier in the evening, when my biggest hope for the night was a Filet-O-Fish, we had talked about noshing after the club. But now I had a more fulfilling offer. I felt bad for ditching my friends, but I didn't think they'd begrudge me this moment. "Sorry. I need to bail."

Mimi, who was aware of my virgin status, glanced over to check out Mark. Under the streetlight, he looked to be in his mid-twenties, just slightly older than me. He was leaning against his car, trying not to appear too eager. My friend had high standards. From the frown on her face, I could tell she wasn't too impressed. "Aren't you leaving Monday?"

"That's why this is perfect. If the sex is bad, we'll never have to see each other again."

Mimi chuckled, but I was serious. I had faced a lot of personal challenges the past four years. This would be my last test in college. My goal had been to find a relationship, but I would happily settle for sex. And despite my friend's pessimism, I did like the guy.

Alicia pointed to the bouncer who was urging the crowds to step away from the door. "We should go. I'm not putting up with any lines."

Mimi turned back to me. She looked me in the eye. "You sure about this?"

I had already made my decision in the club when Mark asked, but I paused just to let her think I was open to hearing her out. "Yeah. I'll be fine."

"You sure?" she asked again.

I appreciated my friend's protectiveness, but growing up in the Corridor, I had developed some street smarts. I knew how to take care of myself. My instincts told me Mark, despite his large hands and feet, wasn't some serial killer. I nodded. "Don't worry. I'm not going to do anything stupid."

"Good. I don't wanna see your face on any milk cartons."

Alicia patted my shoulder. "Be safe. We mean it."

"I will," I said.

Mimi took one last look at Mark. She sighed. "This is it, then."

"Thanks. For everything. I really appreciate it." I was sincere, but I was also trying to wrap this up. As much as I was going to miss my old friends, I couldn't wait to make a new one.

"You better call when you get to New York."

"Okay. I will. I will."

As Alicia helped Mimi wobble off, I took a deep breath to reassess the path ahead. My body remained full of anticipation. I felt like Mary Lou Retton standing on the edge of the floor mat seconds before racing toward the vault. This was it. I was going for my Olympic gold.

Twenty minutes later, we were at Mark's place. I don't remember much of the decor. But then again, I wasn't there to do a home inspection. As we stumbled through his door, our lips were locked and then we were on the ground, ripping off each other's shirts and pants. There were so many firsts for me that night. A lot of seconds too. Kissing. Nipple play. Blow jobs. More kissing. My mouth stayed open the whole time, like I was pigging out at an all-you-can-eat buffet and I was already on my fifth plate.

After we'd fully explored each other's bodies—he was a bit taller and wider than me—Mark positioned his hips behind mine. I froze.

"Wait." It wasn't Mark's size that scared me; it was all the safe-sex pamphlets filling my head. The two of us had already gone way past what Princess Diana had said was safe. I put my foot on the brake. "We don't have to."

"Don't worry. I have a condom." He leaned over and pulled a box from the nightstand.

I looked at the shiny tinfoil in his hand. The silver sparkled. It reminded me of jewelry. As he placed the corner in his mouth to rip it open with his teeth, I grabbed his wrist. "It's okay. I'm fine. No."

Mark looked at me. He had a mischievous grin. "Is this your first time?"

I answered with silence. His smile widened. "I know what I'm doing." He took out the condom and lowered his hand between his legs.

"It's okay. I said no."

Mark tried to push the issue a couple of more times, hoping I would let the moment carry me away, but there was nothing he could say or do to make me change my mind. Coming out in the age of AIDS might have messed me up, but not everything damaged needed to be fixed. I was two days away from my future life. I wasn't taking any chances.

Mother's Day was the busiest day of the year at Chung's. I had promised my family I would come back to help, so after the late night with Mark, I forced myself to get up early. As soon as the alarm rang, I jumped into the shower. Mark joined me and we extended our fun just a little bit more. As I stood under the steaming water with Mark sliding his hands along the small of my back, I realized that this was my graduation ceremony.

As promised, Mark drove me back to my place. We held hands

the whole way, making stupid googly eyes. Having sex for the first time didn't make me feel older. In fact, it made me feel younger. I had turned twenty-two a week earlier, but I felt like a teenager. I wondered if this was how all my straight friends had felt when they were in middle school or high school and got to experience these same milestones.

As we stood in the driveway, Mark tried his best to turn our one-night stand into a thing. "Maybe I can come visit you in New York."

As much as I liked the guy—and he was a nice guy—a new life was waiting for me. It was important for me to have a clean start. No loose ends. No looking back. I held my hand to his cheek. "If New York doesn't work out, I could be back here in the fall."

Whether he knew that was a lie or not, I couldn't tell. We didn't know each other well enough for me to make that assessment. Either way, he let me go. I ran up the stairs and grabbed the rest of my things. One bag sat on my deserted bed. After loading up the car, I dropped the keys into the mailbox and said goodbye to the maize and blue.

By the time I got to Chung's, a little after opening, there was a line out the door. Our dining room was packed. Big parties spanning multiple generations, people dressed in their Sunday best. With so many corsages and bouquets in the house, the place smelled like a florist shop. Compared to our business on Father's Day, it was clear which parent got more love.

Despite the blocked windows, our dining room had recaptured its magic. The guests were extra-loud and chatty, catching up on their lives. The special day brought back family members from far-off homes in the booming Sun Belt: Florida, Arizona, and Texas. It occurred to me that on my next trip home, I would be one of those former Detroiters trekking back for the holidays. It was nice to know that I would have a home to come back to.

Like a well-oiled machine, my family ricocheted around the room. My dad was in front, schmoozing with his old friends. Chris was helping seat people. Even Calvin, Cindy, and Clifford were pitching in as managers and bussers. My mom was shuttling between the kitchen and dining room with takeout orders. I threw down my bag and picked up some menus. I slipped right in. It turns out the boy had never really left Chinatown.

As my mom passed by, she noticed me chuckling. "What's wrong?"

"Nothing," I said, still in the afterglow.

"So what was that noise?"

I had one more chance to come out, to tell my mom what was really going on, why I was so happy, but I decided against it. In addition to this being Mother's Day, I just wasn't ready. It didn't feel right. I still wanted to come out to my family and knew I eventually would, but this was not the moment.

One of the most important lessons I learned at the restaurant was about timing—when to bring out the soup and egg rolls, when to pick up the dirty plates, when to put out the bill. Everything had an order. Nothing could be rushed. I had already come out to my friends and coworkers at Drake's and even to my favorite professor, Charles Baxter. Now I needed a breather.

Eventually, that time would be right, and when it happened, I would know it. At least I had come out to the single most important person—myself. That was more than enough for me.

I looked around the dining room at the crowded tables, the line of customers, the orders waiting to be picked up, our hurrying workers. All was good. The world was as it should be. I looked at my mom. "Happy Mother's Day. Sorry I didn't get you anything."

"You got your degree, didn't you?"

I smiled. We had all been too busy working to attend that year's official graduation ceremony. Too bad, since I later heard that the speaker, former Wolverine Lawrence Kasdan, the cowriter of *The Empire Strikes Back*, *Raiders of the Lost Ark*, and *The Big Chill*, had done a great job. "Don't worry. They're gonna send it. I'll show it to you then."

She waved her hand, signaling it was fine, then continued refilling the water pitchers.

The rest of the day was nonstop running between the dining room and main kitchen. I hadn't worked that hard in months. Drake's was never this busy, not even on game days. By early evening, my muscles were beginning to ache, but I didn't care. This was what I called work. And it was infinitely satisfying.

By nine p.m., the place had mostly cleared out except for a few stragglers with a late seating or the parties with long-winded dads and uncles. The place was a wreck, but the piles of crumpled table-cloths and napkins and stacks of dirty dishes would have to wait. My family and our staff were all famished. Now it was our turn to eat.

My dad decided to throw an impromptu family celebration in honor of Mother's Day and my imminent departure. He even wheeled in Ngin-Ngin from the back kitchen. It had been three years since her stroke and not much had improved. One of my mom's frequent sayings popped into my head: "People only change when they're ready to die." Given my grandma's stubbornness, it was obvious that she would be with us for a long, long time.

My siblings and I set up a big round table in the middle of the room. By the time my dad was done cooking, all of our greatest hits—pan-fried chicken chow mein, sizzling beef, mixed Chinese vegetables with kreplach—covered the table. We barely had room for the teapot or soy sauce bottle. It had been ages since we'd feasted like this, but no one minded. My parents lived by the adage that it was better to have leftovers than to leave the table hungry.

The feast included one of my own creations. Having tried every dish on the menu over the years, one night, in the summer before my junior year, I was craving something different. In a bit of inspiration, being resourceful and using whatever stock I had at my disposal, I combined the breast from our almond boneless chicken with the orange sauce from our worr dipp harr, then topped it off with a sprinkle of sesame seeds. I called it tangy chicken. The dish tasted awesome, if I do say so myself. My parents liked it enough to put it on the menu. It was a pretty decent seller too.

Savoring each bite off my chopsticks, I perused the menu, reviewing all the other dishes that had nourished me throughout my childhood. I considered myself lucky to have such a varied palate. With so many ingredients floating around our kitchen, it taught me that life was full of endless possibilities. I only had to be brave enough to try new recipes.

As my family dove into the plates, the last party of customers got up from their seats. It was another multigenerational group. My dad stood and pushed back his chair. "Everyone sit."

I put down my chopsticks and held up my hands. "That's okay. I've got this."

He paused. "Are you sure?"

"Yeah. You stay and eat."

With that, I dashed into the lobby. I took my spot standing by the display case as the last guest family exited out our red front door.

I smiled and waved with my usual parting words: "Thanks for coming. See you again soon."

THE FORTUNE COOKIE

The sky was dark when our packed car—my parents in front and me and my younger siblings in back—pulled into the dirt and gravel lot of the Michigan Central Train Depot. The offices of the thirteen-story tower, once the tallest train station in the world, had long been abandoned, but a few months earlier, the city had erected a chain-link fence in preparation for the building's planned demolition. Trains now stopped at a makeshift platform adjacent to the ghostly complex. It felt strange to me that a city that had once made so much noise—from its factories to its music—could now be so quiet.

In just sixteen hours and one overnight train ride, New York City would be my new home. On our quick visit to the city over spring break, Mimi and I had swung by Greenwich Village to check out the gay scene. Safer-sex PSAs shouted from all the billboards; every phone booth was tagged with homemade flyers for groups named ACT UP and Queer Nation. My gut response had been selfish relief: "Thank God I missed all this." For the past four years, I had been tucked away in the relatively safe Ann Arbor. Whether my parents knew it or not, their decision to pressure me into going to college nearby, away from the epicenter of the AIDS crisis, may have saved my life.

As my drift away from the GOP continued, I realized that my differences with my former party were no longer just about policies, but about approach. The influx of the religious right changed how they conducted politics. You were either right or wrong, good or evil. That call to arms may have worked for a church, but a democracy requires a balance, even a debate. It needs compromise, like yin and yang. Until those hard-line factions were expunged from the party—hopefully sooner rather than later—I would devote my energies toward AIDS activism. At least the sinners had more compassion than the saints.

At the same time, I was looking forward to finding more creative opportunities. In my final semester at Michigan, I had taken a playwriting class with an enthusiastic instructor named OyamO. He happened to be Black. What a welcome contrast from the previous semester. For the first time in my sixteen years in the American public school system, I had a teacher who was not white. I felt uplifted. My perspective opened up as we read writers like Ntozake Shange and August Wilson. In New York, I hoped to meet more writers of color, especially other Asian Americans. I wondered what new worlds I might discover.

In the shadowy parking lot, a few late-model vehicles dotted the landscape. Thanks to the full moon, the silhouettes of the drivers and passengers could be seen waiting for their transit. My family and I bided our time in the car as well, as the steady voice of the Tigers' Ernie Harwell filled the space. Competing with the play-by-play on the radio, my mom peppered me with questions: "Do you have your train ticket?" "Did you call to see if it's on time?" "Did you check the weather in New York?"

I answered with confidence, but there were still major holes in my plot. My job and housing were both temporary. My pockets weren't deep, and other than my aunt Margaret and her family, whom I had seen only a few times in my life and who were letting me house-sit while they were out of town, I knew no one in the city.

But none of these uncertainties could stop me. It was time to move on.

Cramped in the back seat, my siblings were finishing their home-work. For the past few months, I had been trying to build up our bonds. I wanted us to connect before I left their lives. In addition to trips to Dave's Comics and Astro Lanes Bowling, we'd gone to the local Blockbuster to pick up films that transported them from the conservative Midwest to *Brazil, Manhattan,* and *Another Country.* I hoped I was planting the seeds for when I returned. They seemed to respond to all of it, even the campy musicals, so there was room for optimism.

My eyes turned to the surrounding city. The parking lot was near the site of Detroit's first Chinatown—the one that had been de-molished to build a freeway. Any physical reminders were long gone. The neighborhood and its memories existed only in the retelling of its stories.

After taking a steamer across the Pacific and then a train from Seattle to Chicago to Ohio and on to Detroit, my ancestors had set foot on this sacred ground of the Huron and Odawa people over a century ago. How excited and scared had my great-great-grandpa been when he'd first arrived, poor and alone? Had he been more excited or more scared than I was now as I prepared to leave the same way, by train?

My dad checked the clock on the car's dashboard. He'd left my grandpa in charge of the dining room so he could drive me to the station. Yeh-Yeh had never been good at small talk, especially not in English, so I was sure my dad was anxious to get back to the customers. I patted him on the shoulder. "If you need to go, I'm fine."

"We can wait."

"Don't you have some big orders for tomorrow?" I asked, referring to the slips of paper I had seen posted by the phone in the kitchen before we left.

My family's physical safety remained a concern, but their financial security seemed more solid. Thanks to changes in federal law, an army of drug reps were now ordering large party trays of sweet-and-sour pork and almond boneless chicken to lure hungry doctors and administrators at the nearby hospitals to their sales pitches. With my parents back in the black, making hundreds more each week, they had become part of the American drug trade.

My mom chimed in: "Don't worry. We're fine."

My dad, who was still looking at the clock, turned to my mom. "Another big order did come in as we were leaving." The restaurant was like his seventh child, the neediest one.

"The train's almost here."

As my parents squabbled, my head ping-ponged between the two sides. Once again, the two people—born on opposite sides of the world, under different conditions—had different answers for dealing with the situation. I could see both sides. If being a dreaded middle child meant I was equal parts my mom and my dad, then I was okay with that.

Just then, the doors to the other parked cars began to swing open. The light from the oncoming train that was pulling into the station appeared. We all piled out into the night. Calvin, Cindy, and Clifford and I nudged one another as my dad popped open the trunk. When I reached for my bags, my dad, looking like a hotel porter in his red waiter's jacket, pushed me aside. "I got this."

I ignored him, yanking out my big green duffel bag, the one I'd picked up at the army surplus store during my high-school days.

My mom watched me hoisting my bag. "You have everything?"

I did a quick mental check: clothes, books, portable typewriter, bottles of Wite-Out. I'd left my prized boom box behind but had made a few mixtapes for the ride. High school seemed so far in the past. Even college felt like a closed chapter. Hopefully, I had done enough to make my parents proud. I flung the strap of the bag over my shoulder. "I think so."

My dad reached into his pocket and pulled out his wallet, the old one held together with yellowed Scotch tape. I watched him count out bills. No matter how much he had—or didn't have—he was always happy to give his children whatever was in there. This time was no different. He emptied the entire billfold, probably all the tip money from that night. "Here. In case you get hungry on the train."

My dad must have forgotten that just an hour ago, he had prepared one more family meal where I had once again eaten all my favorites. I was feeling the early stages of a food coma and was ready for the overnight ride. "I'm going to sleep."

My dad pushed the money in my face. "Take it."

Normally, his offer would have come off as a challenge to my independence, but with only a few hundred dollars to my name, I put aside my pride and took the money. The extra cushion might come in handy. "Thanks. I'll pay you back when I come home."

"It's yours," he said. My dad beamed in the parking-lot shadows, happy to still be needed. "I'm proud of you, son."

I smiled. Before I could properly respond, the intercom garbled its next announcement. My siblings wished me luck and gave me a list of possible souvenirs. They jumped back into the car, and my dad followed. My mom waited for everyone else to be loaded up before approaching me. I tried to think of what to say, but instead, her mantra, the one she had given to me as I first boarded the yellow school bus and had used throughout all my schooling, kept ringing in my head: *Work hard. Be quiet. Obey your elders.*

My mom handed me the item she had been holding this whole time. Instead of a shiny red envelope—the kind we got during New Year's—it was a red-and-silver tinfoil bag. The egg rolls were still warm. I could taste the plum sauce blended in with the cabbage and filling. I couldn't wait to have my snack. All I could think to say was "Thanks."

My mom gave me several quick pats on the back. It felt like I was a baby and she was trying to burp me. She then pointed toward the train. "Go." I managed to sneak in one last peck on the cheek, to which she added a few more *Go, go, go*s.

Go, go, go. My family's final words to me that night, confirmation that I was making the right choice.

The other passengers boarded as I joined the end of the shrinking queue. With one foot placed on the train's first step, I turned to give my family one last wave, to thank them for all they had given and taught me. With the parking lot emptied out, I could see their red taillights pulling onto Michigan Avenue on their way back to the restaurant, back to home.

Acknowledgments

Writing a book takes days—okay, years. There are so many people to thank.

First, to Jeff, aka Mr. Yale-Michigan-Law-School-off-to-Japan, thanks for being by my side through my journey, reading drafts, giving me your candid opinion, and taking care of our beloved Lisa and Boycat. This book wouldn't have happened without you.

Thanks to my mom, Shui Kuen Chin, for supporting me through the years and for always taking the time to refresh my memory about our family. Your advice to work hard, be quiet, and obey your editors—I mean elders—was invaluable.

Much love to my siblings and their partners: Craig, Chris, Nadine, Calvin, Angie, Cindy, Clifford, and Biyun—as well as my nephews and nieces, Zachary, Zia, Zoe, Spencer, Sloane, and Eleanor—for supporting me in telling our family's story. Hopefully, I got more of this right than wrong. Apologies in advance.

Thank you, Dad. We still miss you.

Deep appreciation to my agents, Erin Harris and Sonali Chanchani, and Folio Literary for believing in me and helping my story get noticed. I also consider myself very lucky—eight-eight-eight lucky—to have Vivian Lee as my editor. Her insight and guidance have been invaluable. Additional thanks to Morgan Wu, Karen Landry, Tracy Roe, and the outstanding marketing team at Little, Brown—Katharine Myers and Mariah Dwyer and Bryan Christian and Anna Brill—as well as to Lucy Kim for the jacket design. You made the process so easy.

I turned to fellow writers for insights, and those who generously read multiple drafts have earned my deep eternal gratitude: Christina Chiu, David L. Eng, Jon Higham, Makiko Hirata, Marie Myung-Ok Lee, Keri Mickelson, Gayla Wigal Robinson, Richard Sedgwick, Lisa Simmons, Stee Tate, Matthew Wirta, Adam Harris Wolman, Alex Zoubine.

Thanks so much to others who provided creative feedback and encouragement that came at key points in the writing process: Keiko Agena, Timothy K. August, George Balarezo, Zoe Blaylock, Leland Cheuk, Evelyn Chi'en, Sylvia Clare, Francisco Delgado, Gary James Erwin, Cristina Grau, Terry Hong, Chris Keelty, David Ledain, Krys Lee, Martin F. Manalansan, Dwight Okita, Derville Quigley, Julia Rampen, Michael Robison, Brian Schrier, Bryant Simon, Jo Somerset, Robert Turley, Terry Wolverton, Jeff Yang, Paula Yoo, Vincent Young.

Many friends offered additional support and guidance, providing input on the proposal, allowing me to discuss my work with their students, sharing insights on publishing, and helping me to prepare for my book launch. Heartfelt appreciation to you all: Robin Blackwood, Jef Blocker, Kyung-Sook Boo, Jonathan A. Brantley, Lynn Liao Butler, Susan Chan, Grace Chan McKibben, Alexandra Chang, Alexander Chee, Debbie Chen, Ken Chen, Lily Chen, Nancy Chen, Laura Chen-Schultz, Li-Chen Chin, Susan Chinsen, Albert Choi, Lawrence-Minh Bùi Davis, Kenneth Eng, Jenn Fang, Lee Flamand,

Wyman M. Fong, Jamie Ford, Zosette Guir, Jimin Han, Jennifer Ho, Gordon Jee, Elizabeth Kim, James Kim, Jeanney Kim, Owen Kim, Sue J. Kim, Bill Kubota, Chrisna Kuon, Derik Leong, Carolyn Lett, Nancy Lim-Yee, Richard Lui, Matt Madden, Stephanie McClure, Deborah Meadows, Bino Realuyo, Mark Takano, Simon Tam, Lisa Thong, Naomi Tacuyan Underwood, Frances Kai-Hwa Wang, Shu-wen Wang, Carlos Wiley, Betty Wong, Carla Young, Mary Yu Danico, Chien-An Yuan.

Over the years, and especially during COVID, writing workshops around the globe were a source of real support. I am thankful to the organizers for opening up their spaces and to members for welcoming me so warmly: Caversham Writers (England), Central Phoenix Writing Workshop, Gay Men's Writing Group (New York City), Glasgow Writers Group (Scotland), Happy Writing (Germany), Lake St. Clair Creative Writers, London Writers' Salon, Los Angeles Writers Critique Group, MAPID Writers Group (Los Angeles), Memoir Mentors (Germany), Metro Detroit Writing Workshop, New York City Writers Critique Group, Original Writers Group (England), Out on the Page (England), Strange Birds (Netherlands), Vicious Circle Writers Group (Atlanta), Write Out Loud (Los Angeles), Writers Together (England).

Finally, a huge hat tip to the Asian American Writers' Workshop and all the volunteers, staff, board members, and, especially, writers who came through its doors. Over three decades ago, a small group of us found one another, organized our community to create a welcoming space to nurture our aspirations, and began sharing our work in camaraderie and solidarity. Over the years, the success of those who realized their dreams inspired me to keep writing. And now, I join my literary brothers and sisters as a published author. We made it. Thank you.

About the Author

A cofounder of the Asian American Writers' Workshop, Curtis Chin served as the nonprofit's first executive director. He went on to write for network and cable television before transitioning to social-justice documentaries. Chin has screened his films at more than six hundred venues in sixteen countries. His essays have appeared on CNN and in the *Boston Globe*'s *Emancipator* and *Bon Appétit*, as well as in *The Best American Food Writing 2023*. A graduate of the University of Michigan and a former visiting scholar at New York University, Chin has received awards from ABC/Disney Television, the New York Foundation for the Arts, the National Endowment for the Arts, and more. He can be found at CurtisfromDetroit.com.